THE ENCYCLOPEDIA OF
MEXICAN FOOD

THE ENCYCLOPEDIA OF
MEXICAN FOOD

OVER 300 RECIPES FROM THE BELOVED CUISINE

Encyclopedia of Mexican Food

Copyright © 2025 by Cider Mill Press Book Publishers LLC. • This is an officially licensed book by Cider Mill Press Book Publishers LLC. • All rights reserved under the Pan-American and International Copyright Conventions. • No part of this book may be reproduced in whole or in part, scanned, photocopied, recorded, distributed in any printed or electronic form, or reproduced in any manner whatsoever, or by any information storage and retrieval system now known or hereafter invented, without express written permission of the publisher, except in the case of brief quotations in critical articles and reviews. • The scanning, uploading, and distribution of this book via the internet or via any other means without permission of the publisher is illegal and punishable by law. Please support authors' rights, and do not participate in or encourage piracy of copyrighted materials. • 13-Digit ISBN: 978-1-40034-640-0 • 10-Digit ISBN: 1-40034-640-1 • This book may be ordered by mail from the publisher. Please include $5.99 for postage and handling. Please support your local bookseller first! • Books published by Cider Mill Press Book Publishers are available at special discounts for bulk purchases in the United States by corporations, institutions, and other organizations. For more information, please contact the publisher. • Cider Mill Press Book Publishers • "Where good books are ready for press" • 501 Nelson Place • Nashville, Tennessee 37214 • cidermillpress.com • Typography: Hansief, Freight Sans, Freight Serif • Image Credits: Pages 14, 17, 20–21, 23, 25, 29, 31, 33, 36–37, 42–43, 45, 47, 50–51, 54–55, 69, 78–79, 83, 88–89, 93, 95, 97, 100–101, 106–107, 134–135, 140–141, 143, 149, 153, 157, 167, 170–171, 174–175, 189, 196–197, 200–201, 203, 213, 221, 227, 238–239, 246–247, 250, 263, 271, 273, 278–279, 282–283, 285, 288, 291, 314–315, 319, 322–323, 329, 339, 346, 369, 373, 374, 377, 381, 385, 387, 389, 393, 397, 405, 409, 411, 413, and 417 courtesy of Cider Mill Press. Pages 66–67, 81, 177, 209, 215, 337, 349, 353, 359, 361, 363, and 432 courtesy of Unsplash. All other photos used under official license from Shutterstock. • Printed in Malaysia • 24 25 26 27 28 COS 5 4 3 2 1 • First Edition

CONTENTS

Introduction | 8

Appetizers, Salads & Sides | 15

Entrees | 91

Soups & Stews | 219

Sauces & Condiments | 251

Desserts | 289

Beverages | 347

Appendix | 433

Index | 467

INTRODUCTION

The phrase "Mexican food" means many things to people. For a lot of folks, any and all discussion of the cuisine centers around tacos. For the people who call Mexico home, the country's cuisine is a vibrant mélange of ingredients, techniques, and cultures.

To start, Mexico's cuisine is grounded in indigenous ingredients, dishes, and techniques. Despite efforts to erase indigenous practices and ways of life during the colonial era, many indigenous peoples of the region have maintained strong traditions, passing down family recipes from generation to generation.

The intricacy, beauty, and flavors of Mexican cuisine are a result of an insistence that all parts be used—every bit of livestock and produce, even the fungus that grows on corn (known as huitlacoche, or corn smut). Those pieces that others disregard are considered essential in Mexican cuisine, such as the pork tripe in the comforting menudo (see page 226), where it adds texture and a sense of adventure.

Prior to the arrival of the Spanish, the use of meats in Mexican dishes was uncommon, and corn, beans, and squash formed the foundation of most dishes. The Conquest introduced livestock such as cows, pigs, chicken, goats, and sheep to the country, and these were then incorporated into the existing dishes, resulting in the recipes we recognize as Mexican cuisine today.

From 1519 to 1580, the Spanish brought the first African slaves, from Angola and the Congo, to the two main ports in Veracruz and Campeche. The demand for slaves in Mexico continued until the early 1800s. Consequently, Mexican cuisine includes traces of African cooking. Ingredients native to Africa include rice, plantains, sesame seeds, hibiscus flower (which is used to make the popular agua de jamaica, see page 423), and watermelon. Afro-Mexican communities continue to thrive in the Costa Chica of southern Guerrero and Oaxaca, and also in Veracruz.

It is believed that produce from Asia arrived in Mexico starting in the sixteenth century. During these years mango, tamarind, dried, salted plums and apricots, and chamoy were introduced and became commonly used, particularly in northern Mexico.

During the eighteenth and early nineteenth centuries, people from Lebanon migrated to Mexico, initially arriving in Veracruz and later settling in towns throughout the republic. While Lebanese immigrants only accounted for a small percentage of the overall population of Mexico, their culinary traditions became intertwined with native dishes. Tacos al pastor is one result of the collision between these two cultures. The red marinade that contributes much to making these tacos what they are is a combination of Middle Eastern and Mexican spices. The method of cooking the meat, where it is placed on a vertical spit (trompo) and slowly cooked is an adaption of the shawarma that is featured in Middle Eastern cooking.

The occupation of Mexico by the French during the 1800s introduced French culinary techniques into the existing culture. There were efforts by those with higher socioeconomic status to view native dishes, like tamales, as lower class and unrefined. While efforts to erase the existing cuisine ultimately failed, French inspiration can still be found in the sweet breads and empanadas that are popular throughout the country.

The geography, topography, and climate of Mexico heavily influences the ingredients that are accessible to people in its various regions. Many dishes, like tacos and tamales, can be found in every state in Mexico. But each region has its own take on these dishes. Mole, a sauce or paste that is made out of ground chocolate, nuts, and spices, is a prime example of the country's regional diversity. While the sweeter moles featuring rich, velvety chocolate, are more widely known, in central and southern Mexico mole can be spicy and/or textured.

In addition to their own takes on the traditional dishes, every state within Mexico has dishes that are unique to it. The northern states of Mexico are arid and dry. In this region dried meats are commonly incorporated into dishes. Chilorio, dried pork, is wrapped in flour tortillas to make burritos. Machaca, dried beef, is frequently served with scrambled eggs or sautéed with onion, tomatoes, and fresh chile peppers, and served with refried pinto beans. The use of dried meats hints at the past scarcity of animal protein in the region, with curing and drying used to make the most of what was available.

Baja California is recognized for its mariscos, or seafood, like the lightly battered and fried fish tacos, and ceviche, raw fish or shrimp cured in lime juice. And Puerto Nuevo lobster has become iconic thanks to its fresh flavor.

In Jalisco, a state in central Mexico, the bolillo is a sour and salted bread similar to a baguette. Its crunchy outer layer is ideal for making tortas ahogada, a sandwich made with lean pork and topped with a red chile sauce. Bolillos can replace spoons when eating beans and birria (see page 92), a rich meat stew made with goat, beef, or mutton. Carne en su jugo, beef in its juice (see page 133), is the typical dish of Guadalajara, the capital of Jalisco. On hot days, it's customary to drink tejuino (see page 427), a cold drink made out of fermented masa.

The central state of Michoacán is the birthplace of carnitas, cuts of pork braised in lard. Pork shoulder is the cut of choice in carnitas because of its fattiness, but it is common to add all cuts of the pork, like the liver and intestines, to the brass cauldron, the traditional vehicle for cooking the preparation. The tender meat that results is served in tacos fashioned from double tortillas and garnished with finely chopped cilantro, onion, radish, lime, and red salsa.

Puebla is renowned for its mole poblano (see page 154), chiles en nogada (see page 132), and rompope, a type of eggnog spiked with white rum.

The diversity of Mexico's cuisine is most apparent in its southern states, a result of both the ethnic diversity in the region, and the preservation of its indigenous cultures. Oaxaca, for example, has seven ethnic regions, each with its own language, culture, and cuisine. Similarly, in the Yucatan, Mayan cooking techniques and ingredients can still be found in modern-day kitchens.

As one moves south, and draws closer to the equator, the geography and climate drastically change, becoming lush and tropical. The climate of the region has lent itself to the cultivation of coffee and an assortment of tropical fruits, such as guanabana (soursop), papaya, starfruit, and mango.

The food hailing from Oaxaca, the land of the seven moles, is one of the most recognized internationally, an appreciation that is in part due to the preservation of indigenous cooking techniques and native crop cultivation. Common ingredients found in Oaxacan cuisine include huitlacoche (corn smut), chocolate, hoja santa (Mexican pepperleaf), black beans, the aromatic herb epazote, and flor de calabaza (squash blossom).

Further south is the state of Chiapas, another ethnically diverse area with high regard for its native customs and ways. The subtropical climate and lush vegetation foster the various fruits and vegetables used in the region's recipes.

The Yucatan's gastronomy is unique because it preserves the Mayan cooking traditions, but combines them with Spanish, Dutch, and Lebanese influences, a marriage that leads to a unique combination of flavors and aromas. The core of Yucatecan cuisine is formed by achiote, habanero chiles, citrus, like the sour orange, and smoke, which is created either by roasting or barbecuing ingredients. Deer, turkey, pork, quail, armadillos, and other game meats are the proteins of choice in the Yucatan.

The quintessential dish of the Yucatan is cochinita pibil, a slow-roasted pork marinated in a red chile sauce (see page 99). To maximize the rich, smoky flavor of the chiles and spices, pibil is cooked in an underground pit and covered with banana leaves. The pork is served with pickled red onions and habanero chiles, and handmade corn tortillas. The use of banana leaves for roasting protein, or for wrapping and steaming tamales, adds a subtle sweetness and earthiness. Recados, or spice mixes used as pastes or rubs for protein or vegetables, are uniquely Yucatecan and are responsible for the rich flavor palette of some regional dishes. Preparing recado rojo, a popular paste, requires roasting achiote (or using a premade achiote paste), combining it with lime, orange, and grapefruit juices, oregano, marjoram, habanero chiles, garlic, cinnamon, and salt (see page 272).

The resulting paste features a delicate balance of citrus and spice that Yucatecans have mastered better than most.

Veracruz, the vibrant southern state known for its coffee, is a tropical region with its coastline on the Gulf of Mexico, resulting in gastronomy that is rich in flavors and textures. The Spanish Conquest began in Veracruz, and its ports quickly became important. European ships would dock along the coast and bring spices and other goods, like the olives found in arroz a la tumbada, a popular dish similar to Spain's famed paella. The seafood sourced from the coast of Veracruz consists of shrimp, crab, oysters, snails, red snapper, and cod, among others.

APPETIZERS, SALADS & SIDES

Lobster & Street Corn Salad

YIELD: 4 SERVINGS / **ACTIVE TIME:** 25 MINUTES / **TOTAL TIME:** 50 MINUTES

FOR THE SALAD

¼ CUP MAYONNAISE

¼ CUP SOUR CREAM

1 TEASPOON FRESH LIME JUICE

¼ TEASPOON HOT SAUCE

½ CUP GRATED QUESO ENCHILADO

SALT AND PEPPER, TO TASTE

KERNELS FROM 5 EARS OF CORN

2 TABLESPOONS UNSALTED BUTTER, MELTED

FOR THE LOBSTER

½ CUP UNSALTED BUTTER

1 LB. LOBSTER TAILS

2 TABLESPOONS TAJÍN

FRESH CILANTRO, CHOPPED, FOR GARNISH

1. To begin preparations for the salad, preheat the oven to 375°F. Place the mayonnaise, sour cream, lime juice, hot sauce, queso enchilado, salt, and pepper in a salad bowl, stir to combine, and set it aside.

2. Place the corn kernels in a small mixing bowl along with the butter and toss to combine. Place the corn kernels in an even layer on a baking sheet, place them in the oven, and roast until the corn is golden brown, 15 to 20 minutes.

3. Stir the corn into the salad bowl and let it cool. Chill the salad in the refrigerator.

4. To begin preparations for the lobster, place the butter in a skillet and warm over medium-low heat.

5. Remove the meat from the lobster tails using kitchen scissors. Add the meat to the pan and poach until it turns a reddish orange, 4 to 5 minutes. Remove the lobster meat from the pan with a slotted spoon and let it cool.

6. Slice the lobster into small medallions. To serve, spoon the corn salad onto each plate and arrange a few lobster medallions on top of each portion. Sprinkle the Tajín over the dishes, garnish with cilantro, and serve.

Pig Ear Salad

YIELD: 4 SERVINGS / **ACTIVE TIME:** 30 MINUTES / **TOTAL TIME:** 1 HOUR AND 30 MINUTES

4 CUPS CHICKEN STOCK (SEE PAGE 438)

2 CHIPOTLE MORITA CHILE PEPPERS, STEMMED AND SEEDED

½ WHITE ONION, SLICED

4 GARLIC CLOVES, 2 LEFT WHOLE, 2 DICED

1 BAY LEAF

1½ LBS. PIG EARS, TRIMMED

CANOLA OIL, AS NEEDED

2 CUPS RICE FLOUR

SALT AND PEPPER, TO TASTE

¼ RED ONION, SLICED

2 TABLESPOONS TOASTED RICE POWDER (SEE PAGE 438)

15 CURRY LEAVES

10 CHERRY TOMATOES, HALVED

JUICE OF 3 LIMES

2 TABLESPOONS EXTRA-VIRGIN OLIVE OIL

1 TABLESPOON GINGER JUICE

1 TABLESPOON EPAZOTE POWDER

1. Place the stock in a medium saucepan and add the chiles, white onion, whole cloves of garlic, and bay leaf. Bring to a simmer, add the pig ears, and gently simmer until they are very tender. You want to be able to pass a knife through the pig ears with ease. Drain the pig ears and let them cool. When cool, slice them into ½-inch-thick pieces.

2. Add canola oil to a Dutch oven until it is about 2 inches deep and warm it to 350°F.

3. Place the rice flour in a bowl, dredge the pig ears in the flour until coated, and then gently slip them into the hot oil. Fry until the pig ears are crispy on the outside, about 45 seconds. Transfer to a paper towel–lined plate to drain and season the pig ears with salt.

4. Place all of the remaining ingredients, except for the epazote powder, in a mixing bowl, add the fried pig ears, and toss to combine. Top with the epazote powder and serve.

Guanajuato Strawberry & Beet Salad

YIELD: 4 SERVINGS / **ACTIVE TIME:** 20 MINUTES / **TOTAL TIME:** 2 HOURS

3 LARGE GOLDEN BEETS

½ CUP EXTRA-VIRGIN OLIVE OIL

SALT AND PEPPER, TO TASTE

CILANTRO PESTO (SEE PAGE 434)

12 STRAWBERRIES, HULLED AND HALVED

2 CUPS SHREDDED QUESO FRESCO (SEE PAGE 287)

4 OZ. BABY ARUGULA

2 TABLESPOONS ANNATTO OIL

1. Preheat the oven to 375°F. Rinse the beets under cold water and scrub them to remove any excess dirt. Pat dry and place them in a baking dish.

2. Drizzle the olive oil over the beets and season them generously with salt and pepper. Place them in the oven and roast until tender, about 1 hour.

3. Remove the beets from the oven and let them cool.

4. When the beets are cool enough to handle, peel and dice them. Place them in a bowl with the pesto and toss to coat. Add the strawberries, cheese, arugula, and annatto oil, toss until evenly distributed, and serve.

Aguachile Verde

YIELD: 4 SERVINGS / **ACTIVE TIME:** 20 MINUTES / **TOTAL TIME:** 30 MINUTES

1¾ CUPS FRESH LIME JUICE

3 SERRANO CHILE PEPPERS, STEMMED AND SEEDED

1 CUP FRESH CILANTRO, CHOPPED, PLUS MORE FOR GARNISH

3 TABLESPOONS EXTRA-VIRGIN OLIVE OIL

2 TABLESPOONS APPLE JUICE

1 TEASPOON HONEY

SALT, TO TASTE

1 LB. SHRIMP, SHELLS REMOVED, DEVEINED

¼ RED ONION, SLICED

1 CUCUMBER, SLICED

FLESH OF 1 AVOCADO, DICED

TORTILLA CHIPS, FOR SERVING

1. Place the lime juice, serrano peppers, cilantro, olive oil, apple juice, and honey in a blender and puree until smooth. Season the aguachile with salt and set it aside.

2. Slice the shrimp in half lengthwise and place them in a shallow bowl. Cover with the red onion, cucumber, and avocado.

3. Pour the aguachile over the shrimp and let it cure for 5 to 7 minutes before garnishing with additional cilantro and serving with tortilla chips.

Guanajuato Strawberry & Beet Salad

SEE PAGE 19

Ensalada de Nopales

YIELD: 4 SERVINGS / **ACTIVE TIME:** 30 MINUTES / **TOTAL TIME:** 45 MINUTES

3 LARGE NOPALES, SPINES REMOVED

1 TABLESPOON KOSHER SALT, PLUS MORE TO TASTE

½ WHITE ONION, FINELY DICED

2 LARGE TOMATOES, FINELY DICED

½ BUNCH OF FRESH CILANTRO, CHOPPED

JUICE OF 1 LEMON

QUESO FRESCO (SEE PAGE 287), CRUMBLED, FOR GARNISH

COTIJA CHEESE, CRUMBLED, FOR GARNISH

1. Place the nopales in a small bowl and sprinkle the salt over them. Let the nopales rest for 15 minutes.

2. Combine the onion, tomatoes, and cilantro in a separate bowl.

3. Place the nopales and 1 tablespoon of water in a large skillet, cover it, and cook over medium heat until the nopales are tender, about 12 minutes. Remove from the pan and let cool. When cool enough to handle, cut the nopales into ¼-inch-thick strips.

4. Stir the nopales into the tomato mixture, add the lemon juice, and season the salad with salt. If desired, sprinkle Queso Fresco or cotija cheese over the top and enjoy.

Esquites con Longaniza

YIELD: 4 SERVINGS / **ACTIVE TIME:** 25 MINUTES / **TOTAL TIME:** 45 MINUTES

6 CUPS CANNED CORN, DRAINED

SALT, TO TASTE

2 TABLESPOONS EXTRA-VIRGIN OLIVE OIL

1 LB. LONGANIZA, CHOPPED

2 TABLESPOONS UNSALTED BUTTER

1 JALAPEÑO CHILE PEPPER, STEMMED, SEEDED, AND DICED

2 TABLESPOONS MAYONNAISE

2 TEASPOONS GARLIC POWDER

¼ CUP SOUR CREAM

½ TEASPOON CAYENNE PEPPER

½ TEASPOON CHILI POWDER

3 TABLESPOONS FETA CHEESE

3 TABLESPOONS GOAT CHEESE

1 TABLESPOON FRESH LIME JUICE

½ CUP FINELY CHOPPED FRESH CILANTRO

6 CUPS LETTUCE OR ARUGULA, FOR SERVING (OPTIONAL)

1. Preheat the oven to 375°F. Divide the corn among two baking sheets, season it with salt, and place it in the oven. Roast the corn until it is starting to brown, 20 to 25 minutes.

2. While the corn is in the oven, place the olive oil in a mixing bowl and warm it over medium heat. Add the longaniza and cook until it is browned all over and cooked through, 8 to 10 minutes, stirring as necessary. Transfer the cooked longaniza to a large bowl.

3. Remove the corn from the oven and transfer it to the bowl containing the longaniza. Add the remaining ingredients, except for the lettuce or arugula (if using), one at a time, stirring until each one is thoroughly incorporated before adding the next.

4. Taste, adjust the seasoning as necessary, and serve with the lettuce or arugula (if desired).

Striped Sea Bass Ceviche

YIELD: 4 SERVINGS / **ACTIVE TIME:** 1 HOUR AND 15 MINUTES / **TOTAL TIME:** 24 HOURS

5 OZ. TOMATILLOS, HUSKED AND RINSED

1 TABLESPOON COCONUT OIL

5-INCH PIECE OF FRESH GINGER, PEELED AND DICED

2½ SHALLOTS, DICED

6 GARLIC CLOVES, DICED

5 TABLESPOONS SOY SAUCE

1½ TABLESPOONS FISH SAUCE

3½ CUPS COCONUT MILK

1 LEMONGRASS STALK, PEELED AND BRUISED

1 BUNCH OF SCALLIONS, TRIMMED AND SLICED

1 LARGE BUNCH OF FRESH CILANTRO, CHOPPED, PLUS MORE FOR GARNISH

7 TABLESPOONS FRESH LEMON JUICE

2 SERRANO CHILE PEPPERS, STEMMED, SEEDED, AND SLICED, PLUS MORE FOR GARNISH

SALT, TO TASTE

FRESH LIME JUICE, TO TASTE

LIME ZEST, TO TASTE

¼ LB. SEA BASS FILLET, SLICED

2 SHALLOTS, JULIENNED

2 TABLESPOONS SHAVED FRESH COCONUT

¼ CUP TOASTED PEANUTS

COCONUT DRESSING (SEE PAGE 435)

1. Preheat a gas or charcoal grill to medium-high heat (450°F). Place the tomatillos on the grill and grill until charred all over, about 6 minutes, turning occasionally. Remove the tomatillos from the grill and set them aside. When the tomatillos are cool enough to handle, chop them.

2. Place the coconut oil in a skillet and warm it over medium heat. Add the ginger, shallots, and garlic and cook until the shallots are translucent, about 3 minutes, stirring frequently.

3. Add the tomatillos to the skillet and cook until all of the liquid has evaporated. Deglaze the pan with the soy sauce and fish sauce, scraping up any browned bits from the bottom of the pan.

4. Add the coconut milk and lemongrass and bring the mixture to a boil. Remove the pan from heat and let the mixture cool. Store in the refrigerator overnight.

5. Remove the lemongrass and add the scallions, cilantro, and lemon juice to the mixture. Place it in a blender and puree until smooth.

6. Place the serrano peppers in a mixing bowl and season with salt, lime juice, and lime zest. Strain the puree into the bowl, add the sea bass, and chill in the refrigerator for 40 to 50 minutes.

7. Drain the sea bass and season it with salt, lime juice, and lime zest. Combine the shallots, coconut, and toasted peanuts in a mixing bowl and season with the Coconut Dressing. Arrange the salad as a line in the middle of a plate.

8. Place the sea bass in a line next to the salad, garnish with additional cilantro and serrano, and serve.

Coctel de Camarón

YIELD: 4 SERVINGS / **ACTIVE TIME:** 35 MINUTES / **TOTAL TIME:** 1 HOUR AND 35 MINUTES

SALT, TO TASTE

1 LB. SHRIMP, DEVEINED, SHELLS ON

2 LARGE TOMATOES, SEEDED AND FINELY DICED

¼ WHITE ONION, FINELY DICED

1 CUCUMBER, PEELED, SEEDED, AND FINELY DICED

½ CUP KETCHUP OR CLAMATO

JUICE OF 3 LIMES

2 SERRANO CHILE PEPPERS, STEMMED, SEEDED, AND FINELY CHOPPED

1 BUNCH OF FRESH CILANTRO, FINELY CHOPPED

TOSTADAS OR SALTINES, FOR SERVING

LIME WEDGES, FOR SERVING

1. Prepare an ice bath and bring water to a boil in a medium saucepan. Add salt and the shrimp and poach until the shrimp turn bright pink. Plunge them into the ice bath and then peel them. Let the poaching liquid cool and place the shrimp in the refrigerator.

2. When the poaching liquid is cool, place half of it in a bowl. Add the tomatoes, onion, cucumber, and ketchup and stir to combine.

3. Cut the shrimp into ½-inch pieces and add them to the vegetable mixture. Stir in the lime juice, serrano peppers, and cilantro, taste, and season with salt if necessary.

4. Chill the shrimp cocktail in the refrigerator for 1 hour before serving with tostadas and lime wedges.

APPETIZERS, SALADS & SIDES

Shrimp Aguachile with Avocado Panna Cotta

YIELD: 4 SERVINGS / **ACTIVE TIME:** 15 MINUTES / **TOTAL TIME:** 1 HOUR

½ ENGLISH CUCUMBER

1 GARLIC CLOVE

½ CUP FRESH CILANTRO, CHOPPED

½ JALAPEÑO CHILE PEPPER, STEMMED, SEEDED, AND SLICED

¾ CUP FRESH LIME JUICE

SALT AND PEPPER, TO TASTE

½ LB. MEXICAN GULF ROCK SHRIMP, SHELLED AND DEVEINED

AVOCADO PANNA COTTA (SEE PAGE 435), FOR SERVING

1. Place the cucumber, garlic, cilantro, jalapeño, lime juice, salt, and pepper in a blender and puree until smooth.

2. Strain the puree into a bowl, pressing down to push as much of it through as possible.

3. Add the shrimp to the bowl, cover it with plastic wrap, and chill in the refrigerator until the shrimp turns pink, 40 to 50 minutes.

4. Serve alongside the Avocado Panna Cotta.

Coctel de Marisco

YIELD: 4 SERVINGS / **ACTIVE TIME:** 5 MINUTES / **TOTAL TIME:** 1 HOUR AND 5 MINUTES

1 CUP SHELLED AND DEVEINED SHRIMP

1 CUP CRAB KNUCKLE MEAT

1 CUP OCTOPUS, COOKED AND DICED

1½ CUPS CLAMATO

1 CUP KETCHUP

1 TABLESPOON FRESH LEMON JUICE

1 CUCUMBER, DICED

FLESH OF 2 AVOCADOS, DICED

2 TOMATOES, DICED

1 RED ONION, DICED

1 CUP FRESH CILANTRO, CHOPPED, PLUS MORE FOR GARNISH

2 JALAPEÑO CHILE PEPPERS, STEMMED, SEEDED, AND DICED

1 TEASPOON TAJÍN

SALT AND PEPPER, TO TASTE

CORN TORTILLAS (SEE PAGE 65), FOR SERVING

LIME WEDGES, FOR SERVING

1. Place all of the ingredients, except the tortillas and lime wedges, in a large mixing bowl and gently stir until combined.

2. Cover the bowl with plastic wrap and chill in the refrigerator for 1 hour.

3. Garnish with additional cilantro and serve with tortillas and lime wedges.

Ceviche de Pescado

YIELD: 6 SERVINGS / **ACTIVE TIME:** 25 MINUTES / **TOTAL TIME:** 2 HOURS AND 30 MINUTES

2 LBS. HALIBUT OR RED SNAPPER FILLETS, DICED

SALT, TO TASTE

1 JALAPEÑO CHILE PEPPER, STEMMED, SEEDED, AND FINELY DICED

2 SERRANO CHILE PEPPERS, STEMMED, SEEDED, AND FINELY DICED

½ BUNCH OF FRESH CILANTRO, FINELY CHOPPED, PLUS MORE FOR SERVING

JUICE OF 6 LARGE LIMES

TOSTADAS OR SALTINES, FOR SERVING

¼ RED ONION, SLICED THIN, FOR SERVING

½ LB. CHERRY TOMATOES, PEELED AND DICED, FOR SERVING

FLESH OF 1 AVOCADO, DICED, FOR SERVING

1 CUCUMBER, PEELED AND FINELY DICED, FOR SERVING

HOT SAUCE, FOR SERVING

1. Place the fish in a bowl and season with salt. Add the peppers, cilantro, and lime juice, stir to combine, and chill the ceviche in the refrigerator for 2 hours, allowing the fish to cure.

2. Pile the ceviche on top of tostadas or saltines and serve with the onion, tomatoes, avocado, cucumber, hot sauce, and additional cilantro.

Masa-Crusted Sardines with Pickled Manzano

YIELD: 2 SERVINGS / **ACTIVE TIME:** 10 MINUTES / **TOTAL TIME:** 30 MINUTES

½ LB. SARDINES, CLEANED AND HEADS REMOVED

SALT, TO TASTE

1 CUP MASA HARINA

¼ CUP ALL-PURPOSE FLOUR

1 TABLESPOON MOLE SPICE (SEE PAGE 436)

½ TEASPOON CUMIN

1 TEASPOON PAPRIKA

2 CUPS EXTRA-VIRGIN OLIVE OIL

¼ CUP CHILE TOREADO MAYONNAISE (SEE PAGE 439)

¼ CUP PICKLED MANZANO PEPPERS (SEE PAGE 77)

LIME WEDGES, FOR SERVING

1. Rinse the sardines and pat them dry with a paper towel. Season lightly with salt.

2. Place the masa harina, flour, half of the Mole Spice, the cumin, and paprika in a mixing bowl and stir to combine.

3. Dredge the sardines in the masa mixture until completely coated. Set them on paper towels and let them rest for 5 minutes.

4. After 5 minutes, dredge the sardines in the masa mixture again until coated. The resting period allows the sardines to release a bit of moisture, which will help more of the masa stick to them, producing a lighter and crispier result.

5. Place the olive oil in a deep skillet and warm it to 325°F. Working in batches, gently slip the sardines into the hot oil and fry until they are crispy and golden brown, about 4 minutes, turning them over once. Place the fried sardines on a paper towel–lined plate to drain and sprinkle the remaining Mole Spice over them.

6. To serve, spread some of the chile mayo on each serving plate, arrange a few sardines and pickled peppers on top, and serve with lime wedges.

Koji-Marinated Sweet Potatoes with Salsa Macha

YIELD: 4 SERVINGS / **ACTIVE TIME:** 5 MINUTES / **TOTAL TIME:** 1 HOUR AND 45 MINUTES

4 SATSUMA SWEET POTATOES

¼ CUP SHIO KOJI

SALSA MACHA (SEE PAGE 286), FOR SERVING

1. Preheat the oven to 275°F. Wash the sweet potatoes, pat them dry, and poke a few holes in them with a paring knife.
2. Place the sweet potatoes in a baking dish, pour the shio koji over them, and turn the potatoes so that they are completely covered.
3. Place the sweet potatoes in the oven and roast until they are very tender, about 1½ hours.
4. Remove the sweet potatoes from the oven, slice, and serve with the Salsa Macha.

Fried Brussels Sprouts with Habanero Agave

YIELD: 4 SERVINGS / **ACTIVE TIME:** 30 MINUTES / **TOTAL TIME:** 30 MINUTES

CANOLA OIL, AS NEEDED

3 CUPS TRIMMED AND HALVED BRUSSELS SPROUTS

¼ CUP HABANERO AGAVE (SEE PAGE 436)

SALT AND PEPPER, TO TASTE

SUNFLOWER SEEDS, ROASTED AND SHELLED, FOR GARNISH

QUESO ENCHILADO, SHREDDED, FOR GARNISH

1. Add canola oil to a Dutch oven until it is about 2 inches deep and warm it to 350°F over medium heat.
2. Working in batches so as not to overcrowd the pot, gently slip the Brussels sprouts into the hot oil and fry until they are crispy and golden brown, 2 to 3 minutes. Transfer them to a paper towel–lined plate and let the Brussels sprouts drain.
3. Place the Brussels sprouts in a bowl, add the Habanero Agave, and stir until the Brussels sprouts are coated.
4. Season with salt and pepper, transfer the Brussels sprouts to a serving dish, garnish with sunflower seeds and queso enchilado, and serve.

Masa-Crusted Sardines with Pickled Manzano

SEE PAGE 34

Puritos de Platano Macho Relleno de Frijoles Negros y Mole Negro

YIELD: 4 SERVINGS / **ACTIVE TIME:** 45 MINUTES / **TOTAL TIME:** 1 HOUR AND 45 MINUTES

4 PLANTAINS, RIPE AND MOSTLY BLACK, UNPEELED

12 CUPS CHICKEN STOCK (SEE PAGE 438)

2 BAY LEAVES

2 PASILLA CHILE PEPPERS, STEMMED AND SEEDED

SALT, TO TASTE

4 PIECES OF BANANA LEAVES, CUT INTO 12 X 6–INCH RECTANGLES, RIBS AND SPINES REMOVED, TOASTED

FRIJOLES NEGROS REFRITOS (SEE PAGE 56)

3 TABLESPOONS EXTRA-VIRGIN OLIVE OIL

2 CUPS MOLE NEGRO (SEE PAGE 252), FOR SERVING

1 CUP CRUMBLED QUESO FRESCO (SEE PAGE 287), FOR SERVING

RED ONION, JULIENNED, FOR SERVING

1. Place the plantains, stock, bay leaves, and chiles in a large saucepan and bring to a simmer. Cook for 15 minutes, until the plantains start to open and are very soft.

2. Remove the plantains from the pan and let them cool. When cool enough to handle, remove them from their peels, place them in a bowl, and discard the peels. Mash the plantains until they are smooth and season with salt.

3. Place one-quarter of the plantains in the center of each banana leaf and form each portion into a ¼-inch-thick rectangle. Leave enough room on each side of the mashed plantain so that the banana leaves can be rolled up.

4. Place ¼ cup of the beans in the center of the plantains. Using the banana leaf to guide, roll the plantains over the black beans so that they completely encase the beans. Roll the banana leaf around the filling so that it completely encases the mixture. Twist the ends of the roll in opposite directions until it is very tight and tie each end with kitchen twine. Place the packets in the refrigerator and chill them for 30 minutes.

5. Place the olive oil in a large cast-iron skillet and warm it over medium heat. Add the packets and cook for approximately 1 minute on each side. Remove them from the pan and then remove the banana leaves.

6. Return the puritos to the pan and cook until caramelized on both sides, 3 to 4 minutes.

7. To serve, ladle ¼ cup of the mole onto each plate and top with the purito, either left whole or sliced. Serve with the Queso Fresco and onion.

Camote con Mole Blanco

YIELD: 4 SERVINGS / **ACTIVE TIME:** 45 MINUTES / **TOTAL TIME:** 1 HOUR AND 45 MINUTES

- 4 LARGE SWEET POTATOES
- ¼ CUP EXTRA-VIRGIN OLIVE OIL
- SALT, TO TASTE
- MOLE BLANCO (SEE PAGE 260), WARM
- PURSLANE, RINSED WELL AND STEMMED, FOR GARNISH

1. Preheat the oven to 450°F. Wash the sweet potatoes, pat them dry, and poke a few holes in each one with a paring knife.

2. Place them in a baking dish, drizzle the olive oil over the sweet potatoes, and season with salt. Stir until the potatoes are covered, place them in the oven, and roast until so tender that a knife can easily be pushed into their centers, about 1 hour.

3. Remove the sweet potatoes from the oven and let them cool slightly. Slice the potatoes open once they are cool enough to handle.

4. Ladle about ¼ cup of the mole onto each plate and top with the sweet potatoes. Garnish with some purslane and enjoy.

Huauzontles Relleno de Queso con Chiltomate

YIELD: 4 SERVINGS / **ACTIVE TIME:** 30 MINUTES / **TOTAL TIME:** 50 MINUTES

SALT, TO TASTE

3½ OZ. HUAUZONTLES, STEMMED

1 TABLESPOON KOSHER SALT, PLUS MORE TO TASTE

3½ OZ. OAXACA CHEESE, SHREDDED

¾ CUP CORNSTARCH

3½ CUPS MASA HARINA

⅓ CUP VODKA

¼ TEASPOON BAKING POWDER

¼ TEASPOON BAKING SODA

⅔ CUP TOPO CHICO, PLUS MORE AS NEEDED

¼ CUP EGG WHITES

CANOLA OIL, AS NEEDED

SALSA DE CHILTOMATE (SEE PAGE 258), FOR SERVING

LIME WEDGES, FOR SERVING

1. Prepare an ice bath and bring water to a boil in a medium saucepan. Add salt and the huauzontles and boil for 2 minutes. Remove the greens from the water and plunge them into the ice bath until they are cool.

2. Place the huauzontles in a kitchen towel and gently wring it to remove as much water as possible from the greens.

3. Place the huauzontles, kosher salt, cheese, cornstarch, masa, vodka, baking powder, and baking soda in the work bowl of a stand mixer fitted with the paddle attachment and beat until combined. Slowly add the Topo Chico and beat until the mixture has the consistency of a thick pancake batter. It should not be runny at all. Let the batter rest for 20 minutes.

4. If the batter looks too dry after resting, incorporate more Topo Chico until the consistency is right.

5. Place the egg whites in a separate bowl and whip them until they hold stiff peaks. Add them to the batter and gently fold until incorporated. The mixture should hold its shape when portioned out.

6. Add canola oil to a Dutch oven until it is 2 inches deep and warm it to 350°F over medium heat. Gently drop ¼-cup portions of the batter into the hot oil and fry until the fritters are golden brown and cooked all the way through, 4 to 5 minutes, turning them as necessary. Transfer the cooked fritters to a paper towel–lined plate to drain.

7. Ladle about ¼ cup of salsa onto each plate, top with the fritters, and serve with lime wedges.

Coffee & Ancho Carrots

YIELD: 4 SERVINGS / **ACTIVE TIME:** 45 MINUTES / **TOTAL TIME:** 45 MINUTES

1 BUNCH OF ORGANIC RAINBOW CARROTS, LEAFY GREENS RESERVED FOR GARNISH

2 TABLESPOONS EXTRA-VIRGIN OLIVE OIL

2 TABLESPOONS INSTANT COFFEE

2 TABLESPOONS ANCHO CHILE POWDER

⅛ TEASPOON CORIANDER SEEDS, TOASTED AND GROUND

1 TABLESPOON SUMAC

SALT, TO TASTE

2 SERRANO CHILE PEPPERS

2 TABLESPOONS SOY SAUCE

2 TABLESPOONS FRESH LIME JUICE

1 CUP MAYONNAISE

1. Preheat the oven to 420°F. Place the carrots in a mixing bowl, add the olive oil, and toss to coat.

2. Combine the coffee, ancho chile powder, toasted coriander seeds, and sumac in a small bowl and then sprinkle the mixture over the carrots. Season with salt and toss until the carrots are evenly coated.

3. Place the carrots in a baking dish, place it in the oven, and roast the carrots until they are charred, cooked through, and al dente, 15 to 20 minutes. Remove from the oven and let the carrots cool.

4. Warm a large cast-iron skillet over high heat. Add the serrano peppers and cook until they are charred all over, turning occasionally. Transfer the charred peppers to a bowl and add the soy sauce and lime juice. Let the peppers marinate for 15 minutes.

5. Place the peppers in a bowl and mash them into a paste. Stir it into the mayonnaise, and then incorporate the soy-and-lime mixture a bit at a time until the taste is to your liking.

6. Spread the mayonnaise on a serving plate, arrange the carrots on top, and garnish with the leafy carrot greens.

APPETIZERS, SALADS & SIDES

Coffee & Ancho Carrots
SEE PAGE 41

Tomato Aguachile

YIELD: 4 SERVINGS / **ACTIVE TIME:** 20 MINUTES / **TOTAL TIME:** 12 HOURS

2 LBS. ROMA TOMATOES

1 GUAJILLO CHILE PEPPER, STEMMED AND SEEDED

4 DRIED CHILES DE ÁRBOL

SALT, TO TASTE

1 CUP FRESH LIME JUICE

½ CUP PREPARED MASA (SEE PAGE 65)

EXTRA-VIRGIN OLIVE OIL, AS NEEDED

1 LB. CHERRY TOMATOES, HALVED

1 CUP PEELED AND DICED CUCUMBER

2 CUPS CRUMBLED QUESO FRESCO (SEE PAGE 287)

1 SMALL RED ONION, JULIENNED

1 SERRANO CHILE PEPPER, STEMMED, SEEDED, AND SLICED VERY THIN

1 SMALL BUNCH OF FRESH CILANTRO

1. Place the Roma tomatoes and dried chiles in a blender and pulse until the mixture is a coarse puree. Line a fine-mesh sieve or colander with cheesecloth, place it over a bowl, and pour the puree into the cheesecloth. Let the "tomato water" drip through for a minimum of 8 hours.

2. Season the tomato water with salt, stir in the lime juice, and set it aside. The pulp can be reserved, dehydrated, and turned into a flavorful seasoning powder.

3. Form the masa into small, crouton-sized balls. Add olive oil to a large, deep skillet until it is about 1 inch deep and warm it to 350°F. Working in batches to avoid overcrowding the pan, gently slip the balls of masa into the hot oil and fry until they are very crispy. Transfer the fried masa to a paper towel–lined plate to drain.

4. In a mixing bowl, combine the cherry tomatoes, cucumber, and tomato water and drizzle a bit of olive oil over the mixture.

5. Transfer the mixture to a shallow bowl and top with the Queso Fresco, red onion, serrano pepper, fried masa, and cilantro. Sprinkle a flaky sea salt over the dish, preferably Maldon, and serve.

Betabel with Salsa Macha y Queso Fresco

YIELD: 4 SERVINGS / **ACTIVE TIME:** 15 MINUTES / **TOTAL TIME:** 1 HOUR

1 LB. RED AND GOLDEN BEETS, RINSED WELL AND PATTED DRY

3 TABLESPOONS EXTRA-VIRGIN OLIVE OIL

SALT, TO TASTE

¼ CUP SALSA MACHA (SEE PAGE 286)

2 CUPS CRUMBLED QUESO FRESCO (SEE PAGE 287), FOR GARNISH

2 OZ. SORREL OR OTHER GREENS, FOR GARNISH

1. Preheat the oven to 420°F. If the beets are not similar in size, cut them so that they are. This will help them cook at the same rate. Place them on a large sheet of aluminum foil, drizzle the olive oil over the top, and season with salt.

2. Close the foil up so that it is a packet, with the seam on top. Place the packet on a baking sheet, place it in the oven, and roast until the beets are tender and just cooked through, about 45 minutes. A knife or a cake tester should be able to puncture the beets with minimal effort when they are done.

3. Remove the beets from the oven and let them cool slightly. Peel and dice the beets. To avoid staining your hands when peeling the beets, gloves are recommended.

4. Place the beets in a serving dish, add the Salsa Macha, and toss to combine. Garnish with the Queso Fresco and sorrel and serve.

Verdolagas en Salsa Verde

YIELD: 4 SERVINGS / **ACTIVE TIME:** 30 MINUTES / **TOTAL TIME:** 30 MINUTES

2 TABLESPOONS LARD

1 SMALL WHITE ONION, BRUNOISED

10 GARLIC CLOVES, MINCED

1 LB. PURSLANE, RINSED WELL AND STEMMED

1 CHIPOTLE MORITA CHILE PEPPER, STEMMED, SEEDED, AND MINCED

3 TO 4 FRESH EPAZOTE LEAVES

2 CUPS SALSA CRUDA VERDE (SEE PAGE 284)

SALT, TO TASTE

QUESO FRESCO (SEE PAGE 287), CRUMBLED, FOR SERVING

CORN TORTILLAS (SEE PAGE 65), WARM, FOR SERVING

LIME WEDGES, FOR SERVING

1. Place the lard in a saucepan and warm it over medium heat. Add the onion and cook until it is translucent, about 3 minutes, stirring occasionally.

2. Add the garlic and cook for about 1 minute. Add the purslane and cook for 20 to 30 seconds, stirring to coat. Add the chile, epazote, and salsa verde, reduce the heat, and simmer the mixture for 15 minutes.

3. Season the mixture with salt and serve with Queso Fresco, tortillas, and lime wedges.

Ostiones al Tapesco

YIELD: 4 SERVINGS / **ACTIVE TIME:** 30 MINUTES / **TOTAL TIME:** 45 MINUTES

1 BUNCH OF GREEN ALLSPICE LEAVES

12 OYSTERS, RINSED AND SCRUBBED

1 SMALL BUNCH OF BANANA LEAVES

7 TABLESPOONS EXTRA-VIRGIN OLIVE OIL

7 TABLESPOONS FRESH LIME JUICE

3 SERRANO CHILE PEPPERS, STEMS AND SEEDS REMOVED, MINCED

1 CUP FRESH CILANTRO, CHOPPED

SALTINES, FOR SERVING

1. Prepare a charcoal grill for medium-high heat (about 450°F). When the grill is hot and the coals are glowing and covered with a thin layer of ash, place a grill rack on top of the coals and cover it with the allspice leaves.

2. Place the closed oysters on top of the allspice leaves and cover them with the banana leaves. The leaves will begin to smolder and then catch fire. After 3 to 4 minutes, the oysters will begin to open and absorb the smoke. Using tongs, carefully remove the oysters and arrange them on a plate to serve.

3. Place the olive oil, lime juice, chiles, and cilantro in a bowl and stir until thoroughly combined. Serve this sauce and the saltines alongside the oysters.

Frijol Ayocote with Pasilla Yogurt

YIELD: 8 SERVINGS / **ACTIVE TIME:** 30 MINUTES / **TOTAL TIME:** 24 HOURS

- 1 LB. DRIED RANCHO GORDO AYOCOTE BEANS, SOAKED OVERNIGHT
- 1 TABLESPOON CUMIN SEEDS
- 1 TABLESPOON BLACK PEPPERCORNS
- 2 ALLSPICE BERRIES
- 2 TABLESPOONS EXTRA-VIRGIN OLIVE OIL
- 1 SMALL YELLOW ONION, BRUNOISED
- 10 GARLIC CLOVES
- ¼ CINNAMON STICK, GRATED
- 1 BAY LEAF
- 3 TO 6 FRESH EPAZOTE LEAVES (OPTIONAL)
- CHICKEN OR VEGETABLE STOCK (SEE PAGE 438 OR 439), UNSALTED, AS NEEDED
- 4 PASILLA CHILE PEPPERS, STEMMED AND SEEDED
- 2 CUPS YOGURT
- JUICE OF 1 LIME
- SALT, TO TASTE
- FRESH CILANTRO, CHOPPED, FOR SERVING
- CORN TORTILLAS (SEE PAGE 65), WARM, FOR SERVING
- AVOCADO, DICED, FOR SERVING

1. Discard any floating beans. Drain the beans and remove any small pebbles from them.

2. Place the cumin seeds, peppercorns, and allspice in a dry skillet and toast until fragrant, shaking the pan frequently. Remove the pan from heat.

3. Place the olive oil in a large saucepan and warm it over medium heat. Add the onion and cook until it is translucent, about 3 minutes. Add the garlic, cinnamon, and toasted spices and cook, stirring frequently, for 1 minute. Turn off the heat and add the bay leaf and epazote (if desired).

4. Add the beans and cover by 2 inches with the unsalted stock. Bring to a simmer over medium heat, reduce the heat, and cover the pan. Gently simmer the beans until they are very tender, about 2 hours. A good test for when the beans are done is to remove a spoonful containing five beans and blow on them—if the skin peels back on all of the beans, they are ready.

5. Place the chiles in a dry skillet and toast over medium heat until they are fragrant and pliable. Remove from the pan and let them cool. Using a mortar and pestle or a spice grinder, grind the chiles into a powder.

6. Fold the pasilla powder into the yogurt. Stir in the lime juice and season with salt.

7. Drain the beans and reserve the broth. Ladle the beans into bowls, spoon a bit of the broth over them, and top each portion with a dollop of the pasilla yogurt. Serve with cilantro, tortillas, and diced avocado.

APPETIZERS, SALADS & SIDES

Ostiones al Tapesco
SEE PAGE 48

Quesadillas de Champiñones

YIELD: 6 SERVINGS / **ACTIVE TIME:** 20 MINUTES / **TOTAL TIME:** 45 MINUTES

3 DRIED CHILES DE ÁRBOL, STEMMED AND SEEDED

1 TABLESPOON EXTRA-VIRGIN OLIVE OIL

½ WHITE ONION, SLICED THIN

2 GARLIC CLOVES

2 LARGE TOMATOES, FINELY DICED

6 FRESH EPAZOTE LEAVES

SALT, TO TASTE

1 LB. PREPARED MASA (SEE PAGE 65)

3 CUPS MUSHROOM BARBACOA (SEE PAGE 199)

2 CUPS CRUMBLED QUESO FRESCO (SEE PAGE 287)

2 CUPS SHREDDED OAXACA CHEESE (OPTIONAL)

1. Place the chiles in a bowl of warm water and let them soak for 20 minutes. Drain and chop the chiles.

2. Place the olive oil in a large skillet and warm it over medium heat. Add the onion, garlic, and chiles and cook until the onion has softened, about 5 minutes, stirring frequently.

3. Add the tomatoes and epazote, season the mixture with salt, and cook, stirring occasionally, for another 5 minutes. Remove the pan from heat and set the salsa aside.

4. Working with moist hands, form 4 oz. of the masa into a golf ball–sized sphere. Line a tortilla press with squares of resealable plastic bag. Place the ball on the press and gently press down. Rotate the masa and plastic 180° and press down again. Repeat until you have used all of the masa.

5. Warm a comal or a large cast-iron skillet over medium-high heat. Place a freshly made tortilla on the pan and spoon some of the Mushroom Barbacoa over it. Cover with some of the cheese, place another tortilla on top, and add some cheese on top. Lay another tortilla on top and press down to seal the filling. Cook until the quesadillas are golden brown on both sides and the cheese has melted, about 6 minutes.

6. Repeat until all of the barbacoa has been used and serve with the salsa.

Vuelva a la Vida

YIELD: 4 SERVINGS / **ACTIVE TIME:** 30 MINUTES / **TOTAL TIME:** 30 MINUTES

1 LB. SHRIMP, SHELLED AND DEVEINED, SHELLS RESERVED

1 LEMON, HALVED

¼ CUP KOSHER SALT, PLUS MORE TO TASTE

1 TABLESPOON DRIED MEXICAN OREGANO

2 BAY LEAVES

7 TABLESPOONS FRESH LIME JUICE

1½ TABLESPOONS FRESH LEMON JUICE

5 TABLESPOONS ORANGE JUICE

1 TABLESPOON PREPARED HORSERADISH

14 TABLESPOONS KETCHUP

1¼ TABLESPOONS FISH SAUCE

7 TABLESPOONS VALENTINA MEXICAN HOT SAUCE

7 TABLESPOONS SPICY CLAMATO

2⅔ TABLESPOONS WORCESTERSHIRE SAUCE

1 SMALL RED ONION, JULIENNED

5 GARLIC CLOVES, GRATED

FLESH OF 1 AVOCADO, DICED

2 JALAPEÑO CHILE PEPPERS, STEMMED, SEEDED, AND BRUNOISED

2 ROMA TOMATOES, DICED

FRESH CILANTRO, FOR GARNISH

LIME WEDGES, FOR SERVING

TOSTADAS, FOR SERVING

1. Place water in a medium saucepan, add the shrimp shells, lemon, salt, oregano, and bay leaves, and bring to a boil. Reduce the heat and simmer for 10 minutes.

2. Add the shrimp and turn off the burner. Let the shrimp poach in the hot broth for 1 minute. Remove the shrimp and let it cool.

3. Place the juices, horseradish, ketchup, fish sauce, hot sauce, Clamato, and Worcestershire sauce in a mixing bowl and stir to combine.

4. Add the onion, garlic, avocado, jalapeños, tomatoes, and shrimp and fold to incorporate them. Garnish with cilantro and serve with lime wedges and tostadas.

APPETIZERS, SALADS & SIDES

Vuelva a la Vida
SEE PAGE 53

Frijoles Negros Refritos

YIELD: 6 SERVINGS / **ACTIVE TIME:** 15 MINUTES / **TOTAL TIME:** 15 MINUTES

½ CUP LARD

4 DRIED CHILES DE ÁRBOL, STEMMED AND SEEDED

3 GARLIC CLOVES

4 CUPS COOKED OR CANNED BLACK BEANS

SALT, TO TASTE

LEAVES FROM 3 SPRIGS OF FRESH EPAZOTE

1. Place the lard in a large skillet and warm it over medium heat. Add the chiles and garlic to the pan and cook until fragrant, about 1 minute. Remove them from the pan and set them aside. When cool enough to handle, finely chop the chiles and garlic.

2. Add the black beans and fry for 2 minutes, stirring frequently.

3. Using a fork or wooden spoon, smash the beans to create an uneven mixture of mashed and whole beans. Stir the chiles and garlic back into the pan and season the beans with salt. Top with the epazote and serve.

Frijoles de la Olla

YIELD: 6 SERVINGS / **ACTIVE TIME:** 10 MINUTES / **TOTAL TIME:** 24 HOURS

1 CUP DRIED BLACK BEANS, SOAKED OVERNIGHT AND DRAINED

1 WHITE ONION, QUARTERED

3 GARLIC CLOVES

1 TABLESPOON WHITE VINEGAR

SALT, TO TASTE

5 SPRIGS OF FRESH EPAZOTE

1. Place 8 cups of water in a medium saucepan and bring it to a boil.

2. Add the beans, onion, garlic, and vinegar and cook until the beans are tender, about 1½ hours. To test that the beans are done, remove a spoonful containing five beans from the pan and blow on them—if their skins peel back, they're ready.

3. Season with salt and the epazote and drain, making sure to reserve the broth for another preparation. Serve the beans warm or at room temperature.

Flor de Calabaza con Queso Fresco y Hierbabuena

YIELD: 4 SERVINGS / **ACTIVE TIME:** 20 MINUTES / **TOTAL TIME:** 50 MINUTES

- 10 SQUASH BLOSSOMS, STAMENS REMOVED
- 1 BUNCH OF FRESH HIERBABUENA OR SPEARMINT
- 2 CUPS CRUMBLED QUESO FRESCO (SEE PAGE 287)
- ZEST AND JUICE OF 1 LEMON
- SALT, TO TASTE
- 1 CUP ALL-PURPOSE FLOUR
- 1 TEASPOON BAKING POWDER
- 2 EGG YOLKS
- 1 CUP SELTZER WATER
- 2 CUPS CANOLA OIL
- 2 TABLESPOONS HONEY (OPTIONAL)

1. Place the squash blossoms on a paper towel–lined baking sheet.
2. Finely chop the hierbabuena and combine it with the Queso Fresco. Add the lemon zest and juice, season the mixture with salt, and stir to combine.
3. Stuff the squash blossoms with the mixture, taking care not to tear the flowers.
4. In a small bowl, combine the flour, baking powder, egg yolks, and seltzer water and whisk the mixture until it comes together as a smooth batter. Let the batter rest for 20 minutes.
5. Place the canola oil in a deep skillet and warm to 350°F over medium heat.
6. Fold the tips of the squash blossoms closed and dip them into the batter until completely coated. Gently slip them into the oil and fry until crispy and golden brown all over, about 2 minutes, making sure you only turn the squash blossoms once.
7. Drain the fried squash blossoms on the baking sheet. Season them lightly with salt and, if desired, drizzle honey over them before serving.

Flor de Calabaza con Queso Fresco y Hierbabuena
SEE PAGE 57

Tortitas de Coliflor

YIELD: 4 SERVINGS / **ACTIVE TIME:** 25 MINUTES / **TOTAL TIME:** 45 MINUTES

1 LARGE HEAD OF CAULIFLOWER

SALT, TO TASTE

4 EGG WHITES

4 EGG YOLKS

1 CUP ALL-PURPOSE FLOUR

2 CUPS EXTRA-VIRGIN OLIVE OIL

2 LARGE TOMATOES

2 GARLIC CLOVES

¼ WHITE ONION

1 TEASPOON DRIED MEXICAN OREGANO

1. Bring water to a boil in a medium saucepan and prepare an ice bath.

2. Cut the cauliflower into 3-inch-wide florets. Add these and salt to the water and boil for 5 minutes. Remove the cauliflower from the water and plunge it into the ice bath until it is cool. Drain and place the cauliflower on paper towels to dry.

3. In the work bowl of a stand mixer fitted with the whisk attachment, add the egg whites and whip on high until they hold stiff peaks. Add the egg yolks one at a time, reduce the speed to low, and beat until just incorporated, about 2 minutes. Add 2 tablespoons of the flour and again beat until just incorporated, as you do not want to overwork the batter.

4. Place the olive oil in a large, deep skillet and warm it to 310°F.

5. Bring water to a boil in a medium saucepan. Add the tomatoes, garlic, and onion and cook until tender, about 7 minutes. Drain, place the vegetables in a blender, and puree until smooth. Season the sauce with salt, stir in the oregano, and set it aside.

6. Place the remaining flour in a shallow bowl and dredge the cauliflower in it until coated.

7. Gently slip the cauliflower into the hot oil and fry until it is crispy and golden brown, turning it just once. If necessary, work in batches to avoid overcrowding the pan. Place the cauliflower fritters on a paper towel–lined plate and season them with salt.

8. Serve the sauce alongside the fritters.

Taquitos de Requesón con Rajas

YIELD: 4 SERVINGS / **ACTIVE TIME:** 20 MINUTES / **TOTAL TIME:** 35 MINUTES

2 POBLANO CHILE PEPPERS

2 CUPS REQUESÓN OR FRESH RICOTTA CHEESE

SALT, TO TASTE

8 CORN TORTILLAS (SEE PAGE 65)

¼ CUP EXTRA-VIRGIN OLIVE OIL

GUACAMOLE (SEE PAGE 80), FOR SERVING

SALSA, FOR SERVING

1. Roast the poblano chiles over an open flame, on the grill, or in the oven until they are charred all over. Place the poblanos in a bowl, cover it with plastic wrap, and let them steam for 10 minutes. When cool enough to handle, remove the skins, seeds, and stems from the poblanos and slice the remaining flesh thin.

2. Stir the poblanos into the requesón, season with salt, and set the mixture aside.

3. Place the tortillas in a dry skillet and warm them for 1 minute on each side. Fill the tortillas with the cheese-and-poblano mixture and roll them up tight.

4. Place the olive oil in a large skillet and warm over medium heat. Place the tortillas in the pan, seam side down, and cook for 1 minute before turning them over. Cook the taquitos until brown on all sides and then transfer them to a paper towel–lined plate to drain.

5. Serve the taquitos with Guacamole and salsa.

Taquitos de Papa

YIELD: 4 SERVINGS / **ACTIVE TIME:** 30 MINUTES / **TOTAL TIME:** 45 MINUTES

2 RUSSET POTATOES, PEELED AND QUARTERED

SALT, TO TASTE

2 LARGE TOMATOES, FINELY DICED

½ ONION, FINELY DICED

2 JALAPEÑO CHILE PEPPERS, STEMMED, SEEDED, AND CHOPPED

1 CUP FRESH CILANTRO, CHOPPED

2 CUPS SHREDDED GREEN CABBAGE

2 CUPS CRUMPLED COTIJA CHEESE

12 CORN TORTILLAS (SEE PAGE 65)

1 CUP EXTRA-VIRGIN OLIVE OIL

1. Place the potatoes in a small saucepan and cover with cold water. Bring it to a boil, season the water with salt, and reduce the heat so that the potatoes simmer. Cook until tender, about 18 minutes.

2. Drain the potatoes, place them in a mixing bowl, and mash until smooth. Season with salt, add the remaining ingredients, except for the tortillas and olive oil, and stir to combine.

3. Fill the tortillas with the potato mixture and either roll them up tight or fold them over to form half-moons.

4. Place the olive oil in a large, deep cast-iron skillet and warm it over medium heat. Gently slip the filled tortillas into the hot oil and fry until they are browned and crispy.

5. Place the taquitos on a paper towel–lined plate and let them drain and cool slightly before serving.

Charred Escabeche

YIELD: 6 SERVINGS / **ACTIVE TIME:** 30 MINUTES / **TOTAL TIME:** 24 HOURS

3½ TABLESPOONS WATER

2⅓ TABLESPOONS APPLE CIDER VINEGAR

¼ CUP WHITE VINEGAR

1 TABLESPOON SUGAR

1 TABLESPOON KOSHER SALT

2 SPRIGS OF FRESH THYME

2 GARLIC CLOVES

2 BAY LEAVES

5 OZ. JALAPEÑO CHILE PEPPERS, HALVED

1⅓ LBS. CARROTS, PEELED AND SLICED ON A BIAS

1. Place the water, vinegars, sugar, and salt in a saucepan and bring to a boil, stirring to dissolve the sugar and salt. Pour the mixture into a large, sterilized mason jar and add the thyme, garlic, and bay leaves.

2. Warm a large cast-iron skillet over high heat for 5 minutes.

3. Spray the skillet with nonstick cooking spray and add the jalapeños. Weigh them down with a smaller pan and cook until they are charred, about 5 minutes.

4. Place the jalapeños in the brine, add the carrots to the skillet, and weigh them down with the smaller pan. Cook until the carrots are charred, add them to the brine, and let the mixture cool to room temperature. Cover and refrigerate for at least 1 day before using.

Corn Tortillas

YIELD: 32 TORTILLAS / **ACTIVE TIME:** 30 MINUTES / **TOTAL TIME:** 1 HOUR AND 15 MINUTES

1 LB. MASA HARINA

1½ TABLESPOONS KOSHER SALT

3 CUPS WARM FILTERED WATER, PLUS MORE AS NEEDED

1. In the work bowl of a stand mixer fitted with the paddle attachment, combine the masa harina and salt. With the mixer on low speed, slowly begin to add the water. The mixture should come together as a soft, smooth dough. You want the masa to be moist enough so that when a small ball of it is pressed flat in your hands, the edges do not crack. Also, it should not stick to your hands when you peel it off your palm.

2. Let the masa rest for 10 minutes and check the hydration again. You may need to add more water, depending on environmental conditions. When it is correct, this mixture is the prepared masa called for elsewhere in the book.

3. Warm a cast-iron skillet over high heat. Portion the masa into 1 oz. balls and cover them with a damp linen towel.

4. Line a tortilla press with two 8-inch circles of plastic. You can use a grocery store bag, a resealable bag, or even a standard kitchen trash bag as a source for the plastic. Place a masa ball in the center of one circle and gently push down on it with the palm of one hand to flatten. Place the other plastic circle on top and then close the tortilla press, applying firm, even pressure to flatten the masa into a round tortilla.

5. Open the tortilla press and remove the top layer of plastic. Carefully pick up the tortilla and remove the bottom piece of plastic.

6. Gently lay the tortilla flat in the pan, taking care to not wrinkle it. Cook for 15 to 30 seconds, until the edge begins to lift up slightly. Turn the tortilla over and let it cook for 30 to 45 seconds before turning it over one last time. If the hydration of the masa was correct and the heat is high enough, the tortilla should puff up and inflate. Remove the tortilla from the pan and store in a tortilla warmer lined with a linen towel. Repeat until all of the prepared masa has been made into tortillas.

Corn Tortillas
SEE PAGE 65

Tetelas de Aguacate con Requesón y Nopales

YIELD: 4 SERVINGS / **ACTIVE TIME:** 20 MINUTES / **TOTAL TIME:** 20 MINUTES

½ LB. NOPALES, SPINES REMOVED, CLEANED, AND JULIENNED

SALT, TO TASTE

½ TEASPOON BAKING SODA

1 CUP DISTILLED WHITE VINEGAR

1 TABLESPOON SUGAR

1 TEASPOON DRIED MEXICAN OREGANO

2 GARLIC CLOVES

1 SERRANO CHILE PEPPER, STEMMED, SEEDED, AND SLICED

2 BAY LEAVES

½ LB. PREPARED MASA (SEE PAGE 65)

1 CUP REQUESÓN OR RICOTTA CHEESE

FLESH OF 1 LARGE AVOCADO, SLICED

2 TABLESPOONS LARD

SALSA VERDE TATEMADA (SEE PAGE 262), FOR SERVING

FRESH CILANTRO, CHOPPED, FOR SERVING

1. Place the nopales in a saucepan and cover with water by 2 inches. Season generously with salt, add the baking soda, and bring the water to a simmer. Cook until the cactus is tender, 3 to 5 minutes. Drain, rinse the cactus under cold water, and place it in a mixing bowl.

2. Place the vinegar and sugar in a small saucepan and bring to a boil. Pour the brine over the cactus, add the oregano, garlic, serrano, and bay leaves, and let the mixture cool to room temperature.

3. Divide the masa into 2 oz. balls. Line a tortilla press with plastic, place one of the balls in the press, and place another piece of plastic on top. Apply firm, even pressure and press the masa into a ¼-inch-thick round. Repeat with the remaining balls of masa.

4. Place 2 tablespoons of the cheese in the center of each tortilla along with a couple slices of avocado. Fold one-third of the tortilla over the cheese and avocado. Repeat with two other sides of the tortilla to form a triangle.

5. Place the lard in a comal or large cast-iron skillet and warm it over medium-high heat. Add the tetelas and cook until browned on both sides, about 2 minutes. Serve with salsa and cilantro.

Pork Toro with Salsa Macha

YIELD: 4 SERVINGS / **ACTIVE TIME:** 20 MINUTES / **TOTAL TIME:** 4 HOURS AND 30 MINUTES

1 LB. PORK NECK, CUT INTO ½-INCH-THICK SLICES

4 TEASPOONS THIN SOY SAUCE

2 TABLESPOONS THICK SOY SAUCE

1 TABLESPOON BROWN SUGAR

1 TEASPOON FINE SEA SALT

FRESH CILANTRO, CHOPPED, TO TASTE

3 DRIED CHILES DE ÁRBOL

SALSA MACHA (SEE PAGE 286), FOR SERVING

1. Place all of the ingredients, except for the Salsa Macha, in a mixing bowl and stir until the pork neck is coated. Place the bowl in the refrigerator and let the pork neck marinate for 4 hours.

2. Prepare a gas or charcoal grill for high heat (about 500°F). Place the pork neck on the grill and grill until it is cooked through (the interior is 145°F).

3. Remove the pork neck from the grill and let it rest for 10 minutes before serving with the Salsa Macha.

Queso Fundido

YIELD: 4 SERVINGS / **ACTIVE TIME:** 15 MINUTES / **TOTAL TIME:** 35 MINUTES

1 TABLESPOON EXTRA-VIRGIN OLIVE OIL

½ LB. MEXICAN CHORIZO, CASING REMOVED

¼ WHITE ONION, FINELY DICED

1 CUP GRATED OAXACA CHEESE

½ CUP GRATED MONTEREY JACK CHEESE

FRESH CILANTRO, CHOPPED, FOR GARNISH

CORN TORTILLAS (SEE PAGE 65), WARM, FOR SERVING

1. Preheat the oven to 375°F. Place the olive oil in a medium cast-iron skillet and warm it over medium-low heat. Add the chorizo and cook, breaking it up with a fork, until it is browned and cooked through, 8 to 10 minutes. Transfer the chorizo to a bowl and drain all but 1 tablespoon of fat from the pan.

2. Place the onion in the pan and cook until it is translucent, about 3 minutes, stirring occasionally. Remove the pan from heat.

3. Combine the cheeses and spread half of the mixture over the bottom of the pan. Layer half of the chorizo on top, and then repeat with the remaining cheese and chorizo.

4. Place the skillet in the oven and bake until the cheese is golden brown and bubbling, about 10 minutes. Garnish with cilantro and serve with warm tortillas.

Cured Sardines

YIELD: 4 SERVINGS / **ACTIVE TIME:** 15 MINUTES / **TOTAL TIME:** 24 HOURS

1 LB. FRESH SARDINES

¾ CUP KOSHER SALT

¼ CUP SUGAR

EXTRA-VIRGIN OLIVE OIL, AS NEEDED

TOSTADAS OR SALTINES, FOR SERVING

1. Remove the spines from the sardines and butterfly the sardines. Place them on a Silpat-lined baking sheet, skin side down.

2. Combine the salt and sugar in a mixing bowl and sprinkle some of the mixture over the sardines. Turn the sardines over and sprinkle this side with the salt-and-sugar mixture.

3. Cover the pan with plastic wrap and chill it in the refrigerator for 1 day.

4. Transfer the sardines to a fresh Silpat-lined baking sheet and pat them dry with paper towels. You don't want to rinse the sardines.

5. Place the sardines in a container, cover with olive oil, and store them in the refrigerator until ready to serve. Enjoy with tostadas or saltines.

Koji-Fried Sardines

YIELD: 4 SERVINGS / **TOTAL TIME:** 15 MINUTES / **ACTIVE TIME:** 25 MINUTES

CANOLA OIL, AS NEEDED

2 CUPS PLUS 1½ TABLESPOONS ALL-PURPOSE FLOUR

¾ OZ. KOJI, FINELY GROUND

1 TEASPOON KOSHER SALT

½ TEASPOON BLACK PEPPER

3½ OZ. FRESH SARDINES, CLEANED

1. Add canola oil to a Dutch oven until it is about 2 inches deep and warm it to 350°F.

2. Place the flour, koji, salt, and pepper in a mixing bowl and stir to combine. Dredge the sardines in the mixture, gently slip them into the hot oil, and fry until they are golden brown, about 1 minute.

3. Transfer the sardines to a paper towel–lined plate to drain before serving.

Cured Sardines
SEE PAGE 72

Calabacitas con Elote y Queso Fresco

YIELD: 4 SERVINGS / **ACTIVE TIME:** 15 MINUTES / **TOTAL TIME:** 35 MINUTES

- 2 TABLESPOONS EXTRA-VIRGIN OLIVE OIL
- 3 DRIED CHILES DE ÁRBOL, STEMLESS AND SEEDLESS
- ½ WHITE ONION, DICED
- 3 GARLIC CLOVES, SLICED THIN
- KERNELS FROM 2 EARS OF CORN
- 2 LARGE TOMATOES, SEEDLESS AND DICED
- 4 ZUCCHINI, DICED
- SALT, TO TASTE
- 3 SPRIGS OF FRESH CILANTRO
- 1 CUP CRUMBLED QUESO FRESCO (SEE PAGE 287)

1. Place the olive oil in a skillet and warm it over low heat. Add the chiles and toast lightly until fragrant, taking care not to burn them. Remove the chiles from the pan and set them aside. When cool enough to handle, chop the chiles.
2. Add the onion and garlic to the pan and cook until the onion is translucent, about 3 minutes, stirring frequently.
3. Add the corn and cook for 2 minutes, stirring occasionally. Add the tomatoes and cook until they begin to release their juices.
4. Add the zucchini, season the mixture with salt, and cook until the vegetables are tender, about 10 minutes.
5. Add the cilantro to the pan and cook for 1 minute. Remove the cilantro from the pan, add the chiles, and stir until evenly distributed.
6. To serve, top the salad with the Queso Fresco.

Pickled Pineapple

YIELD: 4 SERVINGS / **ACTIVE TIME:** 40 MINUTES / **TOTAL TIME:** 2 DAYS

- 2 STAR ANISE PODS
- ½ CINNAMON STICK
- 2 DRIED CHILES DE ÁRBOL
- 2¼ CUPS APPLE CIDER VINEGAR
- 7 TABLESPOONS WHITE VINEGAR
- 3 TABLESPOONS SUGAR
- SALT, TO TASTE
- 1 PINEAPPLE, PEELED, CORED, AND SLICED

1. Prepare a gas or charcoal grill for medium heat (about 400°F).
2. Place the star anise, cinnamon stick, and chiles in a saucepan and toast until they are fragrant, about 2 minutes, shaking the pan frequently. Add the vinegars and sugar, generously season with salt, and bring to a boil, stirring to dissolve the sugar.
3. Pour the brine into a sterilized mason jar.
4. Place the pineapple on the grill and grill until it is charred on both sides, about 8 minutes, turning it over halfway through. Add the pineapple to the brine while it is warm and let the mixture cool to room temperature. Cover and refrigerate for 2 days before using.

Pickled Red Onion

YIELD: 2 CUPS / **ACTIVE TIME:** 10 MINUTES / **TOTAL TIME:** 2 HOURS

½ CUP APPLE CIDER VINEGAR

½ CUP WATER

2 TABLESPOONS KOSHER SALT

2 TABLESPOONS SUGAR

1 RED ONION, SLICED THIN

1. Place the vinegar, water, salt, and sugar in a saucepan and bring to a boil, stirring to dissolve the salt and sugar.
2. Place the onion in a bowl, pour the brine over it, and let it cool completely.
3. Transfer the onion and brine to a sterilized mason jar and store in the refrigerator for up to 2 weeks.

Pickled Manzano Peppers

YIELD: 2 CUPS / **ACTIVE TIME:** 5 MINUTES / **TOTAL TIME:** 2 HOURS

4 MANZANO CHILE PEPPERS, STEMMED, SEEDED, AND SLICED THIN

¼ CUP APPLE CIDER VINEGAR

¼ CUP WATER

1 TABLESPOON SUGAR

1 TABLESPOON KOSHER SALT

1. Place the manzano peppers in a small mixing bowl.
2. Place the remaining ingredients in a small saucepan and bring to a boil, stirring to dissolve the sugar.
3. Pour the brine over the peppers and let them cool completely.
4. Place the peppers and brine in a sterilized mason jar and use immediately or store in the refrigerator for up to 1 week.

Calabacitas con Elote y Queso Fresco
SEE PAGE 76

Guacamole

YIELD: 4 SERVINGS / **ACTIVE TIME:** 15 MINUTES / **TOTAL TIME:** 15 MINUTES

1 LARGE TOMATO, FINELY DICED

½ ONION, FINELY DICED

2 SERRANO CHILE PEPPERS, FINELY DICED

1 GARLIC CLOVE, MASHED

4 LARGE AVOCADOS, PITTED AND DICED

6 TABLESPOONS FRESH LIME JUICE

SALT, TO TASTE

½ CUP FRESH CILANTRO, CHOPPED

1. Combine the tomato, onion, and serrano peppers in a small bowl. Place the garlic clove in a medium bowl.

2. Add the avocados to the bowl containing the garlic and stir until the mixture is well combined. Stir in the lime juice and season with salt.

3. Add the tomato mixture and stir until it has been incorporated. Add the cilantro and stir to combine. Taste and adjust the seasoning if necessary.

4. Enjoy with anything you please, at any time of day.

Flour Tortillas

YIELD: 18 TORTILLAS / **ACTIVE TIME:** 45 MINUTES / **TOTAL TIME:** 1 HOUR AND 30 MINUTES

1 LB. ALL-PURPOSE FLOUR, PLUS MORE AS NEEDED

1 TABLESPOON KOSHER SALT

1 TABLESPOON BAKING POWDER

2½ OZ. LARD OR UNSALTED BUTTER, MELTED

8 TO 10 OZ. WARM, FILTERED WATER (105°F)

1. In the work bowl of a stand mixer fitted with the paddle attachment, combine the flour, salt, and baking powder and beat on low speed for 30 seconds.

2. Gradually add the lard and beat until the mixture is a coarse meal.

3. Fit the mixer with the dough hook and set it to low speed. Add the water in a slow stream until the dough begins to come together, 2 to 3 minutes. The dough should begin to pull away from the sides of the mixing bowl, leaving no residue behind. Increase the speed to medium and continue mixing until the dough becomes very soft, shiny, and elastic. Please note that more or less of the water may be required due to environmental conditions and/or variations in the flour.

4. Remove the dough from the work bowl and place it in a mixing bowl. Cover with plastic wrap or a damp kitchen towel and let it rest at room temperature for 30 to 45 minutes.

5. Portion the dough into rounds the size of golf balls, approximately 1½ oz. each. Using the palms of your hands, roll the rounds in a circular motion until they are seamless balls. Place them on a parchment-lined baking sheet and cover with plastic wrap. Let them rest at room temperature for 20 minutes.

6. Working on a very smooth and flour-dusted work surface, roll out the balls of dough until they are between ⅛ and ¼ inch thick and about 8 inches in diameter. Stack the tortillas, separating each one with a piece of parchment paper that has been cut to size.

7. Warm a cast-iron skillet over medium-high heat. Gently place a tortilla in the pan. It should immediately sizzle and start to puff up. Do not puncture it. Cook, turning frequently, for 20 to 30 seconds per side, until the tortilla is lightly golden brown in spots. Place in a linen towel, a tortilla warmer, or a plastic resealable bag so it continues to steam and repeat with the remaining tortillas.

Chulibu'ul

YIELD: 4 SERVINGS / **ACTIVE TIME:** 20 MINUTES / **TOTAL TIME:** 30 MINUTES

- 2 TABLESPOONS LARD
- 3 CUPS CORN KERNELS
- 1 GREEN BELL PEPPER, STEMMED, SEEDED, AND FINELY DICED
- 1 SMALL WHITE ONION, FINELY DICED
- 2 TOMATOES, CHOPPED
- 1 (14 OZ.) CAN OF BLACK-EYED PEAS, DRAINED AND RINSED
- 2 TEASPOONS DRIED MEXICAN OREGANO
- 1 TEASPOON KOSHER SALT
- ½ TEASPOON DRIED SAVORY
- ¼ TEASPOON BLACK PEPPER

1. Place the lard in a large skillet and warm it over medium-high heat. Add the corn and cook until it begins to brown, 3 to 5 minutes, stirring occasionally.
2. Add the bell pepper and onion and cook until they begin to soften, 3 to 5 minutes, stirring occasionally.
3. Add the tomatoes and cook until they collapse, about 7 minutes.
4. Stir in the black-eyed peas, oregano, salt, savory, and black pepper, cook until warmed through, and serve.

Arroz a la Mexicana

YIELD: 4 SERVINGS / **ACTIVE TIME:** 5 MINUTES / **TOTAL TIME:** 35 MINUTES

½ LB. LONG-GRAIN RICE

1 TABLESPOON EXTRA-VIRGIN OLIVE OIL

1 ONION, FINELY DICED

1 GARLIC CLOVE

1 CARROT, PEELED AND FINELY DICED

½ CUP TOMATO PASTE

2¼ CUPS CHICKEN STOCK (SEE PAGE 438)

1 BAY LEAF

1 CUP PEAS (OPTIONAL)

SALT, TO TASTE

1. Preheat the oven to 375°F. Place the rice in a sieve or colander and run it under cold water until the water runs clear. Drain the rice well and set it aside.

2. Place the olive oil in a Dutch oven and warm it over medium heat. Add the onion, garlic, and carrot and cook until the onion is translucent, about 3 minutes, stirring frequently.

3. Add the rice and cook for 2 minutes, stirring continually so that it gets coated by the oil.

4. Add the tomato paste and cook for 1 minute. Add the stock, bring the mixture to a boil, and add the bay leaf.

5. Reduce the heat and add the peas (if desired). Season with salt, cover the pot, and place it in the oven. Bake until the rice is tender, about 20 minutes.

6. Remove the rice from the oven and let it rest for 10 minutes.

7. Uncover the pot. The bay leaf should be on top of the rice. Remove the bay leaf and discard it. Fluff the rice with a fork and serve.

Escabeche

YIELD: 4 CUPS / **ACTIVE TIME:** 10 MINUTES / **TOTAL TIME:** 2 HOURS

3 JALAPEÑO CHILE PEPPERS, STEMMED, SEEDED, AND SLICED

1 CARROT, PEELED AND SLICED

½ WHITE ONION, SLICED THIN

2 GARLIC CLOVES

FLORETS FROM ½ HEAD OF CAULIFLOWER

1 TEASPOON DRIED MARJORAM

1 TEASPOON DRIED MEXICAN OREGANO

1 BAY LEAF

2 TABLESPOONS KOSHER SALT

½ TEASPOON SUGAR

1½ CUPS WHITE VINEGAR

1. Place the jalapeños, carrot, onion, garlic, and cauliflower in a bowl and toss to combine.
2. Place the marjoram, oregano, bay leaf, salt, and sugar in a bowl and stir to combine.
3. Place the spice mixture in a small saucepan along with the vinegar. Bring the mixture to a boil.
4. Pour the hot brine over the vegetables and let it cool completely.
5. Transfer the vegetables and brine to a sterilized mason jar and store it in the refrigerator for up to 1 month.

Sweet Corn & Pepita Guacamole

YIELD: 4 SERVINGS / **ACTIVE TIME:** 15 MINUTES / **TOTAL TIME:** 30 MINUTES

1 EAR OF CORN, HUSK ON

1 OZ. PUMPKIN SEEDS

1 OZ. POMEGRANATE SEEDS

FLESH OF 3 AVOCADOS

½ RED ONION, CHOPPED

½ CUP CHOPPED FRESH CILANTRO

1 TEASPOON FRESH LIME JUICE

SALT AND PEPPER, TO TASTE

1. Prepare a gas or charcoal grill for medium-high heat (about 450°F). Place the corn on the grill and cook until it is charred all over and the kernels have softened enough that there is considerable give in them.

2. Remove the corn from the grill and let it cool. When cool enough to handle, husk the corn and cut off the kernels.

3. Combine the corn, pumpkin seeds, and pomegranate seeds in a small bowl. Place the avocados in a separate bowl and mash until just slightly chunky.

4. Stir in the corn mixture, onion, cilantro, and lime juice, season the mixture with salt and pepper, and work the mixture until the guacamole is the desired texture.

Sweet Corn & Pepita Guacamole
SEE PAGE 87

ENTREES

Birria de Chivo

YIELD: 8 SERVINGS / **ACTIVE TIME:** 4 HOURS AND 35 MINUTES / **TOTAL TIME:** 24 HOURS

5 LBS. GOAT OR LAMB MEAT FROM THE LEG OR SHOULDER

10 GUAJILLO CHILE PEPPERS

1 TEASPOON BLACK PEPPERCORNS

½ CINNAMON STICK

1 TABLESPOON DRIED MEXICAN OREGANO

1 TEASPOON ALLSPICE

½ TEASPOON CUMIN

SALT, TO TASTE

5 GARLIC CLOVES

2 TABLESPOONS WHITE VINEGAR

2 TABLESPOONS EXTRA-VIRGIN OLIVE OIL

1 ONION, FINELY DICED

3 LARGE TOMATOES, DICED

2 BAY LEAVES

CORN TORTILLAS (SEE PAGE 65), WARM, FOR SERVING

FRESH CILANTRO, CHOPPED, FOR SERVING

PICKLED RED ONION (SEE PAGE 77), FOR SERVING

1. Cut the meat into 3-inch cubes and place it in a baking dish.

2. Place the guajillo peppers in a dry skillet and toast over medium heat until they darken and become fragrant and pliable. Submerge them in a bowl of boiling water and let them soak for 15 minutes.

3. Place the peppercorns and cinnamon stick in the skillet and toast until fragrant, about 1 minute, shaking the pan frequently. Combine with the oregano, allspice, and cumin and grind the mixture into a fine powder with a mortar and pestle or a spice grinder.

4. Season the meat with salt and the spice powder. Drain the guajillo peppers and place them in a blender along with the garlic and white vinegar. Puree until smooth and then rub the puree over the meat until it is coated. Let it marinate in the refrigerator overnight.

5. Preheat the oven to 350°F. In a large Dutch oven, warm the olive oil over medium heat, add the onion, and cook, stirring occasionally, until it is translucent, about 3 minutes.

6. Stir in the tomatoes, bay leaves, meat, marinade, and 1 cup of water and bring to a boil. Cover the pot, place it in the oven, and braise until the meat is very tender, about 3 hours. Check the meat every hour to make sure it has enough liquid. You don't want to skim off any of the fat, as this will remove liquid from the pot and flavor from the finished broth.

7. Remove the meat from the pot and shred the pieces that haven't fallen apart. Stir the meat back into the liquid.

8. When serving birria, it is customary to also serve a cup of the strained broth as an appetizer with warm tortillas. The stew can also be served with tortillas, cilantro, and pickled onions.

Chilaquiles Rojos

YIELD: 4 SERVINGS / **ACTIVE TIME:** 30 MINUTES / **TOTAL TIME:** 35 MINUTES

4 LARGE TOMATOES

2 GARLIC CLOVES

½ WHITE ONION, SLICED THIN

2 GUAJILLO CHILE PEPPERS, STEMMED AND SEEDED

2 DRIED CHILES DE ÁRBOL, STEMMED AND SEEDED

2 CUPS CANOLA OIL

1 LB. CORN TORTILLAS (SEE PAGE 65), CUT INTO TRIANGLES

SALT, TO TASTE

2 TABLESPOONS EXTRA-VIRGIN OLIVE OIL

4 LARGE EGGS

2 CUPS QUESO FRESCO (SEE PAGE 287), PLUS MORE FOR SERVING

FRESH CILANTRO, CHOPPED, FOR SERVING

1. Bring water to a boil in a medium saucepan. Add the tomatoes, garlic, and half of the onion and cook, stirring occasionally, until they are tender, about 7 minutes.

2. Place the chiles in a bowl and pour some of the hot water over them. Drain the remaining water, place the vegetables in a blender, and puree until smooth. Leave the puree in the blender. Let the chiles soak for 15 minutes.

3. Place the canola oil in a large, deep skillet and warm it to 350°F. Working in batches to avoid overcrowding the pan, add the tortillas and fry until they are crispy, about 3 minutes. Place the fried tortillas on a paper towel–lined plate and let them drain.

4. Preheat the oven to 350°F. Add the chiles to the puree and blitz until smooth. Season the puree generously with salt and set it aside.

5. Place the olive oil in a large cast-iron skillet and warm it over medium heat. Add the remaining onion and cook until translucent, about 3 minutes, stirring occasionally.

6. Add the sauce and tortillas to the skillet and stir until everything is coated in the sauce. Crack the eggs on top, crumble the Queso Fresco over everything, and place the skillet in the oven.

7. Bake until the eggs are cooked to your liking and the cheese is slightly melted. Remove the chilaquiles from the oven and serve with additional Queso Fresco and cilantro.

Joroches de Chorizo y Frijoles Colados

YIELD: 4 SERVINGS / **ACTIVE TIME:** 30 MINUTES / **TOTAL TIME:** 30 MINUTES

2 LBS. PREPARED MASA (SEE PAGE 65)

3½ TABLESPOONS LARD

2 TEASPOONS KOSHER SALT

½ LB. MEXICAN CHORIZO, COOKED

SOPA DE FRIJOL COLADO (SEE PAGE 235)

4 CUPS CHICKEN STOCK (SEE PAGE 438)

COTIJA CHEESE, FOR SERVING

X'NIPEK (SEE PAGE 268), FOR SERVING

FRESH CILANTRO, CHOPPED, FOR SERVING

1. Place the masa, lard, and salt in a mixing bowl and work the mixture until it is homogeneous and thoroughly kneaded.

2. Divide the masa into 1½ oz. balls. Place them on a baking sheet lined with parchment paper.

3. Using a finger, press a hole into the center of each masa ball. Place some of the chorizo in the indentation and then form the dough over it. Cover the joroches with plastic wrap.

4. Place the soup and stock in a saucepan and bring to a simmer.

5. Add the joroches and cook until they are firm and set, 15 to 20 minutes. Remove the joroches from the pot and cook the soup until it has reduced slightly and thickened.

6. Divide the joroches among the serving bowls, ladle the soup over the top, and serve with cotija, X'nipek, and cilantro.

Chilibul

YIELD: 4 SERVINGS / **ACTIVE TIME:** 30 MINUTES / **TOTAL TIME:** 1 HOUR AND 30 MINUTES

- 2 LBS. SKIRT STEAK, CHUCK ROAST, OR BRISKET
- 1 WHITE ONION, QUARTERED
- 1 HEAD OF GARLIC, HALVED AT ITS EQUATOR
- 2 BAY LEAVES
- 1 TEASPOON DRIED MARJORAM
- 1 TEASPOON DRIED MEXICAN OREGANO
- 1 TEASPOON DRIED THYME
- 2 CHIPOTLE CHILE PEPPERS, STEMMED AND SEEDED
- SALT, TO TASTE
- 1 LB. COOKED OR CANNED BLACK BEANS, MASHED
- ½ LB. CHIPOTLES EN ADOBO, PUREED
- CORN TORTILLAS (SEE PAGE 65), WARM, FOR SERVING
- SALSA DE CHILTOMATE (SEE PAGE 258), FOR SERVING
- ESCABECHE (SEE PAGE 86), FOR SERVING

1. Place the steak in a large saucepan with the onion, garlic, bay leaves, marjoram, oregano, thyme, and chipotles. Season with salt, cover the steak with water by 2 inches, and bring to a gentle simmer.

2. Cover the pan and simmer until the steak is tender and easy to shred with a fork, 1 to 2 hours. Let the steak cool in the liquid.

3. Remove the steak from the cooking liquid and, using two forks, shred it.

4. Place the steak, beans, and pureed chipotles in a saucepan, bring to a gentle simmer, and cook until everything is warmed through, 15 to 20 minutes.

5. Season with salt and serve with tortillas, the salsa, and Escabeche.

Cochinita Pibil

YIELD: 4 TO 6 SERVINGS / **ACTIVE TIME:** 30 MINUTES / **TOTAL TIME:** 3 HOURS

5 TO 7 LBS. PORK SHOULDER, CUBED

SALT, TO TASTE

1¾ LBS. RECADO ROJO (SEE PAGE 272)

1 PACKAGE OF BANANA LEAVES

1 LARGE WHITE ONION, JULIENNED

LIME WEDGES, FOR SERVING

CORN TORTILLAS (SEE PAGE 65), WARM, FOR SERVING

X'NIPEK (SEE PAGE 268), FOR SERVING

FRESH CILANTRO, CHOPPED, FOR SERVING

SALSA DE CHILTOMATE (SEE PAGE 258), FOR SERVING

1. Place the pork shoulder in a large mixing bowl and season generously with salt. Pour the Recado Rojo over the pork and rub it all over. Place the pork in the refrigerator and let it marinate for 1 to 2 hours. If time allows, marinate for up to 24.

2. Preheat the oven to 300°F. Remove the spines from the banana leaves and gently toast the leaves over an open flame until they are pliable and bright green. Line a Dutch oven with the banana leaves, place the pork on top, and cover the pork with the onion. Fold the banana leaves over the pork to create a packet. Cover the Dutch oven, place it in the oven, and roast until the pork is fork-tender, 2 to 3 hours.

3. Remove the lid from the Dutch oven and open up the banana leaf packet. Raise the oven's temperature to 400°F and roast for another 20 minutes. Serve with lime wedges, tortillas, X'nipek, cilantro, and Salsa de Chiltomate.

Cochinita Pibil
SEE PAGE 99

Milanesa de Res y Mole Blanco

YIELD: 4 SERVINGS / **ACTIVE TIME:** 30 MINUTES / **TOTAL TIME:** 1 HOUR

3 EGGS

1 TABLESPOON BLACK PEPPER

2 GARLIC CLOVES, GRATED

SALT, TO TASTE

3 CUPS BREAD CRUMBS

2 CUPS ALL-PURPOSE FLOUR

2 TO 3 LBS. TOP ROUND STEAK, SLICED INTO ¼-INCH-WIDE PIECES

CANOLA OIL, AS NEEDED

MOLE BLANCO (SEE PAGE 260), WARMED

LIME WEDGES, FOR SERVING

SALPICON DE RABANO Y CHILE HABANERO (SEE PAGE 264), FOR SERVING

1. Place the eggs, pepper, and garlic in a mixing bowl, season with salt, and whisk until combined.

2. Place the bread crumbs in a shallow bowl and season with salt. Place the flour in a separate shallow bowl. Dredge the steak in the flour, followed by the egg mixture, and finally the bread crumbs. Repeat until the steak is fully coated and place it on a parchment-lined baking sheet.

3. Add canola oil to a Dutch oven until it is about 1 inch deep and warm it to 350°F over medium heat. Working in batches to avoid overcrowding the pot, gently slip the steak into the hot oil and fry, turning once, until it is cooked through and golden brown, about 6 minutes. Transfer the cooked steak to a paper towel-lined plate to drain.

4. To serve, spread about ½ cup of the Mole Blanco on each plate, top with the steak, and serve with lime wedges and salpicon.

Costilla Corta de Res con Chile Colorado

YIELD: 4 SERVINGS / **ACTIVE TIME:** 30 MINUTES / **TOTAL TIME:** 2 HOURS

4 TO 6 LBS. BONE-IN SHORT RIBS

SALT AND PEPPER, TO TASTE

2 TABLESPOONS EXTRA-VIRGIN OLIVE OIL

1 WHITE ONION, JULIENNED

8 CUPS BEEF STOCK (SEE PAGE 440)

8 CUPS CHILE COLORADO (SEE PAGE 256)

FLOUR TORTILLAS (SEE PAGE 82), WARM, FOR SERVING

LIME WEDGES, FOR SERVING

ESCABECHE (SEE PAGE 86), FOR SERVING

1. Preheat the oven to 300°F. Season the short ribs generously with salt and pepper.

2. Place the olive oil in a Dutch oven and warm it over medium heat. Working in batches to avoid overcrowding the pan, place the short ribs in the skillet and cook, turning occasionally, until they are browned on all sides. Remove the seared short ribs from the pot and set them aside.

3. Add the onion to the pot and cook, stirring frequently, until it is translucent, about 3 minutes. Stir in the stock and half of the Chile Colorado and bring to a simmer. Return the short ribs to the pot, return to a simmer, and cover the pot.

4. Place the Dutch oven in the oven and braise until the short ribs are tender and falling off the bone, about 1½ hours.

5. Remove the short ribs from the pot. Add the remaining chile to the Dutch oven and cook the liquid over high heat until it has reduced by half, skimming off any fat as desired.

6. Return the short ribs to the sauce and serve with tortillas, lime wedges, and Escabeche.

Lomo y Manchamanteles

YIELD: 4 SERVINGS / **ACTIVE TIME:** 30 MINUTES / **TOTAL TIME:** 24 HOURS

SALT, AS NEEDED

1 LB. PORK TENDERLOIN

2 PEACHES, PITTED AND QUARTERED

HONEY, AS NEEDED

2 CUPS MOLE MANCHAMANTELES (SEE PAGE 257), WARM

CORN TORTILLAS (SEE PAGE 65), WARM, FOR SERVING

1. Fill a large saucepan with cold water and add 1¾ oz. of salt for every liter of water. Place the pork in the brine and let it sit in the refrigerator for 24 hours.

2. Remove the pork from the brine, pat it dry, and let it come to room temperature. Prepare a gas or charcoal grill for medium-high heat (about 450°F).

3. Place the tenderloin on the grill and grill until the interior is 145°F, 3 to 4 minutes per side. Remove from the grill and let it rest for about 10 minutes before slicing.

4. Brush the cut sides of the peaches with honey and season them with salt. Grill until deeply charred, but not falling apart, about 6 minutes.

5. Spread ½ cup of the mole on each plate, top with slices of pork and the grilled peaches, and serve with tortillas.

Cecina de Cerdo

YIELD: 6 TO 8 SERVINGS / **ACTIVE TIME:** 30 MINUTES / **TOTAL TIME:** 2 HOURS

7 OZ. GUAJILLO CHILE PEPPERS, STEMMED AND SEEDED

1 TEASPOON CUMIN SEEDS

1 TEASPOON CORIANDER SEEDS

1 BAY LEAF

2 TABLESPOONS EXTRA-VIRGIN OLIVE OIL, PLUS MORE AS NEEDED

4 GARLIC CLOVES, MINCED

10 DRIED CHILES DE ÁRBOL, STEMMED AND SEEDED

7 TABLESPOONS APPLE CIDER OR CHAMPAGNE VINEGAR

SALT, TO TASTE

2 LBS. PORK TENDERLOIN, SLICED AND POUNDED ¼ INCH THICK

CORN TORTILLAS (SEE PAGE 65), WARM, FOR SERVING

LIME WEDGES, FOR SERVING

1. Place the guajillo peppers in a dry skillet and toast over medium heat until they darken and become fragrant and pliable. Submerge them in a bowl of hot water and let them soak for 30 minutes.

2. Place the seeds and bay leaf in the skillet and toast until fragrant, shaking the pan frequently. Grind the mixture into a powder using a mortar and pestle or a spice grinder.

3. Place the olive oil in a Dutch oven and warm it over medium heat. Add the garlic, cook until fragrant, and then add the chiles de árbol. Fry for 30 seconds and then remove the pan from heat.

4. Drain the guajillo peppers and reserve the soaking liquid. Place the guajillo peppers, chiles de árbol, spice powder, and garlic in a blender and puree until smooth, adding the vinegar and soaking liquid as needed to attain a "nappe" consistency, meaning smooth and thick enough to evenly coat the pork. Season the puree with salt.

5. Place the pork tenderloin in a baking dish and pour the puree over it. Stir until coated and let it marinate in the refrigerator for at least 30 minutes. If time allows, marinate the pork for up to 24 hours.

6. Prepare a charcoal or gas grill for medium-high heat (about 450°F). Clean the grates and lightly brush them with olive oil. Place the tenderloin on the grill and grill until the interior is 145°F, 2 to 3 minutes per side.

7. Remove the tenderloin from the grill and serve with tortillas and lime wedges.

Cecina de Cerdo

SEE PAGE 105

Michoacán-Style Carnitas

YIELD: 6 TO 8 SERVINGS / **ACTIVE TIME:** 30 MINUTES / **TOTAL TIME:** 2 HOURS

1 LB. LARD

5 BAY LEAVES

5 AVOCADO LEAVES

3 CUPS MODELO NEGRA BEER

2 YELLOW ONIONS, HALVED AND CHARRED

2 HEADS OF GARLIC, HALVED AT THEIR EQUATORS AND CHARRED

5 TO 7 LBS. PORK SHOULDER, CUBED

SALT, TO TASTE

1 CUP FRESH LIME JUICE

1 CUP ORANGE JUICE

1 WHITE ONION, BRUNOISED, FOR SERVING

CORN TORTILLAS (SEE PAGE 65), WARM, FOR SERVING

LIME WEDGES, FOR SERVING

FRESH CILANTRO, CHOPPED, FOR SERVING

SALSA VERDE TATEMADA (SEE PAGE 262), FOR SERVING

1. Place the lard, bay leaves, and avocado leaves in a Dutch oven and warm the mixture over medium-high heat. When the lard comes to a simmer, stir in the beer, charred onions, and garlic.

2. Warm a large skillet over medium heat and season the pork shoulder liberally with salt. Working in batches to avoid overcrowding the pan, add the pork shoulder to the skillet and sear until it is browned all over, turning it as needed.

3. Add the seared pork to the lard and simmer until it begins to get tender, about 2 hours.

4. Stir in the lime juice and orange juice and continue to cook the pork over low heat until the pork is extremely tender, another 30 to 45 minutes.

5. Remove the pork from the Dutch oven and chop it into bite-size pieces for tacos. Serve with the white onion, tortillas, lime wedges, cilantro, and salsa verde.

Dzik de Res

YIELD: 6 SERVINGS / **ACTIVE TIME:** 30 MINUTES / **TOTAL TIME:** 1 HOUR

2 LBS. BEEF BRISKET, TRIMMED AND QUARTERED

SALT, TO TASTE

8 CUPS BEEF STOCK (SEE PAGE 440)

3 GARLIC CLOVES

2 BAY LEAVES

4 SPRIGS OF FRESH THYME

½ ONION, CHARRED

½ CINNAMON STICK

1 TEASPOON DRIED MEXICAN OREGANO

1 TEASPOON CHOPPED FRESH MARJORAM

1 CUP FRESH LIME JUICE

1 CUP ORANGE JUICE

3 OZ. RADISHES, SLICED THIN

3 TO 4 HABANERO CHILE PEPPERS, STEMMED, SEEDED, AND MINCED

1 LARGE RED ONION, JULIENNED

2 AVOCADOS, PITTED AND SLICED

½ LB. ROMA TOMATOES, SEEDED AND BRUNOISED

1 SMALL BUNCH OF FRESH CILANTRO, CHOPPED, FOR SERVING

CORN TORTILLAS (SEE PAGE 65), WARM, FOR SERVING

LIME WEDGES, FOR SERVING

1. Season the brisket with salt and place it in a large saucepan with the stock. Bring to a simmer over medium heat.

2. Using a piece of cheesecloth, create a sachet with the garlic, bay leaves, thyme, onion, cinnamon stick, oregano, and marjoram. Secure the sachet with kitchen twine and add it to the saucepan.

3. Simmer the brisket until it is very tender, 1 to 2 hours. If time allows, let the meat cool in the broth.

4. Strain the liquid and reserve for another use. Shred the brisket into thin strands, place them in a mixing bowl, add the lime juice and orange juice, and stir to combine. Season with salt and then fold in the radishes, habaneros, red onion, avocados, and tomatoes.

5. Serve with cilantro, tortillas, and lime wedges.

Beef Cheeks with Salsa Verde

YIELD: 4 SERVINGS / **ACTIVE TIME:** 15 MINUTES / **TOTAL TIME:** 2 HOURS AND 30 MINUTES

2 LBS. BEEF CHEEKS

1 WHITE ONION, HALVED

3 GARLIC CLOVES, CHOPPED

6 DRIED CHILES DE ÁRBOL, STEMMED AND SEEDED

4 GUAJILLO CHILE PEPPERS, STEMMED AND SEEDED

SALT, TO TASTE

1 CINNAMON STICK

2 CUPS SALSA CRUDA VERDE (SEE PAGE 284)

CORN TORTILLAS (SEE PAGE 65), WARM, FOR SERVING

FRESH CILANTRO, CHOPPED, FOR SERVING

LIME WEDGES, FOR SERVING

1. Fill a large saucepan with water and add the beef cheeks, onion, garlic, and dried chiles.

2. Season the water very generously with salt, add the cinnamon stick, and bring to a boil. Reduce the heat to low and simmer the beef cheeks until they are very tender, about 2 hours.

3. Remove the beef cheeks and reserve 1 cup of the cooking liquid. Chop the beef cheeks into ½-inch cubes and stir them into the salsa.

4. Stir in the reserved cooking liquid, taste, and adjust the seasoning if necessary. Serve with warm tortillas, cilantro, and lime wedges.

Higados en Salsa Chipotle de Adobo

YIELD: 4 SERVINGS / **ACTIVE TIME:** 30 MINUTES / **TOTAL TIME:** 45 MINUTES

1 LB. CHICKEN LIVERS

3 TABLESPOONS ALL-PURPOSE FLOUR

1 TABLESPOON GARLIC POWDER

1 TABLESPOON CHILI POWDER

1 TABLESPOON CUMIN

SALT AND PEPPER, TO TASTE

1 TABLESPOON LARD

½ WHITE ONION, DICED

2 GARLIC CLOVES, DICED

2 TABLESPOONS CHOPPED CHIPOTLES EN ADOBO

½ CUP CHICKEN STOCK (SEE PAGE 438)

FRESH CILANTRO, CHOPPED, FOR GARNISH

1. Place the chicken livers, flour, garlic powder, chili powder, cumin, salt, and pepper in a mixing bowl and stir until the chicken livers are coated.

2. Place the lard in a skillet and warm it over medium heat. Shake the chicken livers to remove any excess flour, add them to the skillet, and briefly fry for 10 seconds on each side. Add the onion and garlic and cook until the onion is translucent, about 2 minutes.

3. Stir in the chipotles and stock, reduce the heat to medium-low, and let the mixture simmer until the sauce has emulsified and the chicken livers are cooked through, 5 to 10 minutes. Serve immediately and garnish each portion with cilantro.

Higados en Salsa Chipotle de Adobo
SEE PAGE 113

Lengua en Salsa Roja

YIELD: 6 SERVINGS / **ACTIVE TIME:** 20 MINUTES / **TOTAL TIME:** 4 HOURS

3 TO 4 LBS. OX OR BEEF TONGUE

SALT, TO TASTE

1 WHITE ONION

6 GARLIC CLOVES, CHOPPED

1 CINNAMON STICK

6 WHOLE CLOVES

5 LARGE TOMATOES

4 JALAPEÑO CHILE PEPPERS

1 TABLESPOON EXTRA-VIRGIN OLIVE OIL

CORN TORTILLAS (SEE PAGE 65), WARM, FOR SERVING

FRESH CILANTRO, CHOPPED, FOR SERVING

RADISHES, TRIMMED AND SLICED THIN, FOR SERVING

1. Place the tongue in a large pot and cover it with cold water. Season generously with salt, stir in half of the onion and garlic, the cinnamon stick, and cloves and bring to a boil.

2. Reduce the heat to low and simmer until the tongue is very tender, about 3 hours. If necessary, weigh the tongue down with a heavy plate as it simmers to ensure that it remains submerged.

3. While the tongue is simmering, warm a dry skillet over medium heat. Add the tomatoes, jalapeños, and remaining onion and garlic and cook until the mixture is charred (you can also roast these in the oven if that's your preferred method). Transfer the charred vegetables to a blender and puree until smooth.

4. When the beef tongue is tender, remove it from the pan and reserve 2 cups of the cooking liquid. Remove the outer connective membrane from the tongue while it is still warm and then slice the tongue into thin slices or cubes.

5. Place the olive oil in a large skillet and warm over high heat. Add the pureed salsa, season it with salt, and cook for 3 minutes.

6. Stir in the tongue and cook for 5 minutes. Serve with tortillas, cilantro, and radishes.

Tostadas de Cueritos

YIELD: 6 SERVINGS / **ACTIVE TIME:** 15 MINUTES / **TOTAL TIME:** 1 HOUR AND 15 MINUTES

2 TABLESPOONS KOSHER SALT

3 DRIED CHILES DE ÁRBOL

1 CUP WHITE VINEGAR

½ WHITE ONION, SLICED THIN

1 TEASPOON DRIED MEXICAN OREGANO

1 LB. SKIN FROM PORK BELLY, CUT INTO ¼-INCH-WIDE STRIPS

CANOLA OIL, AS NEEDED

CORN TORTILLAS (SEE PAGE 65)

1 CUP FRIJOLES NEGROS REFRITOS (SEE PAGE 56), WARM

1 CUP ESCABECHE (SEE PAGE 86)

½ CUP SHREDDED LETTUCE

1 CUP COTIJA CHEESE (OPTIONAL)

1. Bring a large pot of water to a boil. Add the salt, chiles, vinegar, onion, and oregano, reduce the heat so that the liquid simmers, and add the pork skin. Cook for 30 minutes.

2. Turn off the heat and let the pork skin sit in the pickling liquid for another 30 minutes.

3. The pork skin will have expanded and absorbed some of the liquid. Transfer the skin and remaining pickling liquid to a sterilized mason jar and store it in the refrigerator for up to 2 weeks.

4. Add canola oil to a Dutch oven until it is about 1 inch deep and warm it to 350°F. Add the tortillas, taking care not to crowd the pot, and fry until crispy, about 2 minutes. Transfer the tostadas to a paper towel-lined plate to cool.

5. To assemble the tostadas, spread some of the beans on the tostadas and top with the pickled pork skin, Escabeche, lettuce, and, if desired, cotija.

Carne Asada

YIELD: 4 SERVINGS / **ACTIVE TIME:** 30 MINUTES / **TOTAL TIME:** 2 HOURS AND 30 MINUTES

1 JALAPEÑO CHILE PEPPER, STEMMED, SEEDED, AND MINCED

3 GARLIC CLOVES, MINCED

½ CUP CHOPPED FRESH CILANTRO

¼ CUP AVOCADO OIL

JUICE OF 1 ORANGE

2 TABLESPOONS APPLE CIDER VINEGAR

2 TEASPOONS CAYENNE PEPPER

1 TEASPOON ANCHO CHILE POWDER

1 TEASPOON GARLIC POWDER

1 TEASPOON PAPRIKA

1 TEASPOON KOSHER SALT

1 TEASPOON CUMIN

1 TEASPOON DRIED OREGANO

¼ TEASPOON BLACK PEPPER

2 LBS. FLANK STEAK, TRIMMED

CORN TORTILLAS (SEE PAGE 65), FOR SERVING

1. Place all of the ingredients, except for the steak and tortillas, in a large resealable plastic bag and stir to combine. Add the steak, place the bag in the refrigerator, and let the steak marinate for 2 hours.

2. Remove the steak from the marinade, pat it dry, and let it rest at room temperature.

3. Warm a large cast-iron skillet over high heat. Add the steak and cook until it is medium-rare (the interior registers 130°F) and the exterior is nicely seared, 4 to 6 minutes, turning it over just once.

4. Remove the steak from the pan and let it rest for 2 minutes before slicing it thin against the grain and serving it with tortillas.

Chicharron en Salsa Roja

YIELD: 6 SERVINGS / **ACTIVE TIME:** 25 MINUTES / **TOTAL TIME:** 1 HOUR AND 45 MINUTES

1 LB. PORK BELLY, CUT INTO 1-INCH-WIDE AND 6-INCH-LONG STRIPS

1½ TABLESPOONS KOSHER SALT

4 CUPS LARD OR CANOLA OIL

4 LARGE TOMATOES

3 SERRANO CHILE PEPPERS

3 GARLIC CLOVES

CORN TORTILLAS (SEE PAGE 65), WARM, FOR SERVING

1. Place a wire rack in a rimmed baking sheet. Season the pork belly with the salt.

2. Place the lard in a Dutch oven, making sure it doesn't reach more than halfway up the side of the pot, and warm it over medium-high heat. Add the pork belly and cook until it is golden brown and very crispy, about 1 hour.

3. Place the pork belly on the wire rack and let it drain. When the pork is cool enough to handle, chop it into ½-inch cubes.

4. Fill a medium saucepan with water and bring to a boil. Add the tomatoes, serrano peppers, and garlic and cook until they are tender, about 10 minutes. Drain, transfer the vegetables to a blender, and puree until smooth.

5. Return the puree to the saucepan, add the pork belly, and simmer for about 20 minutes, so that the chicharron absorbs some of the sauce. Serve with tortillas.

Costillitas de Puerco en Chile Rojo

YIELD: 6 SERVINGS / **ACTIVE TIME:** 25 MINUTES / **TOTAL TIME:** 1 HOUR AND 25 MINUTES

SALT, TO TASTE

4 LBS. PORK RIBS, CUT INTO 3-INCH-WIDE PIECES

1 WHITE ONION

4 GARLIC CLOVES

2 BAY LEAVES

4 GUAJILLO CHILE PEPPERS, STEMMED AND SEEDED

2 PASILLA CHILE PEPPERS, STEMMED AND SEEDED

4 CHIPOTLE MORITA CHILE PEPPERS, STEMMED AND SEEDED

2 TABLESPOONS CUMIN SEEDS

1 TABLESPOON DRIED THYME

½ CUP LARD OR EXTRA-VIRGIN OLIVE OIL

CORN TORTILLAS (SEE PAGE 65), WARM, FOR SERVING (OPTIONAL)

WHITE RICE, COOKED, FOR SERVING (OPTIONAL)

FRIJOLES DE LA OLLA (SEE PAGE 56), FOR SERVING (OPTIONAL)

1. Fill a large saucepan with water, season it generously with salt, add the ribs, onion, garlic, and bay leaves, and bring the water to a boil.

2. Reduce the heat to medium and cook until the ribs are tender but not falling apart, about 1 hour.

3. Place the chile peppers in a dry skillet and toast over medium heat until they darken and become fragrant and pliable. Submerge them in a bowl of hot water and let them sit for 20 minutes.

4. Place the cumin seeds in the dry skillet and toast until fragrant, about 1 minute. Transfer them to a small dish.

5. Drain the chiles, place them in a blender, and add the thyme, toasted cumin seeds, onion, garlic, and 2 cups of the cooking liquid. Puree until smooth, taste the puree, and season with salt.

6. When the pork is tender but still intact, remove the ribs and drain them on paper towels.

7. Place the lard in a deep skillet and warm over medium heat. Add the ribs and sear, turning occasionally, until they are browned all over.

8. Drain any excess fat from the pan, strain the puree over the ribs, and cook over low heat for 10 minutes. Serve with warm tortillas or rice and beans.

Costillitas de Puerco en Chile Rojo
SEE PAGE 121

Pierna de Puerco

YIELD: 6 SERVINGS / **ACTIVE TIME:** 30 MINUTES / **TOTAL TIME:** 2 HOURS AND 30 MINUTES

2 ANCHO CHILE PEPPERS, STEMMED AND SEEDED

1 DRIED CASCABEL CHILE PEPPER, STEMMED AND SEEDED

1 CHIPOTLE MORITA CHILE PEPPER, STEMMED AND SEEDED

1 GUAJILLO CHILE PEPPER, STEMMED AND SEEDED

½ TEASPOON BLACK PEPPERCORNS

1½ TEASPOONS CORIANDER SEEDS

1 TEASPOON CUMIN SEEDS

½ TEASPOON CINNAMON

½ TEASPOON GROUND CLOVES

8 GARLIC CLOVES

½ CUP WHITE VINEGAR

1 CUP MEZCAL

SALT, TO TASTE

8 LBS. PORK SHOULDER

½ WHITE ONION, CHOPPED

4 BAY LEAVES

1 TABLESPOON ALL-PURPOSE FLOUR

WHITE RICE, COOKED, FOR SERVING

1. Place the chiles in a bowl of hot water and let them sit for 20 minutes.

2. Place the black peppercorns, coriander, and cumin in a dry skillet and toast until they are fragrant, shaking the pan frequently.

3. Drain the chiles and place them in a blender along with the toasted spices, cinnamon, cloves, garlic, vinegar, and mezcal. Puree until smooth and season the puree generously with salt.

4. Place the pork shoulder in a large baking dish, rub the puree over it, and let it marinate in the refrigerator for 1 hour.

5. Place the pork shoulder and marinade in a large saucepan, add water until the pork is completely covered, and add the onion and bay leaves. Bring the water to a boil, reduce the heat so that the water simmers, and cook the pork until it is fork-tender, about 1 hour.

6. Stir in the flour and cook until the sauce has thickened slightly. Taste, adjust the seasoning as needed, and serve with white rice.

Picadillo de Res

YIELD: 4 SERVINGS / **ACTIVE TIME:** 10 MINUTES / **TOTAL TIME:** 35 MINUTES

2 TABLESPOONS EXTRA-VIRGIN OLIVE OIL

2 LBS. GROUND BEEF

SALT, TO TASTE

1 TEASPOON CUMIN

1½ TEASPOONS DRIED MEXICAN OREGANO

1½ TEASPOONS CHILI POWDER

1 TABLESPOON TOMATO PASTE

1 ONION, FINELY DICED

2 SERRANO CHILE PEPPERS, STEMMED, SEEDED, AND CHOPPED

2 BAY LEAVES

1 LB. YUKON GOLD POTATOES, PEELED AND DICED

½ LB. CARROTS, PEELED AND FINELY DICED

3 LARGE TOMATOES, FINELY DICED

½ CUP PEAS (OPTIONAL)

FRESH CILANTRO, CHOPPED, FOR SERVING

1 CUP SOUR CREAM, FOR SERVING

1. Place the olive oil in a large skillet and warm it over medium heat. Add the ground beef, season it with salt, and cook, breaking the meat up with a wooden spoon, until it has browned, about 6 minutes.

2. Stir in the cumin, oregano, and chili powder, cook for 1 minute, and then stir in the tomato paste, onion, and peppers. Cook until the onion is tender, about 5 minutes.

3. Add the bay leaves, potatoes, carrots, and tomatoes and cook until the potatoes are tender and the flavors have developed to your liking, about 20 minutes. If using peas in the dish, add them during the last 5 minutes of cooking the potatoes.

4. Serve with cilantro and sour cream.

Puerco en Pipian Verde

YIELD: 6 SERVINGS / **ACTIVE TIME:** 35 MINUTES / **TOTAL TIME:** 1 HOUR AND 45 MINUTES

¼ CUP EXTRA-VIRGIN OLIVE OIL

½ CUP RAW PEANUTS

½ CUP RAW ALMONDS

1 LB. GREEN PUMPKIN SEEDS

2 LBS. PORK SHOULDER, CUT INTO 3-INCH CUBES

1 WHITE ONION, QUARTERED

6 GARLIC CLOVES

SALT, TO TASTE

1 LB. TOMATILLOS, HUSKED, RINSED, AND QUARTERED

3 SERRANO CHILE PEPPERS, STEMMED, SEEDED, AND FINELY DICED

1 JALAPEÑO CHILE PEPPER, STEMMED, SEEDED, AND FINELY DICED

1 PASILLA CHILE PEPPER, STEMMED, SEEDED, AND CHOPPED

1 CUP PACKED FRESH SPINACH

½ BUNCH OF FRESH CILANTRO, CHOPPED

1 CUP CHOPPED ROMAINE LETTUCE

3 SPRIGS OF FRESH EPAZOTE

1 BUNCH OF GREEN ONIONS, TRIMMED AND CHOPPED

1 TABLESPOON CUMIN SEEDS

2 TABLESPOONS SESAME SEEDS, PLUS MORE FOR GARNISH

CORN TORTILLAS (SEE PAGE 65), WARM, FOR SERVING

1. Place the olive oil in a large saucepan and warm it over medium heat. Add the peanuts and almonds and fry until they are fragrant and browned, about 4 minutes. Place the pumpkin seeds in the skillet and cook, stirring frequently to make sure that they don't burn, until they are golden brown. Place the nuts and pumpkin seeds in a blender. Set the pan aside and leave the olive oil in it.

2. Place the pork in a saucepan with three-quarters of the white onion and 3 garlic cloves. Cover with water, bring to a boil, and then reduce the heat so that the pork simmers gently. After 45 minutes, season generously with salt. Cook the pork until tender, about 1 hour.

3. Gradually add the tomatillos, chile peppers, spinach, cilantro, lettuce, and epazote to the blender and puree until smooth. When all of these have been incorporated, add the green onions, cumin seeds, sesame seeds, and remaining onion and garlic and puree until incorporated. If necessary, add some of the pork's cooking liquid to the puree to get the desired consistency.

4. Warm the olive oil left in the large saucepan and pour in the sauce. Season with salt, bring the sauce to a boil, and cook for 5 minutes. Reduce the heat so that the sauce simmers gently and cook for another 30 minutes.

5. Add the pork to the sauce and cook for 5 minutes. Serve with warm tortillas and garnish with additional sesame seeds.

Classic Carnitas

YIELD: 6 SERVINGS / **ACTIVE TIME:** 15 MINUTES / **TOTAL TIME:** 2 HOURS AND 15 MINUTES

4 LBS. PORK SHOULDER OR PORK BELLY, CUT INTO 3-INCH CUBES

SALT AND PEPPER, TO TASTE

1 TABLESPOON CUMIN

4 CUPS LARD

1 ONION, QUARTERED

1 HEAD OF GARLIC, HALVED AT ITS EQUATOR

JUICE OF 2 ORANGES

1 CINNAMON STICK

1 (12 OZ.) CAN OF COLA

SALSA VERDE TATEMADA (SEE PAGE 262), FOR SERVING

CORN TORTILLAS (SEE PAGE 65), WARM, FOR SERVING

PICKLED RED ONION (SEE PAGE 77), FOR GARNISH

FRESH CILANTRO, CHOPPED, FOR GARNISH

1. Season the pork with salt, pepper, and the cumin.
2. Place the lard in a Dutch oven and warm it over medium-high heat. Add the pork, onion, garlic, orange juice, and cinnamon stick and cook until the pork is very tender and well browned, about 1½ hours. Adjust the heat as necessary to ensure the pork doesn't brown too quickly.
3. Preheat the oven to 375°F and place a cooling rack in a rimmed baking sheet. When the pork is very tender, add the cola and cook for about 10 minutes.
4. Remove the pork from the pot and place it on the cooling rack. Place it in the oven and roast until the outside is crispy, 10 to 20 minutes.
5. Serve with salsa and tortillas and garnish with pickled onion and cilantro.

Rabo de Res en Salsa Roja

YIELD: 4 SERVINGS / **ACTIVE TIME:** 20 MINUTES / **TOTAL TIME:** 2 HOURS AND 20 MINUTES

- 12 DRIED PUYA CHILE PEPPERS
- 6 LARGE TOMATOES
- 3 GARLIC CLOVES
- ¼ WHITE ONION
- 2 TABLESPOONS EXTRA-VIRGIN OLIVE OIL
- 2 LBS. OXTAIL
- SALT AND PEPPER, TO TASTE
- 1 TEASPOON DRIED MARJORAM
- 1 TABLESPOON GRATED FRESH GINGER
- 2 BAY LEAVES
- WHITE RICE, COOKED, FOR SERVING (OPTIONAL)
- CORN TORTILLAS (SEE PAGE 65), WARM, FOR SERVING (OPTIONAL)

1. Place the chiles in a bowl of hot water and soak them for 20 minutes.

2. Place water in a medium saucepan and bring it to a boil. Add the tomatoes and boil until tender, about 10 minutes. Drain and place them in a blender. Drain the chiles and add them to the blender along with the garlic and onion. Puree until smooth and set the puree aside.

3. Place the olive oil in a Dutch oven and warm it over medium heat. Add the oxtail, season with salt and pepper, and sear until it is browned all over. Remove the oxtail from the pot and set it aside.

4. Strain the puree into the pot and warm over low heat for 5 minutes.

5. Return the oxtail to the pot, add 4 cups of water along with the marjoram, ginger, and bay leaves, and simmer over low heat until the oxtail is very tender, about 1½ hours.

6. Shred the oxtail with two forks and serve it with rice or warm tortillas.

Empanadas de Picadillo

YIELD: 4 SERVINGS / **ACTIVE TIME:** 35 MINUTES / **TOTAL TIME:** 1 HOUR AND 40 MINUTES

3 CUPS PREPARED MASA (SEE PAGE 65)

1 LB. PICADILLO DE RES (SEE PAGE 125)

½ LB. COTIJA CHEESE, PLUS MORE FOR SERVING

2 CUPS EXTRA-VIRGIN OLIVE OIL

½ LB. CABBAGE, FINELY SHREDDED, FOR SERVING

FRESH CILANTRO, CHOPPED, FOR SERVING

PICKLED RED ONION (SEE PAGE 77), FOR SERVING

SALSA, FOR SERVING

½ CUP SOUR CREAM, FOR SERVING

1. Wet your hands. Working with 1 oz. of masa at a time, gently form it into a ball. Place the masa in a tortilla press lined with two sheets of plastic (two squares cut from a 1-gallon plastic bag and a rolling pin can also be used).

2. Press the masa gently to form a ⅛-inch-thick round.

3. Place 2 oz. of picadillo in the center of the round and use one sheet of plastic to fold the round over the picadillo, forming a half-moon. Top with some cotija and press down on the edge to crimp and seal the empanada.

4. Repeat Steps 1–3 with the remaining masa, picadillo, and cotija.

5. Place the olive oil in a deep skillet and warm it over low heat until it is 310°F. Working with one empanada at a time, gently slip them into the hot oil and fry until golden brown, about 5 minutes, adjusting the heat to make sure the oil does not get too hot. Transfer the cooked empanadas to a paper towel–lined plate to drain.

6. Serve with the cabbage, cilantro, pickled onion, your preferred salsas, sour cream, and additional cotija.

Chiles en Nogada

YIELD: 4 SERVINGS / **ACTIVE TIME:** 45 MINUTES / **TOTAL TIME:** 1 HOUR AND 15 MINUTES

4 POBLANO CHILE PEPPERS

1 CUP ALMONDS OR WALNUTS

¼ CUP CRUMBLED QUESO FRESCO (SEE PAGE 287)

2 CUPS SOUR CREAM, PLUS MORE AS NEEDED

½ TABLESPOON SUGAR

SALT, TO TASTE

3 CUPS PICADILLO DE RES (SEE PAGE 125), AT ROOM TEMPERATURE

¼ CUP POMEGRANATE ARILS, FOR GARNISH

FRESH CILANTRO, CHOPPED, FOR GARNISH

1. If you do not have a gas stove, preheat a grill or an oven to 400°F. Roast the poblanos over an open flame, on the grill, or in the oven until the skin is blackened and blistered all over, turning occasionally. Place the poblanos in a heatproof bowl, cover with plastic wrap, and let them sit for 10 minutes.

2. Remove the charred skins from the poblanos. Make a small slit in the peppers and remove the seeds.

3. Place the nuts, Queso Fresco, sour cream, and sugar in a blender and puree until smooth. If the sauce seems too thick, incorporate more sour cream until the sauce is the desired texture. Season the sauce with salt and set it aside.

4. Stuff the peppers with the picadillo.

5. To serve, spoon the sauce over the peppers and garnish with the pomegranate arils and cilantro.

Carne en su Jugo

YIELD: 4 SERVINGS / **ACTIVE TIME:** 15 MINUTES / **TOTAL TIME:** 50 MINUTES

3 TOMATILLOS, HUSKED AND RINSED

4 GARLIC CLOVES

2 SERRANO CHILE PEPPERS, STEMMED, SEEDED, AND MINCED

SALT, TO TASTE

¼ CUP EXTRA-VIRGIN OLIVE OIL

1 LB. BACON, CHOPPED

4 LBS. BEEF CHUCK, CUT INTO 2- TO 3-INCH-LONG STRIPS

1 ONION, FINELY DICED

1 BUNCH OF FRESH CILANTRO, CHOPPED

1 LB. COOKED OR CANNED PINTO BEANS

CORN TORTILLAS (SEE PAGE 65), WARM, FOR SERVING

LIME WEDGES, FOR SERVING

1. In a small saucepan, add 4 cups water, the tomatillos, garlic, and serrano chiles. Bring to a boil and cook until the vegetables are tender, about 10 minutes. Drain, transfer the vegetables to a blender, and puree until smooth. Season the puree with salt and set it aside.

2. Place the olive oil in a Dutch oven and warm it over medium-low heat. Add the bacon and cook until it is golden brown, about 10 minutes. Remove the bacon from the pot and set it aside.

3. Drain the excess fat from the pot, raise the heat to high, and add the beef. Sear until it is browned all over, turning it as necessary. Remove the beef from the pot and set it aside.

4. Add the onion and cook, stirring occasionally, until it starts to soften, about 5 minutes. Return the beef and bacon to the pot, pour the puree over everything, and, if necessary, add water until the meat is covered.

5. Cook over low heat until the meat is very tender, about 40 minutes.

6. Stir in the cilantro and pinto beans and cook until warmed through. Taste, adjust the seasoning as necessary, and serve with warm tortillas and lime wedges.

Chiles en Nogada
SEE PAGE 132

Chilorio

YIELD: 6 SERVINGS / **ACTIVE TIME:** 15 MINUTES / **TOTAL TIME:** 2 HOURS AND 30 MINUTES

4 LBS. BONELESS PORK SHOULDER, CUT INTO 4 PIECES

SALT, TO TASTE

2 TABLESPOONS EXTRA-VIRGIN OLIVE OIL

4 GUAJILLO CHILE PEPPERS, STEMMED AND SEEDED

2 ANCHO CHILE PEPPERS, STEMMED AND SEEDED

6 GARLIC CLOVES

¼ WHITE ONION

2 CUPS ORANGE JUICE

¼ CUP WHITE VINEGAR

1 TABLESPOON DRIED MEXICAN OREGANO

1½ TEASPOONS CUMIN

1½ TEASPOONS BLACK PEPPER

CORN TORTILLAS (SEE PAGE 65), WARM, FOR SERVING (OPTIONAL)

ARROZ A LA MEXICANA (SEE PAGE 85), FOR SERVING (OPTIONAL)

1. Season the pork with salt and let it sit at room temperature while you prepare the sauce.

2. Place the olive oil in a Dutch oven and warm it over medium heat. Add the chiles and fry until fragrant.

3. Transfer the chiles to a blender, add the remaining ingredients, except for the tortillas or rice, and puree until smooth.

4. Working with one piece of pork at a time, place it in the Dutch oven and sear until browned on all sides.

5. Pour the puree over the pork. If the pork is not covered, add water until it is.

6. Cover the Dutch oven and cook the pork over low heat until tender and falling apart, about 2 hours.

7. Serve with the sauce and warm tortillas or rice.

Gorditas de Picadillo de Res

YIELD: 4 SERVINGS / **ACTIVE TIME:** 25 MINUTES / **TOTAL TIME:** 45 MINUTES

4 OZ. CABBAGE, SHREDDED

¾ LB. PREPARED MASA (SEE PAGE 65)

¼ CUP EXTRA-VIRGIN OLIVE OIL

PICADILLO DE RES (SEE PAGE 125), WARMED

4 OZ. COTIJA CHEESE

½ CUP SOUR CREAM

SALSA CRUDA VERDE (SEE PAGE 284), FOR SERVING

PICKLED RED ONION (SEE PAGE 77), FOR SERVING

1. Place the cabbage in a bowl of ice water.

2. Working with 3 oz. of prepared masa at a time, form it into a ball with your hands, place it on a work surface, and press down until it is even. Place the pressed masa in a comal or large cast-iron skillet and cook until it is lightly browned all over, about 3 minutes per side.

3. Add 1 tablespoon of the olive oil to a skillet and warm it over medium heat. Add the gorditas one at a time and fry until golden brown on both sides, about 6 minutes. Transfer the gorditas to a paper towel–lined plate and repeat with the remaining olive oil and gorditas.

4. Drain the cabbage and pat it dry.

5. Cut a small slit in the edge of each gordita, taking care not to cut all of the way through. Stuff the gordita with the picadillo, garnish with the cabbage, cotija, and sour cream, and serve with the salsa verde and pickled onion.

Chicken de Champiñones

YIELD: 4 SERVINGS / **ACTIVE TIME:** 20 MINUTES / **TOTAL TIME:** 20 MINUTES

2 TABLESPOONS EXTRA-VIRGIN OLIVE OIL

1 LB. CHICKEN CUTLETS

SALT AND PEPPER, TO TASTE

6 BUTTON MUSHROOMS, QUARTERED

1 SHALLOT, CHOPPED

1 GARLIC CLOVE, SLICED

¼ CUP WHITE WINE

¼ CUP HEAVY CREAM

¼ CUP SHREDDED OAXACA CHEESE

1 TEASPOON CUMIN

FRESH CILANTRO, CHOPPED, FOR GARNISH

1. Place the olive oil in a skillet and warm it over medium-high heat. Season the chicken with salt and pepper, place it in the pan, and sear for 1 minute on each side.

2. Add the mushrooms and cook for about 30 seconds. Add the shallot and garlic and cook for another 30 seconds, stirring frequently.

3. Deglaze the pan with the white wine and cook until the liquid has reduced by half.

4. Stir in the heavy cream, Oaxaca cheese, and cumin and cook until the chicken is cooked through (the interior is 165°F), about 8 minutes.

5. Garnish with cilantro and serve.

Gorditas de Picadillo de Res

SEE PAGE 138

Muscovy Duck Breast Mole

YIELD: 4 SERVINGS / **ACTIVE TIME:** 1 HOUR / **TOTAL TIME:** 2 HOURS

½ CUP SESAME SEEDS

5 WHOLE CLOVES

1 CINNAMON STICK

½ TEASPOON ANISE SEEDS

¼ TEASPOON CORIANDER SEEDS

6 TABLESPOONS LARD

6 GUAJILLO CHILE PEPPERS, STEMMED AND SEEDED

4 ANCHO CHILE PEPPERS, STEMMED AND SEEDED

¼ CUP RAISINS

¼ CUP BLANCHED ALMONDS

¼ CUP PUMPKIN SEEDS

2 CORN TORTILLAS (SEE PAGE 65), TORN INTO PIECES

4 CUPS CHICKEN OR VEGETABLE STOCK (SEE PAGE 438 OR 439)

1 TABLET OF ABUELITA CHOCOLATE

1 BONELESS, SKIN-ON DUCK BREAST

SALT AND PEPPER, TO TASTE

2 TABLESPOONS CANOLA OIL

FRESH CILANTRO, CHOPPED, FOR GARNISH

1. Place the sesame seeds in a dry skillet and toast over medium heat until they are lightly browned, about 2 minutes, shaking the pan occasionally. Remove the toasted sesame seeds from the pan and place them in a blender.

2. Add the cloves, cinnamon stick, anise seeds, and coriander seeds to the skillet and toast until fragrant, shaking the pan frequently. Transfer the mixture to the blender.

3. Place half of the lard in a large skillet and warm it over medium heat. Add the chiles and fry until they are fragrant and pliable. Transfer them to a bowl of hot water and let them soak for 20 minutes.

4. Place the raisins, almonds, pumpkin seeds, and tortillas in the skillet and cook, stirring frequently, until the seeds turn golden brown, about 3 minutes. Transfer the contents of the skillet to the blender, add the chiles and half of the stock, and puree until smooth.

5. Place the remaining lard in a stockpot and warm over medium heat. Add the puree, cook for 3 minutes, and then stir in the remaining stock and the chocolate. Reduce the heat and simmer for 30 minutes, stirring frequently.

6. Season the duck breast with salt and pepper.

7. Place the canola oil in a medium skillet and warm it over high heat. Place the duck breast in the pan, skin side down, and sear for 2 to 3 minutes. Turn the duck breast over and sear for 2 to 3 minutes. Turn the duck breast over and sear until the skin is crispy and golden brown and the interior is cooked through, while basting the duck with the fat that has rendered.

8. Remove the duck from the pan and let it rest for 5 minutes.

9. To serve, slice the duck breast into medallions. Place the mole in the center of the serving plates, set the duck on top, and garnish with cilantro.

Beef Machaca with Potatoes & Eggs

YIELD: 4 SERVINGS / **ACTIVE TIME:** 15 MINUTES / **TOTAL TIME:** 45 MINUTES

2 TABLESPOONS EXTRA-VIRGIN OLIVE OIL

1 TABLESPOON MINCED WHITE ONION

1 LB. BEEF MACHACA

½ LB. RUSSET POTATOES, PEELED AND FINELY DICED

2 LARGE TOMATOES, FINELY DICED

2 JALAPEÑO CHILE PEPPERS, CHARRED

4 LARGE EGGS, BEATEN

SALT, TO TASTE

4 FLOUR TORTILLAS (SEE PAGE 82), FOR SERVING

FRIJOLES DE LA OLLA (SEE PAGE 56), FOR SERVING

1. Place the olive oil in a large saucepan and warm over medium heat. Add the onion and cook, stirring occasionally, until it is translucent, about 3 minutes. Add the machaca, potatoes, and tomatoes and 1 cup of water and cook until the machaca is rehydrated and the potatoes are tender, about 20 minutes.

2. Place the jalapeños in a dry skillet and cook over medium heat until the skins are charred and the chiles are aromatic, about 10 minutes, turning the peppers as needed. Remove from the pan and let the chiles cool slightly. Slice the chiles thin and stir them into the machaca mixture.

3. When the potatoes are tender, add the beaten eggs to the pan and season with salt. Cook until the eggs are set, about 4 minutes, stirring occasionally.

4. Serve with the Flour Tortillas and Frijoles de la Olla.

Pork Milanesa

YIELD: 4 SERVINGS / **ACTIVE TIME:** 15 MINUTES / **TOTAL TIME:** 15 MINUTES

2 CUPS FINE BREAD CRUMBS

4 LARGE EGGS

1 CUP EXTRA-VIRGIN OLIVE OIL

2 LBS. PORK CUTLETS (¼ INCH THICK)

SALT, TO TASTE

1. Place the bread crumbs in a shallow bowl. Place the eggs in a separate bowl and beat them.

2. Place the olive oil in a large skillet and warm it over medium-high heat until it is hot enough that a bread crumb sizzles gently when added.

3. Season the pork cutlets with salt, dredge them in the beaten eggs and then in the bread crumbs until they are coated all over. Gently press down on the bread crumbs so that they adhere to the pork.

4. Gently slip the cutlets into the hot oil and fry until golden brown on both sides and cooked through, 8 to 10 minutes. Transfer the milanesa to a paper towel–lined plate to drain before serving.

Beef Machaca with Potatoes & Eggs
SEE PAGE 144

Chicken Chorizo

YIELD: 4 SERVINGS / **ACTIVE TIME:** 45 MINUTES / **TOTAL TIME:** 24 HOURS

- 2 OZ. GUAJILLO CHILE PEPPERS
- 2 OZ. PASILLA CHILE PEPPERS
- 2 SKIN-ON, BONELESS CHICKEN THIGHS
- 1 TABLESPOON RECADO ROJO (SEE PAGE 272)
- 2 GARLIC CLOVES, CHOPPED
- 1 TABLESPOON DRIED THYME
- 1 TABLESPOON DRIED MEXICAN OREGANO
- 1 TABLESPOON CUMIN
- 2 TABLESPOONS SMOKED PAPRIKA
- 1 TEASPOON CAYENNE PEPPER
- 1 TEASPOON GROUND CLOVES
- 1 TEASPOON ONION POWDER
- SALT AND PEPPER, TO TASTE
- 2 CUPS TORTILLA CHIPS
- SALSA VERDE TATEMADA (SEE PAGE 262)
- 2 TABLESPOONS UNSALTED BUTTER
- 8 EGGS
- QUESO ENCHILADO, SHREDDED, FOR SERVING
- PICKLED RED ONION (SEE PAGE 77), FOR SERVING
- AVOCADO, SLICED, FOR SERVING
- FRESH CILANTRO, CHOPPED, FOR SERVING
- LIME WEDGES, FOR SERVING
- CREMA OR SOUR CREAM, FOR SERVING

1. Place the chiles in a heatproof bowl, pour boiling water over them, and let them sit for 30 minutes. Drain and let the chiles cool. When cool enough to handle, remove the stems, seeds, and skins from the peppers.

2. Grind the chicken thighs in a meat grinder or food processor. Place the ground meat in a large mixing bowl, add the chiles, Recado Rojo, garlic, thyme, oregano, cumin, paprika, cayenne, ground cloves, onion powder, salt, and pepper and stir to combine. Cover the bowl with plastic wrap and let the chorizo marinate in the refrigerator overnight.

3. Place the chorizo in a large skillet and cook over medium heat until cooked through, about 6 to 8 minutes, stirring occasionally. Add the tortilla chips and salsa verde and cook for another 2 minutes. Transfer the mixture to a serving bowl and tent it with aluminum foil.

4. Melt the butter in a separate skillet, add the eggs, and cook to desired level of doneness. Arrange the eggs over the chorizo-and-tortilla chip mixture and serve with queso enchilado, pickled onion, avocado, chopped cilantro, lime wedges, and crema.

Mixiotes de Pollo

YIELD: 4 SERVINGS / **ACTIVE TIME:** 30 MINUTES / **TOTAL TIME:** 2 HOURS

- 4 ANCHO CHILE PEPPERS, STEMMED AND SEEDED
- 4 GUAJILLO CHILE PEPPERS, STEMMED AND SEEDED
- ½ TEASPOON ALLSPICE BERRIES
- ½ TEASPOON WHOLE CLOVES
- 2 BAY LEAVES
- 1 CINNAMON STICK
- 10 GARLIC CLOVES
- 7 TABLESPOONS APPLE CIDER VINEGAR
- 7 TABLESPOONS ORANGE JUICE
- 7 TABLESPOONS FRESH LIME JUICE
- 3 TO 4 LB. WHOLE CHICKEN, SEPARATED INTO PIECES
- MIXIOTE LEAVES, AS NEEDED
- 1 SMALL WHITE ONION, JULIENNED
- 3½ OZ. CACTUS, SPINES REMOVED, BLANCHED, AND CUT INTO STRIPS
- 2 FRESH HOJA SANTA LEAVES
- SALT, TO TASTE
- CORN TORTILLAS (SEE PAGE 65), WARM, FOR SERVING
- LIME WEDGES, FOR SERVING
- SALSA BORRACHA (SEE PAGE 280), FOR SERVING

1. Warm a cast-iron skillet or comal over medium heat. Add the chiles and toast until they are pliable and fragrant, about 30 seconds. Place the chiles in hot water and let them soak for 20 to 30 minutes.

2. Add the allspice berries, cloves, bay leaves, and cinnamon stick to the skillet and toast until fragrant, shaking the pan frequently. Grind the mixture into a fine powder with a mortar and pestle or spice grinder.

3. Place the chiles, ground spices, garlic, vinegar, orange juice, and lime juice in a blender and puree until smooth.

4. Rub the puree over the chicken and let it marinate in the refrigerator for at least 30 minutes. If time allows, marinate the chicken for up to 24 hours.

5. Place the chicken in the center of the mixiote leaves and cover with the onion, cactus, and hoja santa. Season the mixture with salt. Fold the mixiote leaves over the chicken and use kitchen twine to tie the packet closed.

6. Bring a few inches of water to a boil in a saucepan. Place a steaming basket over the water and place the mixiote packet in it. Steam until the chicken is cooked through (the interior is 165ºF) and very tender, about 1 hour. Make sure to keep an eye on the water level in the pan so that it does not completely evaporate.

7. Remove the packet from the steaming basket and let it rest for 10 minutes. Serve with tortillas, lime wedges, and Salsa Borracha.

Pavo en Escabeche

YIELD: 8 SERVINGS / **ACTIVE TIME:** 1 HOUR / **TOTAL TIME:** 24 HOURS

½ TEASPOON ALLSPICE BERRIES

½ TEASPOON WHOLE CLOVES

3½ OZ. BLACK PEPPERCORNS

1 CINNAMON STICK

1 TEASPOON DRIED MEXICAN OREGANO

1 TEASPOON DRIED MARJORAM

8 GARLIC CLOVES

14 TABLESPOONS WHITE VINEGAR

SALT, TO TASTE

7 TO 8 LB. WHOLE TURKEY

4 TO 5 XCATIC OR ANAHEIM CHILE PEPPERS

1 HEAD OF GARLIC, HALVED AT ITS EQUATOR

3 BAY LEAVES

ESCABECHE (SEE PAGE 86)

LIME WEDGES, FOR SERVING

1. Place the allspice berries, cloves, peppercorns, and cinnamon stick in a dry skillet and toast until fragrant, shaking the pan frequently. Grind the mixture into a fine powder with a mortar and pestle or spice grinder.

2. Place the spice powder, oregano, marjoram, garlic cloves, and three-quarters of the white vinegar in a blender and puree until the mixture is a thick paste. Add the remaining vinegar as needed to get the desired consistency. Season with salt.

3. Coat the turkey with the recado blanco paste and let it marinate in the refrigerator overnight. If time is a factor, marinate for at least 1 to 2 hours.

4. Prepare a charcoal or gas grill for medium-high heat (about 450°F). Season the turkey with salt and grill until it is deeply charred all over, but not cooked all the way through. Take care not to move the turkey too much on the grill so that the skin stays intact. Remove the turkey from the grill and set it aside.

5. Place the chiles on the grill and cook, turning occasionally, until they are blistered and black on both sides. Place them in a heatproof mixing bowl, cover it with plastic wrap, and let the chiles steam for 5 to 10 minutes. When they are cool enough to handle, remove the skin from the chiles, cut the chiles into strips, and set them aside.

6. Place the turkey in a stockpot or a saucepan that is deep enough to allow it to be covered with water by 2 to 3 inches. Add the head of garlic, bay leaves, and ½ cup of the recado blanco paste. Cover the turkey with water and bring to a simmer. Cook until the turkey is cooked through and just beginning to fall apart.

7. Add the Escabeche to the stew and season it with salt. Simmer for an additional 10 minutes.

8. Serve the turkey in large bowls, either on or off the bone with good amounts of the Escabeche, lime wedges, and the strips of roasted chiles.

Codorniz a la Parrilla

YIELD: 4 SERVINGS / **ACTIVE TIME:** 30 MINUTES / **TOTAL TIME:** 24 HOURS

8 CUPS WATER

¼ CUP KOSHER SALT, PLUS MORE TO TASTE

4 SEMIBONELESS QUAIL

1 TABLESPOON ALLSPICE BERRIES

1 CINNAMON STICK

3 TABLESPOONS CORIANDER SEEDS

2 TABLESPOONS CUMIN SEEDS

½ TEASPOON WHOLE CLOVES

2 TABLESPOONS BLACK PEPPERCORNS

1½ TEASPOONS WHITE PEPPERCORNS

3 BAY LEAVES

1 TEASPOON DRIED MEXICAN OREGANO

1 TEASPOON DRIED MARJORAM

1 TABLESPOON ANCHO CHILE POWDER

3½ TABLESPOONS ORANGE JUICE

3½ TABLESPOONS FRESH LIME JUICE

2 TABLESPOONS EXTRA-VIRGIN OLIVE OIL

LIME WEDGES, FOR SERVING

CORN TORTILLAS (SEE PAGE 65), WARM, FOR SERVING

SALSA, FOR SERVING

1. Place the water and salt in a saucepan and warm over low heat, stirring until the salt has dissolved. Remove the pan from heat and let the brine cool completely. Place the quail in the brine and let them sit in the refrigerator for 12 to 24 hours.

2. Remove the quail from the brine and let them air-dry in the refrigerator for 1 to 2 hours.

3. Place the allspice berries, cinnamon stick, coriander seeds, cumin seeds, cloves, peppercorns, and bay leaves in a dry skillet and toast until fragrant, shaking the pan frequently so that they do not burn. Grind the mixture into a fine powder with a mortar and pestle or spice grinder.

4. Place the toasted spice powder, oregano, marjoram, ancho chile powder, orange juice, and lime juice in a blender and puree until the mixture is a smooth paste. Rub the paste over the quail and marinate them in the refrigerator for at least 30 minutes.

5. Prepare a gas or charcoal grill for medium-high heat (about 450°F). Clean the grates and brush them with the olive oil.

6. Place the quail on the grill, breast side down, and cook until they are crispy and caramelized, 2 to 3 minutes. Turn them over and cook until the interior is 140°F, 1 to 2 minutes. Remove the quail from the grill and let them rest for 10 minutes before serving with lime wedges, tortillas, and salsa.

Mole Poblano

YIELD: 4 SERVINGS / **ACTIVE TIME:** 1 HOUR / **TOTAL TIME:** 3 HOURS

3 TO 4 LB. WHOLE CHICKEN

½ WHITE ONION

4 GARLIC CLOVES, UNPEELED

1 TO 2 CINNAMON STICKS

SALT, TO TASTE

1 CUP LARD

4 DRIED CALIFORNIA OR GUAJILLO CHILE PEPPERS, STEMMED AND SEEDED

3 CHIPOTLE MECO CHILE PEPPERS, STEMMED AND SEEDED

3 PASILLA CHILE PEPPERS, STEMMED AND SEEDED

2 CHIPOTLE MORITA CHILE PEPPERS, STEMMED AND SEEDED

2 MULATO OR NEGRO CHILE PEPPERS, STEMMED AND SEEDED

½ CUP SESAME SEEDS, PLUS MORE FOR GARNISH

½ CUP WHOLE ALMONDS

3 SLICES OF BREAD

1 RIPE BANANA

4 OZ. MEXICAN OR DARK CHOCOLATE

SUGAR, TO TASTE

CORN TORTILLAS (SEE PAGE 65), WARM, FOR SERVING

PICKLED RED ONION (SEE PAGE 77), FOR SERVING

FRESH CILANTRO, CHOPPED, FOR GARNISH

1. Place the chicken in a large stockpot, cover it with cold water, and add the white onion, garlic, and cinnamon sticks, along with a pinch of salt. Bring to a boil, lower the heat, and simmer the chicken until the meat pulls away from the bone, about 40 minutes.

2. Carefully remove the chicken and let it cool. When it is cool enough to handle, shred the chicken with two forks and set it aside. Keep the broth simmering while you work on the sauce. Remove the garlic cloves and peel them when they are cool enough to handle.

3. Place the lard in a large skillet and warm over medium heat. Add the chiles and fry until they are fragrant and pliable, about 2 minutes. Transfer them to a blender. Place the sesame seeds, almonds, and bread in the pan and fry until the mixture is just browned, about 2 minutes. Transfer it to the blender.

4. Add the banana and chocolate to the blender. Add 1 cup of the broth and the garlic cloves and blend until the mixture is smooth.

5. Place the puree in a saucepan and warm it over medium-low heat. Taste, season with salt or sugar if necessary, and add the shredded chicken. Warm the chicken through, serve with tortillas and pickled onion, and garnish each portion with cilantro and additional sesame seeds.

Masa-Battered Fried Chicken

YIELD: 4 SERVINGS / **ACTIVE TIME:** 45 MINUTES / **TOTAL TIME:** 1 HOUR AND 15 MINUTES

2 LBS. BONE-IN, SKIN-ON CHICKEN THIGHS

½ TEASPOON KOSHER SALT, PLUS MORE TO TASTE

BLACK PEPPER, TO TASTE

1 LB. MASA HARINA

¾ CUP WATER, PLUS MORE AS NEEDED

CANOLA OIL, AS NEEDED

1. Season the chicken thighs with salt and pepper.
2. Place the masa in a baking dish, add the salt, and then add the water. Stir to combine. Stick a spoon into the batter; you want it to coat the spoon and drip slowly off. Depending on the masa used, you may need to add more water.
3. Dredge the chicken in the masa mixture until it is evenly coated.
4. Add canola oil to a Dutch oven until it is 2 inches deep and warm it to 375°F.
5. Gently slip the chicken into the hot oil, making sure not to overcrowd the pot, which will lower the temperature of the oil. Fry until the chicken is cooked through (the interior is 165°F), golden brown, and crispy, 15 to 18 minutes.
6. Transfer the fried chicken to a paper towel–lined plate and let it drain before serving.

Lobster Mojo de Ajo

YIELD: 4 SERVINGS / **ACTIVE TIME:** 30 MINUTES / **TOTAL TIME:** 1 HOUR

10 OZ. GARLIC CLOVES, UNPEELED

1 CUP PLUS 2 TABLESPOONS UNSALTED BUTTER

2 TABLESPOONS GUAJILLO CHILE POWDER

2 TABLESPOONS CHOPPED FRESH CILANTRO

4 FRESH LOBSTER TAILS, SPLIT IN HALF LENGTHWISE SO THAT THE FLESH IS EXPOSED

LIME WEDGES, FOR SERVING

1. Place the garlic in a dry skillet and toast it over medium heat until it is lightly charred in spots, about 10 minutes, turning occasionally. Remove the garlic from the pan and peel it.

2. Place the butter in a skillet and melt it over medium heat. Add the garlic and continue cooking until the butter begins to foam and brown slightly. Remove the pan from heat and let the mixture cool to room temperature.

3. Place the garlic, butter, guajillo powder, and cilantro in a blender and puree until smooth. Transfer three-quarters of the mojo de ajo to a large mixing bowl. Place the remaining mojo de ajo in a small bowl and set it aside. Let the mojo cool completely.

4. Add the lobster tails to the mojo in the large mixing bowl and let them marinate for 15 to 20 minutes.

5. Prepare a gas or charcoal grill for medium-high heat (about 450°F). Place the small bowl containing the reserved mojo de ajo beside the grill. Place the lobster tails on the grill, flesh side down, and grill until they are caramelized and almost cooked through, 3 to 4 minutes.

6. Flip the lobster tails over and brush them with some of the reserved mojo de ajo. Grill until completely cooked through, 1 to 2 minutes. Serve with lime wedges and any of the remaining reserved mojo de ajo.

Pollo Veracruzano

YIELD: 4 SERVINGS / **ACTIVE TIME:** 15 MINUTES / **TOTAL TIME:** 45 MINUTES

4 BONE-IN, SKIN-ON CHICKEN LEGS

4 BONE-IN, SKIN-ON CHICKEN THIGHS

SALT AND PEPPER, TO TASTE

3 TABLESPOONS EXTRA-VIRGIN OLIVE OIL

2 RED BELL PEPPERS, STEMMED, SEEDED, AND SLICED THIN

1 WHITE ONION, SLICED THIN

2 GARLIC CLOVES, MINCED

½ CUP WHITE WINE

2 CUPS CHICKEN STOCK (SEE PAGE 438)

2 TABLESPOONS CAPER BRINE

2 TABLESPOONS CAPERS, CHOPPED

½ CUP CHOPPED GREEN OLIVES

4 CUPS CHOPPED CANNED TOMATOES

¼ CUP DRIED MEXICAN OREGANO (OPTIONAL)

1. Season the chicken with salt and pepper. Place the olive oil in a Dutch oven and warm it over medium heat. Add the chicken and sear until it is golden brown on both sides, about 10 minutes, turning it as necessary. Remove the chicken from the pan and set it aside.

2. Add the peppers, onion, and garlic, reduce the heat to low, and cook until the peppers have softened, about 8 minutes, stirring occasionally.

3. Return the chicken to the pan and deglaze the pan with the white wine, stock, and caper brine, scraping up any browned bits from the bottom of the pot. Add the capers, olives, tomatoes, and oregano (if using), bring to a simmer, and cook until the chicken is cooked through (the interior is 165°F), about 15 minutes.

4. To serve, arrange the chicken on a plate, place some of the vegetables on top, and spoon some of the pan sauce over everything.

Enchiladas de Mole

YIELD: 4 SERVINGS / **ACTIVE TIME:** 10 MINUTES / **TOTAL TIME:** 35 MINUTES

2 CUPS MOLE NEGRO (SEE PAGE 252)

2 TABLESPOONS EXTRA-VIRGIN OLIVE OIL

8 CORN TORTILLAS (SEE PAGE 65)

1 LB. LEFTOVER CHICKEN, SHREDDED

1 CUP PICKLED RED ONION (SEE PAGE 77), FOR SERVING

QUESO FRESCO (SEE PAGE 287), CRUMBLED, FOR SERVING

FRESH CILANTRO, CHOPPED, FOR SERVING

1. Preheat the oven to 350°F. Place the mole in a small saucepan and warm it over low heat.

2. Place some of the olive oil in a skillet and warm it over low heat. Warm the tortillas one at a time and set them aside. Replenish the olive oil in the pan as needed.

3. Dip the warmed tortillas in the mole until completely coated and transfer them to a plate.

4. Fill the tortillas with the shredded chicken and roll them up. Place them in a square baking dish, seam side down, and pour more mole over the top.

5. Place the dish in the oven and bake until the enchiladas are warmed through. Remove them from the oven and serve with pickled onion, Queso Fresco, and cilantro.

Enchiladas de Mole

SEE PAGE 159

Milanesa de Pollo

YIELD: 4 SERVINGS / **ACTIVE TIME:** 10 MINUTES / **TOTAL TIME:** 30 MINUTES

2 LBS. BONELESS, SKINLESS CHICKEN BREASTS

2 CUPS BREAD CRUMBS

4 LARGE EGGS

1 CUP EXTRA-VIRGIN OLIVE OIL

SALT, TO TASTE

ENSALADA DE NOPALES (SEE PAGE 22), FOR SERVING

CORN TORTILLAS (SEE PAGE 65), FOR SERVING

WHITE RICE, COOKED, FOR SERVING

1. Ask your butcher to pound the chicken breasts until they are no more than ¼ inch thick. You can also do this at home, placing the chicken between pieces of plastic wrap and using a cast-iron skillet or mallet.

2. Place the bread crumbs in a shallow bowl. Place the eggs in a separate bowl and beat until scrambled.

3. Place the olive oil in a deep skillet and warm it over medium heat until it is hot enough that a bread crumb sizzles gently when added.

4. Season the chicken breasts with salt, dredge them in the beaten eggs and then in the bread crumbs until coated all over. Gently press down on the bread crumbs so that they adhere to the chicken.

5. Working with one breast at a time, add the chicken to the hot oil and fry until golden brown on both sides and cooked through, about 10 minutes, turning it over just once. Transfer the cooked chicken breasts to a paper towel–lined plate to drain.

6. When all of the chicken has been cooked, serve with the Ensalada de Nopales, tortillas, and rice.

Camarones en Adobo

YIELD: 4 SERVINGS / **ACTIVE TIME:** 30 MINUTES / **TOTAL TIME:** 45 MINUTES

- 4 GUAJILLO CHILE PEPPERS, STEMMED AND SEEDED
- 6 GARLIC CLOVES
- 2 SMALL ROMA TOMATOES
- 3 TABLESPOONS CHIPOTLES EN ADOBO
- SALT, TO TASTE
- 1 LB. LARGE SHRIMP, SHELLED AND DEVEINED
- ¼ CUP LARD
- CORN TORTILLAS (SEE PAGE 65), FOR SERVING
- WHITE ONION, CHOPPED, FOR SERVING
- FRESH CILANTRO, CHOPPED, FOR SERVING
- LIME WEDGES, FOR SERVING

1. Place the dried chiles in a dry skillet and toast them over medium heat until they darken and become fragrant and pliable. Submerge them in a bowl of hot water and let them soak for 15 to 20 minutes.

2. Drain the chiles and reserve the soaking liquid. Add the chiles to a blender along with the garlic, tomatoes, chipotles, and a small amount of the soaking liquid and puree until the mixture is a smooth paste. Season the adobo marinade with salt and let it cool completely.

3. Place the shrimp in the adobo and let it marinate in the refrigerator for at least 30 minutes.

4. Place some of the lard in a large skillet and warm it over medium-high heat. Working in batches to avoid overcrowding the pan, add the shrimp and cook until they are just firm and turn pink, 2 to 3 minutes. Add more lard to the pan if it starts to look dry.

5. Serve the shrimp in tortillas with onion, cilantro, and lime wedges.

Camarones en Adobo
SEE PAGE 163

Pulpo al Pastor

YIELD: 4 TO 6 SERVINGS / **ACTIVE TIME:** 30 MINUTES / **TOTAL TIME:** 4 HOURS

1 HEAD OF GARLIC, HALVED AT ITS EQUATOR

1 WHITE ONION, QUARTERED

3 ALLSPICE BERRIES

2 WHOLE CLOVES

½ CINNAMON STICK

3 CHIPOTLE MORITA CHILE PEPPERS

2 DRIED CHILES DE ÁRBOL

7 GUAJILLO CHILE PEPPERS

2 TABLESPOONS FRESH LIME JUICE

2 TABLESPOONS ORANGE JUICE

2 TABLESPOONS GRAPEFRUIT JUICE

7 TABLESPOONS PINEAPPLE JUICE

½ CUP RECADO ROJO (SEE PAGE 272)

5 GARLIC CLOVES

⅛ TEASPOON DRIED OREGANO

SALT, TO TASTE

6 TO 8 LB. OCTOPUS, BEAK REMOVED AND HEAD CLEANED

1 SMALL BUNCH OF FRESH EPAZOTE

3 BAY LEAVES

8 CUPS CHICKEN STOCK (SEE PAGE 438)

CORN TORTILLAS (SEE PAGE 65), FOR SERVING

LIME WEDGES, FOR SERVING

FRESH CILANTRO, CHOPPED, FOR SERVING

1. Place the garlic and onion in a dry skillet and cook them over medium heat until they are lightly charred. Remove them from the pan and set them aside.

2. Add the allspice, cloves, and cinnamon stick to the skillet and toast until fragrant, shaking the pan frequently. Grind to a powder using a mortar and pestle or a spice grinder.

3. Place the chiles in the skillet and toast over medium heat until they darken and become fragrant and pliable. Submerge them in a bowl of hot water and let them soak for 30 minutes.

4. Drain the chiles and reserve the liquid. Add the chiles, toasted spice powder, juices, Recado Rojo, garlic cloves (not the charred head of garlic), and oregano to a blender and puree until smooth. Season the al pastor marinade with salt and set it aside.

5. Bring water to a boil in a large saucepan. Place the octopus in the boiling water and poach it for 3 minutes. Remove the octopus from the water and let it cool.

6. Preheat the oven to 300°F. Place the octopus, epazote, bay leaves, head of garlic, and onion in a Dutch oven and add stock until half of the octopus is submerged. Cover the Dutch oven, place it in the oven, and braise the octopus for 2 to 3 hours, until the thickest parts of the tentacles are very tender. Remove the octopus from the braising liquid and let it cool.

7. Place the octopus in the al pastor marinade and let it marinate in the refrigerator for a minimum of 30 minutes.

8. Prepare a gas or charcoal grill for high heat (about 500°F). Remove the octopus from the marinade and shake to remove any excess. Place the octopus on the grill and grill until it is caramelized and crispy on all sides, 5 to 7 minutes, taking care not to let the octopus burn. Serve with tortillas, lime wedges, and cilantro.

Tinga de Pollo

YIELD: 6 SERVINGS / **ACTIVE TIME:** 20 MINUTES / **TOTAL TIME:** 1 HOUR AND 20 MINUTES

2 BONE-IN, SKIN-ON CHICKEN LEGS

2 BONE-IN, SKIN-ON CHICKEN THIGHS

2 TABLESPOONS KOSHER SALT, PLUS MORE TO TASTE

2 BAY LEAVES

1 TABLESPOON EXTRA-VIRGIN OLIVE OIL

1 WHITE ONION, SLICED THIN

1 GARLIC CLOVE, SLICED THIN

3 LARGE TOMATOES, DICED

2 CHIPOTLE CHILE PEPPERS, STEMMED AND SEEDED

TOSTADAS, FOR SERVING (OPTIONAL)

CORN TORTILLAS (SEE PAGE 65), WARM, FOR SERVING (OPTIONAL)

PICKLED RED ONION (SEE PAGE 77), FOR SERVING

QUESO FRESCO (SEE PAGE 287), FOR SERVING

1. Place the chicken in a large pot and cover it with cold water by at least an inch. Add the salt and bay leaves and bring to a simmer. Cook the chicken until the meat pulls away from the bone, about 40 minutes.

2. While the chicken is simmering, place the olive oil in a large skillet and warm it over medium heat. Add the onion and garlic and cook, stirring frequently, until the onion is translucent, about 3 minutes. Reduce the heat to low and cook until the onion has softened.

3. Add the diced tomatoes and cook for another 5 minutes.

4. Shred the chicken and reserve 2 cups of the cooking liquid. Place the chiles in a bowl with 1 cup of the cooking liquid and let them sit until tender, about 20 minutes.

5. Chop the chiles, add them to the skillet along with the shredded chicken, and cook, stirring occasionally, until the flavor has developed to your liking, about 8 minutes. Add the remaining cooking liquid to the pan if it becomes too dry.

6. Season with salt and serve over tostadas or tortillas with pickled onion and Queso Fresco.

Mextlapique de Callo de Hacha

YIELD: 4 SERVINGS / **ACTIVE TIME:** 40 MINUTES / **TOTAL TIME:** 40 MINUTES

12 SCALLOPS, RINSED

SALT, TO TASTE

2 PASILLA CHILE PEPPERS, GROUND

2 ANCHO CHILE PEPPERS, GROUND

3 ROMA TOMATOES, DICED

¾ SMALL YELLOW ONION, DICED

3 JALAPEÑO CHILE PEPPERS, DICED

8 TO 12 CORN HUSKS, DRIED AND REHYDRATED

6 FRESH EPAZOTE LEAVES

EXTRA-VIRGIN OLIVE OIL, TO TASTE

LIME WEDGES, FOR SERVING

1. Season the scallops with salt and the ground chiles.
2. Place the tomatoes, onion, and jalapeños in a mixing bowl and stir to combine. Season the mixture with salt.
3. Place three scallops in each corn husk and cover with some of the vegetable mixture and epazote. Drizzle olive oil over the top.
4. Tie the corn husks at both ends by using a piece of torn corn husk. Add more corn husks as needed to fully enclose the scallops.
5. Prepare a gas or charcoal grill for medium heat (about 400°F) or warm a cast-iron skillet over medium heat. Place the packets of scallops on the cooking surface and cook until the husks begin to char, 3 to 4 minutes. The scallops should be cooked through.
6. Serve with lime wedges.

Tinga de Pollo
SEE PAGE 168

Pan de Cazon

YIELD: 4 SERVINGS / **ACTIVE TIME:** 40 MINUTES / **TOTAL TIME:** 40 MINUTES

4 HABANERO CHILE PEPPERS

SALT, TO TASTE

1 SMALL BUNCH OF FRESH EPAZOTE

1 LB. DOGFISH, COD, OR MONKFISH FILLETS

¼ CUP LARD

1 WHITE ONION, CHOPPED

5 GARLIC CLOVES, MINCED

1 TEASPOON DRIED MEXICAN OREGANO

ZEST AND JUICE OF 1 LIME

ZEST AND JUICE OF 1 ORANGE

4 ROMA TOMATOES, QUARTERED

1 CUP CANNED OR COOKED BLACK BEANS

16 CORN TORTILLAS (SEE PAGE 65), WARMED AND WRAPPED IN FOIL

FRESH CILANTRO, CHOPPED, FOR SERVING

1. Place the habaneros in a dry skillet and cook over medium heat until they are charred, turning them frequently. Set the charred habaneros aside and let them cool. When they are cool enough to handle, remove the stems and seeds from the peppers and chop the remaining flesh. Gloves are recommended for handling the habaneros, as their liquid can prove severely irritating to skin.

2. Bring a saucepan of water to a boil. Season very generously with salt and add a few sprigs of epazote.

3. Add the fish and poach until just cooked through, 2 to 3 minutes. Remove the fish, let it cool, and shred it with a fork once it is cool enough to handle.

4. Place some of the lard in a large skillet and warm it over medium-high heat. Add half of the onion and garlic and cook, stirring the occasionally, until the onion is translucent, about 3 minutes. Season the mixture with salt and the oregano, add the fish and the citrus juices to the pan, and cook until the flavors are combined, 1 to 2 minutes. Remove the pan from heat and set it aside.

5. In a separate skillet, add the remaining lard and warm it over medium-high heat. Add the remaining onion and garlic along with a few sprigs of epazote and cook, stirring occasionally, until the onion is translucent, about 3 minutes. Add to a blender along with the tomatoes and black beans and puree until smooth.

6. Place the black bean puree in a saucepan and bring it to a boil. Reduce the heat and simmer until it has reduced by one-quarter, about 15 minutes.

7. Working quickly, dip the tortillas one at a time into the black bean puree until they are coated lightly on both sides. Place a tortilla in the center of a plate. Top with about 2 oz. of the fish mixture. Repeat with three more tortillas. For the fourth tortilla, spread the black bean puree only on one side and place it, coated side down, on top of the stack.

8. Cover the stack with about ¼ cup of the puree and garnish with some of the charred habanero and cilantro. Repeat with the remaining tortillas, fish mixture, puree, habanero, and cilantro and serve.

Tikin Xic

YIELD: 2 TO 4 SERVINGS / **ACTIVE TIME:** 30 MINUTES / **TOTAL TIME:** 1 HOUR

1 WHOLE RED SNAPPER, CLEANED AND DESCALED

1½ CUPS RECADO ROJO (SEE PAGE 272)

BANANA LEAVES, AS NEEDED

2 HABANERO CHILE PEPPERS, STEMS AND SEEDS REMOVED, SLICED

1 BUNCH OF FRESH CILANTRO

SALT, TO TASTE

CORN TORTILLAS (SEE PAGE 65), WARMED, FOR SERVING

LIME WEDGES, FOR SERVING

SALSA DE CHILTOMATE (SEE PAGE 258), FOR SERVING

1. Preheat the oven to 450°F. Rub the inside and outside of the snapper with the Recado Rojo. Let the fish marinate for at least 30 minutes. If time allows, marinate the snapper for up to 24 hours in the refrigerator.

2. Remove any stiff spines from the banana leaves and cut the leaves into pieces large enough to wrap up the fish completely. Toast the banana leaves over an open flame or in a dry cast-iron skillet until bright green and very pliable.

3. Place the fish in the banana leaves and top with the sliced habaneros and cilantro. Season with salt, fold the banana leaves over so that they completely cover the fish, and tie the packet closed with kitchen twine.

4. Place the packet on a baking sheet, place it in the oven, and roast until just cooked through, 15 to 20 minutes, depending on the thickness of the fish. Remove from the oven and let the fish rest in the packet for 5 minutes.

5. Open the packet, divide the snapper between the serving plates, and serve with tortillas, lime wedges, and Salsa de Chiltomate.

Tikin Xic
SEE PAGE 173

Carnitas de Atun

YIELD: 4 SERVINGS / **ACTIVE TIME:** 15 MINUTES / **TOTAL TIME:** 40 MINUTES

- 1 LB. TUNA LOIN, SLICED
- SALT, TO TASTE
- 3 TABLESPOONS GUAJILLO CHILE POWDER
- ¼ CUP FRESH LIME JUICE
- ¼ CUP ORANGE JUICE
- 1 BAY LEAF
- ¼ CUP LARD
- CRISPY TACO SHELLS, WARMED, FOR SERVING
- CABBAGE, FINELY SHREDDED, FOR SERVING
- LIME WEDGES, FOR SERVING
- SALSA, FOR SERVING
- AVOCADO, DICED, FOR SERVING
- SESAME SEEDS, FOR SERVING

1. Season the tuna with salt and the guajillo powder. Combine the juices in a mixing bowl, add the tuna and bay leaf, and marinate for 15 minutes.

2. Place the lard in a skillet and warm over high heat. Add the tuna and pan-fry until the outside is crispy and caramelized and the inside is rare, 2 to 3 minutes.

3. Serve the tuna in crispy taco shells with cabbage, lime wedges, salsa, avocado, and sesame seeds.

Smoked Trout Tostadas

YIELD: 4 SERVINGS / **ACTIVE TIME:** 10 MINUTES / **TOTAL TIME:** 15 MINUTES

½ CUP EXTRA-VIRGIN OLIVE OIL, PLUS MORE AS NEEDED

1 LARGE WHITE ONION, SLICED THIN

4 GARLIC CLOVES, SLICED

1 LB. SMOKED TROUT, SHREDDED

2 TEASPOONS ACHIOTE POWDER

½ LB. CARROTS, PEELED AND GRATED

½ CUP SAUERKRAUT

2 TABLESPOONS CHOPPED CASTELVETRANO OLIVES

2 TABLESPOONS FRESH LEMON JUICE

2 TABLESPOONS KOSHER SALT

TOSTADAS, FOR SERVING

1. Coat a large skillet with olive oil and warm over medium heat. Add the onion and garlic and cook until the onion is translucent, about 3 minutes, stirring frequently.

2. Stir the trout and achiote into the pan and cook, stirring to break up the trout, until it is warmed through, about 3 minutes.

3. Turn off the heat, stir in the remaining ingredients, and let the mixture sit for a minute or two before serving with tostadas.

Pescado Veracruz

YIELD: 2 SERVINGS / **ACTIVE TIME:** 15 MINUTES / **TOTAL TIME:** 45 MINUTES

1 TO 2 LBS. RED SNAPPER, SCALED, CLEANED, AND GUTTED, HEAD AND TAIL LEFT ON

SALT AND PEPPER, TO TASTE

4 LARGE TOMATOES, SEEDED AND FINELY DICED

4 OZ. GREEN OLIVES, PITTED AND QUARTERED

¼ CUP CAPERS

2 TABLESPOONS EXTRA-VIRGIN OLIVE OIL

1 WHITE ONION, SLICED THIN

1 RED BELL PEPPER, STEMMED, SEEDED, AND SLICED THIN

5 GARLIC CLOVES, SLICED THIN

1 TABLESPOON CAPER BRINE

1. Using a sharp knife, score the fish three to four times on each side, making each cut about ¼ inch deep. Lightly season the snapper with salt and pepper and set aside.

2. Combine the tomatoes, olives, and capers in a mixing bowl.

3. Place the olive oil in a large skillet and warm it over medium-high heat. Add the onion, bell pepper, and garlic and cook until they have softened, about 7 minutes, stirring frequently.

4. Stir in the tomato mixture. Place the fish on top of the vegetables, add the caper brine, and cover the pan. Cook over low heat until the fish is fully cooked through, 15 to 20 minutes.

5. To serve, divide the vegetables between the serving plates and top each one with a piece of the red snapper.

Camarones a la Diabla

YIELD: 4 SERVINGS / **ACTIVE TIME:** 20 MINUTES / **TOTAL TIME:** 35 MINUTES

- 10 GUAJILLO CHILE PEPPERS
- 4 DRIED CHILES DE ÁRBOL
- 3 GARLIC CLOVES, CHOPPED
- 4 LARGE TOMATOES, QUARTERED
- ½ WHITE ONION, CHOPPED
- 1 TABLESPOON KOSHER SALT
- 2 TABLESPOONS EXTRA-VIRGIN OLIVE OIL
- 1 LB. SHRIMP, SHELLS REMOVED, DEVEINED
- WHITE RICE, COOKED, FOR SERVING

1. Place the chile peppers in a bowl of boiling water and let them soak for 10 minutes. Drain, reserve the soaking liquid, and place the chiles in a blender.

2. Add the garlic, tomatoes, and onion to the blender and puree until smooth, adding the reserved liquid as needed to get the desired texture. Season the puree with the salt.

3. Place the olive oil in a large skillet and warm it over medium-high heat. Add the puree and cook for 5 minutes, stirring occasionally.

4. Add the shrimp, reduce the heat to medium, and cook until the shrimp turn pink and curl up slightly.

5. To serve, ladle the sauce and shrimp over white rice.

Masa-Battered Fish Tacos

YIELD: 4 SERVINGS / **ACTIVE TIME:** 30 MINUTES / **TOTAL TIME:** 1 HOUR

2 LBS. TILAPIA, CUT INTO SMALLER PIECES

½ TEASPOON KOSHER SALT, PLUS MORE TO TASTE

BLACK PEPPER, TO TASTE

1 LB. MASA HARINA

¾ CUP WATER, PLUS MORE AS NEEDED

CANOLA OIL, AS NEEDED

CORN TORTILLAS (SEE PAGE 65), WARMED, FOR SERVING

CABBAGE, FINELY SHREDDED, FOR SERVING

SOUR CREAM, FOR SERVING

SALSA, FOR SERVING

1. Season the tilapia with salt and pepper. Place the masa in a baking dish, add the salt, and then add the water. Stir to combine. Stick a spoon into the batter; you want it to coat the spoon and drip slowly off. Depending on the masa used, you may need to add more water.

2. Dredge the tilapia in the masa mixture until it is evenly coated.

3. Add canola oil to a Dutch oven until it is 2 inches deep and warm it to 375°F. Gently slip the tilapia into the hot oil, making sure not to crowd the pot, which will lower the temperature of the oil. Fry until cooked through, golden brown, and crispy, 8 to 10 minutes. Remove and transfer to a paper towel–lined plate to drain.

4. Chop the fish into bite-size pieces and serve in tortillas along with cabbage, sour cream, and salsa.

Masa-Battered Fish Tacos
SEE PAGE 181

Pescado Adobado en Hoja de Plátano

YIELD: 4 SERVINGS / **ACTIVE TIME:** 20 MINUTES / **TOTAL TIME:** 2 HOURS AND 10 MINUTES

6 GUAJILLO CHILE PEPPERS, STEMMED AND SEEDED

2 SERRANO CHILE PEPPERS

3 GARLIC CLOVES

2 TABLESPOONS RECADO ROJO (SEE PAGE 272)

2 TABLESPOONS WHITE VINEGAR

¼ CUP EXTRA-VIRGIN OLIVE OIL

SALT AND PEPPER, TO TASTE

2 BANANA LEAVES

2 LBS. SEA BASS OR RED SNAPPER FILLETS

3 BAY LEAVES

PICKLED RED ONION (SEE PAGE 77), FOR GARNISH

FRESH CILANTRO, CHOPPED, FOR GARNISH

CORN TORTILLAS (SEE PAGE 65), WARM, FOR SERVING

1. Place the guajillo peppers in a bowl of hot water and let them soak for 15 minutes.

2. Drain the guajillo peppers and place them in a blender. Add the serrano peppers, garlic, Recado Rojo, vinegar, and olive oil and puree until smooth. Season the adobo marinade with salt, reserve ¼ cup for serving, and set the rest aside.

3. Remove any stiff spines from the banana leaves and cut the leaves into pieces large enough to wrap up the fish completely. Toast the banana leaves over an open flame or in a dry cast-iron skillet until they are bright green and very pliable.

4. Season the fish with salt and pepper and place it in the banana leaves. Pour the adobo over the fish and place the bay leaves on top. Fold the banana leaves over so that they completely cover the fish and tie the packet closed with kitchen twine.

5. Transfer the fish to the refrigerator and let it marinate for at least 1 hour. If time allows, you can marinate the fish overnight.

6. Preheat the oven to 375°F. Place the packet containing the fish in a roasting pan, place it in the oven, and roast until it is cooked through, about 12 minutes. Remove from the oven and let the fish rest for 5 minutes.

7. Cut open the banana leaves and brush the fish with the reserved adobo. Garnish with pickled onion and cilantro and serve with warm tortillas.

Pescado Zarandeado

YIELD: 4 SERVINGS / **ACTIVE TIME:** 10 MINUTES / **TOTAL TIME:** 40 MINUTES

2 WHOLE RED SNAPPER, SCALED, CLEANED, GUTTED, AND BUTTERFLIED

SALT, TO TASTE

½ TEASPOON DRIED MEXICAN OREGANO

1 TEASPOON CUMIN

3 GUAJILLO CHILE PEPPERS, STEMMED AND SEEDED

2 ANCHO CHILE PEPPERS, STEMMED AND SEEDED

3 GARLIC CLOVES

2 TABLESPOONS MAGGI SEASONING OR WORCESTERSHIRE SAUCE

¼ CUP FRESH LIME JUICE

CORN TORTILLAS (SEE PAGE 65), WARM, FOR SERVING

1. Using a sharp knife, score each side of the fish four times. Season them with salt, the oregano, and cumin and place them in a large roasting pan.

2. Place the chile peppers in a bowl of boiling water and let them soak for 10 minutes. Drain the chiles, reserve the soaking liquid, and place the chiles in a blender.

3. Add the garlic and Maggi sauce and puree until smooth, adding the reserved liquid as needed to get the desired texture.

4. Pour the puree over the fish and let it marinate for 20 minutes.

5. Prepare a gas or charcoal grill for medium-high heat (about 450°F) and coat the grates with nonstick cooking spray.

6. Place the fish on the grill and cook for 4 minutes. Turn the fish over and cook until it is cooked through, another 4 minutes.

7. Remove the fish from the grill and pour the lime juice over it. Serve immediately with warm tortillas.

Pescado Adobado en Hoja de Plátano

SEE PAGE 184

Chayote en Pipian Rojo

YIELD: 4 SERVINGS / **ACTIVE TIME:** 30 MINUTES / **TOTAL TIME:** 45 MINUTES

2 TO 3 LARGE CHAYOTES

CHICKEN STOCK (SEE PAGE 438), AS NEEDED

SALT, TO TASTE

2 TABLESPOONS LARD

1½ CUPS PIPIAN ROJO (SEE PAGE 266), WARMED

FRESH CILANTRO, CHOPPED, FOR GARNISH

FRESH PARSLEY, CHOPPED, FOR GARNISH

TOASTED PUMPKIN SEEDS, FOR GARNISH

1. Quarter the chayotes and remove the pits.
2. Place the chayotes in a saucepan and cover with stock by 1 or 2 inches. Season the stock generously with salt and bring it to a simmer. Cook the chayotes until they are al dente. Remove and let them cool in the refrigerator.
3. Place the lard in a large cast-iron skillet and warm it over medium-high heat. Place the chayotes in the pan, cut side down, and sear until they are caramelized all over. Repeat with the other cut sides.
4. Ladle about a ¼ cup of the Pipian Rojo onto each serving plate, top with some of the chayote, and sprinkle flaky sea salt over the top, preferably Maldon. Garnish with cilantro, parsley, and toasted pumpkin seeds and enjoy.

Chiles Rellenos

YIELD: 6 SERVINGS / **ACTIVE TIME:** 1 HOUR / **TOTAL TIME:** 2 HOURS

6 LARGE POBLANO CHILE PEPPERS

1 LB. OAXACA OR MONTEREY JACK CHEESE

4 EGG WHITES

4 EGG YOLKS

2 CUPS ALL-PURPOSE FLOUR

2 CUPS CANOLA OIL

2 LARGE TOMATOES

2 GARLIC CLOVES

¼ WHITE ONION

SALT, TO TASTE

1 TEASPOON DRIED MEXICAN OREGANO

1. Roast the poblanos over an open flame, on the grill, or in the oven until they are charred all over. Place them in a bowl, cover it with plastic wrap, and let them steam for 5 minutes.

2. Remove the chiles from the bowl and remove the charred skin with your hands.

3. Using a sharp paring knife, make a cut close to the stems of the peppers. Remove the seed pod, but leave the stems attached.

4. Stuff the chiles with 1 to 2 oz. of cheese (the amount depends on the size of the chile) and use toothpicks to close up the small cuts you've made.

5. In the work bowl of a stand mixer fitted with the whisk attachment, add the egg whites and whip on high until they hold stiff peaks.

6. Add the egg yolks, reduce the speed to low, and beat until just incorporated, about 30 seconds. Add ½ cup of flour and again beat until just incorporated, as you do not want to overwork the batter.

7. Place the canola oil in a large, deep skillet and warm it to 325°F.

8. Bring water to a boil in a medium saucepan. Add the tomatoes, garlic, and onion and cook until tender, about 7 minutes. Drain, place the vegetables in a blender, and puree until smooth. Season the sauce with salt, stir in the oregano, and set it aside.

9. Place the remaining flour on a baking sheet. Dredge the chiles in the flour until they are completely coated. Dip the chiles into the batter until they are coated and gently slip them into the hot oil.

10. Fry the chiles until crispy and golden brown, about 5 minutes, making sure you turn them just once. Transfer the fried chiles to a paper towel–lined plate to drain.

11. When all of the chiles have been fried, serve them alongside the tomato sauce.

Huaraches with Wild Mushrooms & Epazote

YIELD: 4 SERVINGS / **ACTIVE TIME:** 45 MINUTES / **TOTAL TIME:** 1 HOUR

¼ CUP EXTRA-VIRGIN OLIVE OIL

2 DRIED CHILES DE ÁRBOL, STEMMED AND SEEDED

1 LB. WILD MUSHROOMS, CHOPPED

½ WHITE ONION, SLICED THIN

3 GARLIC CLOVES, SLICED THIN

1 SMALL BUNCH OF FRESH EPAZOTE, TORN

SALT, TO TASTE

2 LBS. PREPARED MASA (SEE PAGE 65)

2 CUPS FRIJOLES NEGROS REFRITOS (SEE PAGE 56)

2 CUPS SHREDDED QUESO FRESCO (SEE PAGE 287)

½ CUP SALSA

FRESH CILANTRO, CHOPPED, FOR GARNISH

PICKLED RED ONION (SEE PAGE 77), FOR SERVING

1. Place the olive oil in a skillet and warm it over medium-high heat. Add the chiles and fry until fragrant and pliable. Remove the chiles from the pan and let them cool slightly. When cool enough to handle, finely dice the chiles.

2. Add the mushrooms to the pan and cook, stirring occasionally, until well browned, about 12 minutes. Transfer the mushrooms to a bowl.

3. Add the onion to the pan and cook, stirring frequently, until well browned, about 10 minutes. Add the garlic, cook for 1 minute, and then stir in the chiles and mushrooms. Add the epazote, season the mixture with salt, and transfer it to a bowl.

4. Working with 2 oz. of masa at a time, form it into a cup that fits into the palm of your hand. Place some of the refried beans in the center and close the cup of masa, sealing the beans. Gently form the masa into a flat patty and then shape it into an oval.

5. Line a tortilla press with plastic. Place one of the ovals in the press and place another piece of plastic on top. Apply firm, even pressure and press the oval until flat and about ¼ inch thick. Repeat with the remaining masa.

6. Warm the pan over medium heat. Add the huaraches one at a time and cook until golden brown on both sides, about 2 minutes per side.

7. Place a layer of the mushroom mixture on top of the huaraches and top with the cheese, salsa, cilantro, and pickled onion.

Chiles Rellenos
SEE PAGE 190

Abuela's Sopes

YIELD: 1 SERVING / **ACTIVE TIME:** 20 MINUTES / **TOTAL TIME:** 20 MINUTES

3 OZ. PREPARED MASA (SEE PAGE 65)

½ TEASPOON WATER

1 CUP CANOLA OIL

3 TABLESPOONS FRIJOLES NEGROS REFRITOS (SEE PAGE 56)

3 TABLESPOONS CHICKEN CHORIZO (SEE PAGE 148)

¼ CUP FINELY SHREDDED ICEBERG LETTUCE

2 CHERRY TOMATOES, HALVED

AVOCADO, SLICED

QUESO ENCHILADO, SHREDDED, FOR SERVING

SALSA, FOR SERVING

1. Place the masa and water in a mixing bowl and work the mixture until it is soft and pliable. Form into a small ball and gently flatten until it resembles a thick tortilla. Pinch the edge to raise it slightly, so that the masa becomes a shallow bowl.

2. Place the oil in a small saucepan and warm it to 375°F. Place the masa bowl in the oil and fry until golden brown, about 3 minutes. Transfer to a paper towel–lined plate and let it drain.

3. Layer the beans, chorizo, lettuce, tomatoes, and avocado atop the bowl and serve with the cheese and salsa.

Tortilla Gruesa de Hoja Santa y Queso

YIELD: 4 SERVINGS / **ACTIVE TIME:** 30 MINUTES / **TOTAL TIME:** 30 MINUTES

2 LBS. PREPARED MASA (SEE PAGE 65)

3 TABLESPOONS FINELY CHOPPED FRESH HOJA SANTA

1 CUP SHREDDED OAXACA CHEESE (CAN SUBSTITUTE MUENSTER OR SIMILAR CHEESE)

2 TEASPOONS KOSHER SALT

LIME WEDGES, FOR SERVING

SALSA DE ÁRBOL (SEE PAGE 269), FOR SERVING

1. Place the masa, hoja santa, cheese, and salt in a mixing bowl and work the mixture until it is smooth. Form the masa into four balls.

2. Line a tortilla press with plastic, place one of the balls in the press, and place another piece of plastic on top. Apply firm, even pressure and press the masa into a ½-inch-thick tortilla. Cover the tortilla with a moist linen towel and repeat with the remaining balls.

3. Warm a comal or large cast-iron skillet over medium-high heat. Working with one tortilla at a time, place it in the skillet and cook for 2 minutes. Turn it over and cook for another 2 minutes. Turn the tortilla over one last time and cook until it starts to char, about 2 minutes.

4. Remove from the pan and let the tortilla cool slightly. When all of the tortillas have been cooked, serve with lime wedges and salsa.

Molotes de Frijol y Queso

YIELD: 4 SERVINGS / **ACTIVE TIME:** 20 MINUTES / **TOTAL TIME:** 20 MINUTES

CANOLA OIL, AS NEEDED

½ LB. PREPARED MASA (SEE PAGE 65)

½ CUP FRIJOLES NEGROS REFRITOS (SEE PAGE 56)

1 CUP OAXACA OR CHIHUAHUA CHEESE

1 SMALL BUNCH OF FRESH EPAZOTE

FRESH CILANTRO, CHOPPED, FOR SERVING

CREMA OR SOUR CREAM, FOR SERVING

SALSA CRUDA VERDE (SEE PAGE 284), FOR SERVING

LIME WEDGES, FOR SERVING

1. Add canola oil to a Dutch oven until it is 2 inches deep and warm it to 350°F.

2. Divide the masa into four balls and line a tortilla press with plastic. Working with one ball at a time, place it in the center of the plastic and gently push down with the palm of one hand to flatten it. Cover with another piece of plastic and then close the tortilla press. Apply firm, even pressure to flatten the masa to about ¼ inch thick. Open the tortilla press and remove the top piece of plastic. Carefully remove the other piece of plastic.

3. Place some of the beans and cheese in the center of the round and add 1 to 2 leaves of epazote. Fold the round into a half-moon and press down on the edge to seal. Cover with a damp linen towel and make the rest to molotes.

4. Working in batches of one or two, gently slip the molotes into the hot oil and fry until they are golden brown and crispy, about 4 minutes. Transfer the fried molotes to a paper towel–lined plate to drain.

5. When all of the molotes have been fried, serve with cilantro, crema, salsa verde, and lime wedges.

Abuela's Sopes
SEE PAGE 194

Tamales de Chulibu'ul

YIELD: 6 SERVINGS / **ACTIVE TIME:** 30 MINUTES / **TOTAL TIME:** 1 HOUR AND 30 MINUTES

1 PACKAGE OF BANANA LEAVES

MASA FOR TAMALES (SEE PAGE 434)

4 CUPS CHULIBU'UL (SEE PAGE 84)

SALSA DE CHILTOMATE (SEE PAGE 258), FOR SERVING

1. Remove the spines from the banana leaves, taking care not to crack the leaves. Place the banana leaves in a dry skillet and toast them briefly so that they become pliable.

2. Cut the banana leaves into 8 x 10–inch rectangles.

3. Take a banana leaf and lay it, shiny side down, on a flat surface with the short side parallel to you. Place 3½ oz. of the masa in the center of the leaf and form it into a rectangle.

4. Place about ¼ cup of Chulibu'ul in the center of the masa. Fold the banana leaf over itself in thirds so that the masa encloses the filling. Fold the banana leaf over again in the same manner, creating a long packet. Fold the two open edges of the banana leaf toward the center. Press down on the edges of the masa until the packet is compact. Repeat with the remaining masa, Chulibu'ul, and banana leaves.

5. Bring water to a simmer in a saucepan and place a steaming basket over it. Place the tamales in the basket, seam side down, and steam for 1 hour.

6. To test if the tamales are done, remove one and unwrap it. If the banana leaf easily comes away from the masa, they are ready. If the masa is still sticking to the banana leaf, steam for another 10 to 20 minutes.

7. When the tamales are done, remove them from the steamer and let them cool for 5 minutes before serving with the salsa. To reheat after cooling completely, steam them, or place them in a banana leaf and toast in a hot cast-iron skillet.

Mushroom Barbacoa

YIELD: 4 SERVINGS / **ACTIVE TIME:** 1 HOUR / **TOTAL TIME:** 8 HOURS

1 TABLESPOON CORIANDER SEEDS

½ TEASPOON WHOLE CLOVES

½ TEASPOON ALLSPICE BERRIES

½ TEASPOON CUMIN SEEDS

1½ TABLESPOONS BLACK PEPPERCORNS

1 ANCHO CHILE PEPPER, STEMMED AND SEEDED

1 GUAJILLO CHILE PEPPER, STEMMED AND SEEDED

1 CHIPOTLE CHILE PEPPER, STEMMED AND SEEDED

1 PASILLA CHILE PEPPER, STEMMED AND SEEDED

1 ONION, SLICED, PLUS MORE FOR SERVING

1 CUP ORANGE JUICE

1 CUP FRESH LIME JUICE

SALT, TO TASTE

2¼ LBS. MUSHROOMS, JULIENNED

BANANA LEAVES, SPINES REMOVED, TOASTED, AS NEEDED

5 GARLIC CLOVES

2 BAY LEAVES

CORN TORTILLAS (SEE PAGE 65), FOR SERVING

SALSA VERDE TATEMADA (SEE PAGE 262), FOR SERVING

FRESH CILANTRO, CHOPPED, FOR SERVING

1. Place the coriander, cloves, allspice, cumin, and peppercorns in a dry skillet and toast until fragrant, shaking the pan frequently. Use a mortar and pestle or a spice grinder to grind the mixture into a powder.

2. Place the chiles in the skillet and toast until they are fragrant and pliable. Transfer the chiles to a bowl of hot water and soak for 20 minutes.

3. Drain the chiles and reserve the soaking liquid. Place the chiles, onion, and some of the soaking liquid in a blender and puree until smooth. Add the toasted spice powder, orange juice, and lime juice and pulse until incorporated.

4. Season the mixture with salt and place it in a mixing bowl. Add the mushrooms and let them marinate for at least 6 hours.

5. Preheat the oven to 420°F. Remove the mushrooms from the marinade and place them in the banana leaves. Layer the garlic and bay leaves on top, fold the banana leaves over to form a packet, and tie it closed with kitchen twine.

6. Place the packet on a parchment-lined baking sheet, place it in the oven, and roast for 20 minutes.

7. Remove from the oven and open the packet. Return to the oven and roast for an additional 10 to 15 minutes to caramelize the mushrooms.

8. Remove the mushrooms from the oven and serve with tortillas, salsa, additional onion, and cilantro.

Mushroom Barbacoa
SEE PAGE 199

Tlacoyos de Hongos

YIELD: 4 SERVINGS / **ACTIVE TIME:** 45 MINUTES / **TOTAL TIME:** 45 MINUTES

1 LB. PREPARED MASA (SEE PAGE 65)

1 TABLESPOON EXTRA-VIRGIN OLIVE OIL

½ LB. MUSHROOMS, JULIENNED

1 SMALL WHITE ONION, BRUNOISED

SALT, TO TASTE

2 TABLESPOONS LARD

SALSA DE AGUACATE (SEE PAGE 274), FOR SERVING

RED ONION, JULIENNED, FOR SERVING

CREMA, FOR SERVING

FRESH CILANTRO, CHOPPED, FOR SERVING

1. Form the masa into 4 oz. balls and cover them with a damp linen towel.

2. Place the olive oil in a skillet and warm it over medium-high heat. Add the mushrooms and cook, stirring occasionally, until they are well browned, about 12 minutes.

3. Add the onion, season the mixture with salt, and cook until the onion is translucent, about 3 minutes, stirring occasionally. Remove the pan from heat and set the mixture aside.

4. Line a tortilla press with plastic, place one of the balls in the press, and place another piece of plastic on top. Apply firm, even pressure and press the masa into a ¼-inch-thick round. Cover with a damp linen towel and repeat with the remaining balls.

5. Place the mushroom mixture in the center of each round and fold the masa over it to form a half-moon. Pinch the edges to seal and flatten the tlacoyos.

6. Place the lard in a comal or cast-iron skillet and warm over medium-high heat. Add the tlacoyos and cook until browned on both sides, about 2 minutes.

7. Serve the tlacoyos with salsa, onion, crema, and cilantro.

Tacos Dorados de Frijol, Chorizo y Camote

YIELD: 4 SERVINGS / **ACTIVE TIME:** 45 MINUTES / **TOTAL TIME:** 45 MINUTES

1 LB. SWEET POTATOES, PEELED AND DICED

2 TABLESPOONS LARD

SALT, TO TASTE

2 TEASPOONS GUAJILLO CHILE POWDER

2 TEASPOONS DRIED MEXICAN OREGANO

1 LB. PREPARED MASA (SEE PAGE 65)

3 TABLESPOONS EXTRA-VIRGIN OLIVE OIL

1 CUP FRIJOLES NEGROS REFRITOS (SEE PAGE 56)

4 OZ. CHORIZO, COOKED

1 SMALL RED ONION, JULIENNED, FOR SERVING

MORITA SALSA (SEE PAGE 276), FOR SERVING

FRESH CILANTRO, CHOPPED, FOR SERVING

COTIJA CHEESE, CRUMBLED, FOR SERVING

1. Preheat the oven to 400°F. Place the sweet potatoes in a mixing bowl, add the lard, and toss until the potatoes are coated. Season with salt and the chile powder, spread the sweet potatoes in an even layer on a baking sheet, and place in the oven. Roast until the sweet potatoes are cooked through and crispy, about 30 minutes. Remove them from the oven and season with the oregano.

2. Divide the masa into 1 oz. balls. Line a tortilla press with plastic, place one of the balls in the press, and place another piece of plastic on top. Apply firm, even pressure and press the masa into a ¼-inch-thick tortilla. Repeat with the remaining balls of masa.

3. Warm a comal or large cast-iron skillet over medium-high heat. Working with one tortilla at a time, gently lay it in the pan, taking care to not wrinkle it. Cook for 15 to 30 seconds, until the edges begin to lift up slightly. Turn the tortilla over and let it cook for 30 to 45 seconds before turning it over one last time. If the hydration of the masa was correct and the heat is high enough, the tortilla should puff up and inflate. Remove the tortilla from the pan and store it in a tortilla warmer lined with a linen towel.

4. Place the olive oil in a skillet and warm it over medium heat. Fill the tortillas with the beans, chorizo, and sweet potatoes, taking care not to overfill.

5. Place the tacos in the skillet and fry on each side until they are golden brown and crispy. Serve with the onion, salsa, cilantro, and cheese.

Memelas de Chicharron

YIELD: 4 SERVINGS / **ACTIVE TIME:** 1 HOUR / **TOTAL TIME:** 2 HOURS

3 CUPS PREPARED MASA (SEE PAGE 65)

1 CUP FRIJOLES NEGROS REFRITOS (SEE PAGE 56)

CHICHARRON EN SALSA ROJA (SEE PAGE 120)

½ LB. OAXACA CHEESE, SHREDDED

PICKLED RED ONION (SEE PAGE 77), FOR GARNISH

1 BUNCH OF FRESH CILANTRO, CHOPPED, FOR GARNISH

SALSA, FOR SERVING

1. Form the masa into 2 oz. balls. Gently press the balls into an oblong shape and line a tortilla press with plastic. Place one of the ovals in the press and place another piece of plastic on top. Apply firm, even pressure and press the oval until it is flat and about ¼ inch thick. Repeat with the remaining masa.

2. Warm a comal or large cast-iron skillet over medium-high heat. Working with one memela at a time, place it in the pan and cook until it is golden and crispy on each side, about 6 minutes.

3. Spread the beans over the masa, top with the chicarron, and sprinkle the cheese over everything. Garnish with the pickled onion and cilantro and serve with your favorite salsa.

Chicken Tinga Sopes

YIELD: 6 SERVINGS / **ACTIVE TIME:** 35 MINUTES / **TOTAL TIME:** 45 MINUTES

3 CUPS PREPARED MASA (SEE PAGE 65)

1 CUP EXTRA-VIRGIN OLIVE OIL

1 CUP FRIJOLES NEGROS REFRITOS (SEE PAGE 56)

TINGA DE POLLO (SEE PAGE 168)

3 OZ. QUESO FRESCO (SEE PAGE 287), SHREDDED

1 CUP SHREDDED GREEN CABBAGE OR ICEBERG LETTUCE

1 BUNCH OF RADISHES, TRIMMED AND SLICED THIN

SALSA, FOR SERVING

1. Form the masa into 2 oz. balls and flatten them between your hands until each one is a disk. Pinch the edge of each disk to form a raised edge, shaping the masa into a shallow bowl.

2. Place the olive oil in a large, deep cast-iron skillet and warm it to 350°F. Working with one sope at a time, gently slip it into the hot oil and fry until it is golden brown and crispy. Transfer the fried sopes to a paper towel–lined baking sheet to drain.

3. Spoon some beans into each sope and top with the Tinga de Pollo, cheese, cabbage, and radishes. Serve with salsa.

Tacos Dorados de Frijol, Chorizo y Camote

SEE PAGE 204

Huevos Rancheros

YIELD: 4 SERVINGS / **ACTIVE TIME:** 15 MINUTES / **TOTAL TIME:** 20 MINUTES

¾ CUP EXTRA-VIRGIN OLIVE OIL

4 CORN TORTILLAS (SEE PAGE 65)

3 LARGE TOMATOES

¼ ONION

2 SERRANO CHILE PEPPERS, STEMMED, SEEDED, AND SLICED

SALT, TO TASTE

4 EGGS

QUESO FRESCO (SEE PAGE 287), FOR GARNISH

½ CUP CHOPPED FRESH CILANTRO, FOR GARNISH

FRIJOLES DE LA OLLA (SEE PAGE 56), FOR SERVING

1. Place half of the olive oil in a large skillet and warm it over medium-high heat. Add the tortillas and fry for about 1 minute on each side. Transfer to a paper towel–lined plate and let them drain.

2. Place the tomatoes, onion, and chiles in a blender and puree until smooth.

3. Place 2 tablespoons of the remaining olive oil in a small skillet and warm it over medium heat. Carefully add the puree, reduce the heat to low, and cook the salsa for 5 minutes. Season with salt and then set the salsa aside.

4. Place the remaining olive oil in a skillet, add the eggs, season the yolks generously with salt, and cook until they are to your liking.

5. To assemble, place an egg on top of a fried tortilla, spoon the salsa on top, and garnish with the cheese and cilantro. Serve with the Frijoles de la Olla.

Huevos Motuleños

YIELD: 4 SERVINGS / **ACTIVE TIME:** 20 MINUTES / **TOTAL TIME:** 30 MINUTES

3 LARGE TOMATOES

¼ WHITE ONION

1 GARLIC CLOVE

2 HABANERO CHILE PEPPERS, STEMMED, SEEDED, AND SLICED

SALT, TO TASTE

¾ CUP EXTRA-VIRGIN OLIVE OIL

2 PLANTAINS, PEELED AND SLICED INTO ¼-INCH ROUNDS

4 OZ. CHORIZO, CHOPPED (OPTIONAL)

6 CORN TORTILLAS (SEE PAGE 65)

8 WHOLE EGGS

2 CUPS FRIJOLES NEGROS REFRITOS (SEE PAGE 56)

1 CUP CRUMBLED QUESO FRESCO (SEE PAGE 287)

1. Place the tomatoes, onion, garlic, and one of the habaneros in a blender and puree until smooth. Season the salsa with salt.

2. Place 2 tablespoons of the olive oil in a small saucepan and warm it over medium-high heat. Carefully add the salsa and cook for 2 minutes. Reduce the heat to low, cook for another 5 minutes, and remove the pan from heat.

3. Place the remaining olive oil in a large skillet and warm it over medium heat. Add the plantains and cook until they are golden brown on both sides, about 5 minutes. Transfer the plantains to a paper towel–lined plate to drain.

4. If using chorizo, add it to the pan and cook until it is crispy and cooked through, about 5 minutes. Remove the chorizo from the pan and set it aside.

5. Working with one tortilla at a time, place them in the pan and fry until they are golden brown on both sides, about 1 minute per side. Transfer the fried tortillas to a paper towel–lined plate to drain.

6. Remove any excess olive oil from the pan, add the eggs, generously season the yolks with salt, and cook the eggs to your liking.

7. To assemble, divide the tortillas among the serving plates. Spread the beans over the tortillas, top them with two eggs, and spoon the salsa over the top. Sprinkle the cheese and chorizo (if using) over everything and serve with the fried plantains.

Tortas de Lomo

YIELD: 4 SERVINGS / **ACTIVE TIME:** 10 MINUTES / **TOTAL TIME:** 1 HOUR AND 25 MINUTES

1 LB. PORK TENDERLOIN

½ WHITE ONION, CHOPPED

3 GARLIC CLOVES

SALT, TO TASTE

½ CUP MAYONNAISE

4 BOLILLOS, SPLIT OPEN

2 TABLESPOONS EXTRA-VIRGIN OLIVE OIL

1 CUP ESCABECHE (SEE PAGE 86)

½ LB. QUESO PANELA, SLICED

1. Bring water to a boil in a medium saucepan. Add the pork, onion, and garlic, season generously with salt, and reduce the heat to low. Cook until the pork is tender, about 45 minutes.

2. Remove the pork from the pan and let it rest for 10 minutes.

3. Spread the mayonnaise on the cut sides of the bread.

4. Place the olive oil in a skillet and warm it over medium-high heat. Slice the pork thin, add it to the pan, and sear until it is crispy and golden brown on both sides, about 4 minutes. Remove the pork from the pan and set it aside.

5. Drain the excess oil from the pan, place the bread in the pan, mayonnaise side down, and cook until it is golden brown. Remove the bread from the pan and assemble the tortas, layering the pork, Escabeche, and cheese. Cut the sandwiches in half and enjoy.

Beef Barbacoa Tacos

YIELD: 4 SERVINGS / **ACTIVE TIME:** 30 MINUTES / **TOTAL TIME:** 24 HOURS

5 LBS. BEEF SHOULDER, TRIMMED AND CUBED

SALT AND PEPPER, TO TASTE

1 TEASPOON GRATED FRESH GINGER

2 WHOLE CLOVES

1 TEASPOON ALLSPICE

¼ CUP RED WINE VINEGAR

2 GARLIC CLOVES

½ (4 OZ.) BAG OF PICKLING SPICES

4 DRIED NEW MEXICO CHILE PEPPERS, STEMMED AND SEEDED

1 TEASPOON SESAME SEEDS

¾ CUP WATER

¼ CUP ALL-PURPOSE FLOUR

⅓ CUP CHILI POWDER

6 BAY LEAVES

OAXACA CHEESE, SHREDDED, FOR SERVING

ONION, CHOPPED, FOR SERVING

FRESH CILANTRO, CHOPPED, FOR SERVING

12 CORN TORTILLAS (SEE PAGE 65), WARM, FOR SERVING

PICKLED RED ONION (SEE PAGE 77), FOR SERVING

1. Place the beef in a large mixing bowl and season it with salt and pepper.

2. Place the ginger, cloves, allspice, red wine vinegar, garlic, pickling spices, chiles, sesame seeds, water, flour, and chili powder in a blender and puree until smooth.

3. Pour the puree over the beef and stir until it is coated. Cover the bowl with plastic wrap and let the beef marinate in the refrigerator overnight.

4. Preheat the oven to 350°F. Place the beef in a large roasting pan and add the bay leaves and about 6 cups water. Cover the pan with aluminum foil, place in the oven, and braise until the meat is falling apart, about 4 hours.

5. Remove the beef from the oven, use two forks to shred it, and serve with cheese, fresh onion, cilantro, the tortillas, and pickled onion.

Chilaquiles Verdes

YIELD: 4 SERVINGS / **ACTIVE TIME:** 15 MINUTES / **TOTAL TIME:** 30 MINUTES

4 CUPS HUSKED, RINSED, AND CHOPPED TOMATILLOS

1 TABLESPOON CHOPPED PEQUIN CHILE PEPPER

1 ONION, CHOPPED

4 CUPS GARLIC CLOVES

2 JALAPEÑO CHILE PEPPERS, STEMMED, SEEDED, AND MINCED

4 CUPS CHICKEN STOCK (SEE PAGE 438)

1 TEASPOON CUMIN

2 CUPS FRESH CILANTRO, CHOPPED

SALT AND PEPPER, TO TASTE

2 TABLESPOONS UNSALTED BUTTER

8 EGGS

2 CUPS TORTILLA CHIPS

1 CUP CHICKEN CHORIZO (SEE PAGE 148)

FRIJOLES NEGROS REFRITOS (SEE PAGE 56), FOR SERVING

1. Place the tomatillos, pequin chile, onion, garlic, jalapeños, stock, and cumin in a medium saucepan and bring to a simmer over medium heat. Cook until the tomatillos have collapsed, about 20 minutes.

2. Stir the cilantro into the mixture, season it with salt and pepper, and set it aside.

3. Place the butter in a skillet and melt it over medium heat. Add the eggs, salt the yolks generously, and cook until they are to your liking. Remove the eggs from the pan.

4. Add the tortilla chips and chorizo to the pan and cook until warmed through.

5. To serve, layer the tortilla chips, chorizo, and beans on the serving plates, top with the eggs, and ladle the sauce over everything.

Tortas Ahogadas

YIELD: 4 SERVINGS / **ACTIVE TIME:** 15 MINUTES / **TOTAL TIME:** 1 HOUR AND 25 MINUTES

1 LB. PORK TENDERLOIN

SALT, TO TASTE

5 LARGE TOMATOES, CHOPPED

10 DRIED CHILES DE ÁRBOL, STEMMED AND SEEDED

2 GARLIC CLOVES, MINCED

1 TABLESPOON DRIED MEXICAN OREGANO

2 TABLESPOONS WHITE VINEGAR

2 TABLESPOONS EXTRA-VIRGIN OLIVE OIL

4 BAGUETTES

PICKLED RED ONION (SEE PAGE 77), FOR SERVING

1. Bring water to a boil in a medium saucepan. Add the pork, season generously with salt, and reduce the heat to low. Cook until the pork is tender, about 45 minutes.

2. Bring water to a boil in a medium saucepan and add the tomatoes, chiles, and garlic. Cook until they are tender, about 10 minutes. Drain, place the mixture in a blender, and puree until smooth. Strain the sauce into a bowl and season with salt. Stir in the oregano and white vinegar.

3. Place the olive oil in a skillet and warm it over medium-high heat. Slice the pork thin, add it to the pan, and sear until it is crispy and golden brown on both sides, about 4 minutes. Remove the pork from the pan and set it aside.

4. Slice the bread in half lengthwise and fill it with the pork loin.

5. Place the sauce in a pan large enough that a torta can easily be dipped into it. Bring the sauce to a simmer and dip the tortas in the sauce until they are smothered. Serve the tortas with pickled onion.

SOUPS & STEWS

Pozole Blanco

YIELD: 10 SERVINGS / **ACTIVE TIME:** 1 HOUR / **TOTAL TIME:** 24 HOURS

1½ LBS. DRIED HOMINY, SOAKED OVERNIGHT

16 CUPS WATER, PLUS MORE AS NEEDED

½ OZ. CALCIUM OXIDE

1 TABLESPOON KOSHER SALT, PLUS MORE TO TASTE

2 LBS. BONELESS PORK SHOULDER, CUT INTO 2-INCH CUBES

2 LBS. BONE-IN, SKIN-ON CHICKEN THIGHS

1 ONION, HALVED

1 HEAD OF GARLIC

RADISHES, SLICED THIN, FOR SERVING

GREEN CABBAGE, FINELY SHREDDED, FOR SERVING

LIME WEDGES, FOR SERVING

SALSA OR HOT SAUCE, FOR SERVING

1. Drain the hominy and place it in a large saucepan. Add the water, calcium oxide, and salt and bring to a boil. Cook for 30 minutes.

2. Drain the hominy and run it under cold water, rubbing the hominy between your hands to remove the loosened husks. Set the hominy aside.

3. Place the pork and chicken in a large saucepan. Fill the pan with water until it is no less than 2 inches from the top. Add the onion and garlic, season with salt, and bring to a simmer. Reduce the heat to low and cook until the pork and chicken are so tender they are falling apart, about 2 hours.

4. Remove the chicken from the pot. Remove the bones and skin and reserve the bones for another preparation.

5. Use a strainer to remove the garlic skins from the broth. Return the chicken to the pot, add the hominy, and cook for another 30 minutes.

6. Ladle the pozole into warmed bowls and serve with radishes, cabbage, lime wedges, and salsa.

Sopa de Conchitas

YIELD: 4 SERVINGS / **ACTIVE TIME:** 20 MINUTES / **TOTAL TIME:** 35 MINUTES

- ¼ CUP EXTRA-VIRGIN OLIVE OIL
- ½ LB. SMALL-FORMAT SHELL PASTA
- ½ WHITE ONION, DICED
- 2 GARLIC CLOVES, DICED
- 2 MEDIUM HEIRLOOM TOMATOES
- 6 CUPS CHICKEN STOCK (SEE PAGE 438)
- 2⅓ TABLESPOONS CUMIN
- SALT AND PEPPER, TO TASTE
- FRESH CILANTRO, CHOPPED, FOR GARNISH
- ROASTED BONE MARROW (SEE PAGE 437), FOR GARNISH
- LIME CREMA (SEE PAGE 437), FOR SERVING

1. Place the olive oil, pasta, onion, and garlic in a medium saucepan and cook, stirring occasionally, until the shells are golden brown, 4 to 5 minutes.

2. Place the tomatoes in a blender and add 1 cup of stock. Puree until smooth, add the puree to the pan, and stir in the remaining stock, the cumin, salt, and pepper. Bring to a simmer and cook until the shells are tender, 10 to 12 minutes.

3. Ladle the soup into warm bowls and garnish with cilantro. Spoon the Roasted Bone Marrow onto the soup and serve with Lime Crema.

Sopa de Hongos

YIELD: 4 SERVINGS / **ACTIVE TIME:** 30 MINUTES / **TOTAL TIME:** 1 HOUR AND 15 MINUTES

8 CUPS WATER

1 LB. SHIITAKE MUSHROOMS, STEMS REMOVED AND RESERVED, CAPS QUARTERED

3 TO 4 PASILLA CHILE PEPPERS, STEMMED AND SEEDED

3 TABLESPOONS UNSALTED BUTTER

1 SMALL WHITE ONION, BRUNOISED

7 GARLIC CLOVES, MINCED

3 TO 4 FRESH EPAZOTE LEAVES

1 SMALL BUNCH OF FRESH THYME

1 BAY LEAF

SALT, TO TASTE

1. Place the water in a medium saucepan and bring it to a simmer. Add the mushroom stems and simmer for 10 to 15 minutes to create a flavorful broth. Strain the broth and set it aside.

2. Place the chiles in a dry skillet and toast them for 30 seconds. Remove the chiles from the pan and chiffonade them.

3. Place the butter in a clean medium saucepan and melt it over medium-high heat. Add the mushrooms and cook until they are well browned, about 15 minutes, stirring occasionally.

4. Add the onion and cook until it is translucent, about 3 minutes, stirring occasionally. Add the garlic and chiles and cook until they are fragrant, about 1 minute. Add the mushroom broth and bring to a gentle simmer.

5. Place the epazote, thyme, and bay leaf in a sachet of cheesecloth, secure it with kitchen twine, and add it to the soup. Simmer the soup until the flavor has developed to your liking, 20 to 30 minutes.

6. Season the soup with salt and ladle it into warmed bowls.

Sopa de Chorizo, Ayocotes y Acelgas

YIELD: 4 SERVINGS / **ACTIVE TIME:** 30 MINUTES / **TOTAL TIME:** 24 HOURS

1 LB. DRIED AYOCOTE BEANS (RANCHO GORDO PREFERRED), SOAKED OVERNIGHT

½ LB. MEXICAN CHORIZO, CASING REMOVED

1 LARGE WHITE ONION, BRUNOISED

1 LB. SWISS CHARD, RINSED WELL, LEAVES TORN, STEMS DICED

10 GARLIC CLOVES, MINCED

1 BAY LEAF

1 CHIPOTLE MORITA CHILE PEPPER, STEMMED, SEEDED, AND HALVED

1 GUAJILLO CHILE PEPPER, STEMMED, SEEDED, AND CHIFFONADE

8 CUPS CHICKEN OR VEGETABLE STOCK (SEE PAGE 438 OR 439)

1 SMALL BUNCH OF FRESH EPAZOTE

SALT, TO TASTE

LIME WEDGES, FOR SERVING

BOLILLO OR TELERA, BUTTERED AND TOASTED, FOR SERVING

1. Drain the beans and set them aside.
2. Place the chorizo in a large saucepan and cook it over medium-low heat until the fat has rendered, 2 to 3 minutes.
3. Add the onion and chard stems and cook until the onion is translucent, about 3 minutes, stirring occasionally. Add the garlic, bay leaf, and chiles and cook for 1 minute, until fragrant, stirring frequently.
4. Add the chard leaves and cook, stirring frequently, until they start to wilt, about 2 minutes.
5. Add the stock, epazote, and beans and bring the soup to a gentle simmer. Cook until the beans are tender, 45 minutes to 1 hour.
6. Season with salt, ladle the soup into warm bowls, and serve with lime wedges and toasted bread.

Sere de Pescado

YIELD: 4 SERVINGS / **ACTIVE TIME:** 30 MINUTES / **TOTAL TIME:** 1 HOUR

3 SMALL ROMA TOMATOES

¼ CUP EXTRA-VIRGIN OLIVE OIL

¾ SMALL WHITE ONION, CHOPPED

10 GARLIC CLOVES, MINCED

2 SERRANO CHILE PEPPERS, STEMMED, SEEDED, AND MINCED

1 DRIED CHILE DE ÁRBOL, STEMMED, SEEDED, AND MINCED

⅛ TEASPOON DRIED MEXICAN OREGANO

2 CUPS COCONUT MILK

6 CUPS VEGETABLE STOCK (SEE PAGE 439)

1 BAY LEAF

ZEST AND JUICE OF 1 LIME

2 TEASPOONS HONEY

SALT, TO TASTE

4 HALIBUT FILLETS (ABOUT 1½ LBS.)

LIME WEDGES, FOR SERVING

RADISHES, SLICED THIN, FOR SERVING

SCALLIONS, TRIMMED AND SLICED, FOR SERVING

FRESH CILANTRO, CHOPPED, FOR SERVING

1. Prepare a gas or charcoal grill for medium heat (about 400°F) or warm a cast-iron skillet over medium heat. Place the tomatoes on the cooking surface and cook until charred all over, turning frequently. Remove the tomatoes and let them cool briefly. When cool enough to handle, chop the tomatoes and set them aside.

2. Place half of the olive oil in a large skillet and warm it over medium heat. Add the onion, garlic, serrano peppers, chile de árbol, and oregano and cook until the onion turns translucent, about 3 minutes, stirring frequently.

3. Add the tomatoes and cook until they start to collapse, about 10 minutes, stirring occasionally.

4. Add the coconut milk, stock, and bay leaf and simmer for 20 minutes, stirring occasionally.

5. Stir in the lime zest, lime juice, and honey. Season the broth with salt and remove it from heat.

6. Warm the remaining olive oil in a cast-iron skillet over medium-high heat. Pat the halibut dry with a paper towel and season it generously with salt.

7. Place the halibut in the pan, skin side down, and cook until it is caramelized and crispy, 2 to 3 minutes. Turn the halibut over and cook until it is just cooked through and opaque. Remove it from the pan and let the halibut rest for 3 minutes.

8. Ladle ¼ cup of the broth into each bowl and top each portion with a fillet. Serve with lime wedges, radishes, scallions, and cilantro.

Menudo

YIELD: 10 SERVINGS / **ACTIVE TIME:** 30 MINUTES / **TOTAL TIME:** 3 HOURS

3 LB. HONEYCOMB TRIPE, CUT INTO 2- TO 3-INCH PIECES

1 LB. MARROW BONES, CUT INTO 3-INCH PIECES

SALT, TO TASTE

6 GUAJILLO CHILE PEPPERS, STEMMED AND SEEDED

2 DRIED CHILES DE ÁRBOL, STEMMED AND SEEDED, PLUS MORE FOR GARNISH

1 LARGE TOMATO

3 GARLIC CLOVES

1 TABLESPOON DRIED MEXICAN OREGANO, PLUS MORE FOR GARNISH

1 TEASPOON CUMIN

5 CUPS HOMINY (SEE PAGE 220 FOR HOMEMADE) (OPTIONAL)

WHITE ONION, CHOPPED, FOR GARNISH

FRESH CILANTRO, CHOPPED, FOR GARNISH

CORN TORTILLAS (SEE PAGE 65), WARM, FOR SERVING

LIME WEDGES, FOR SERVING

1. Place the tripe and marrow bones in a large saucepan and fill it with water. Bring to a boil, season generously with salt, and reduce the heat to low. Cook for 2½ hours.

2. Place the chiles in a bowl. Pour 2 cups of the warm broth over the chiles and let them soak for 20 minutes.

3. Place the chiles, soaking liquid, tomato, and garlic in a blender and puree until smooth. Strain the sauce into the saucepan, stir in the oregano and cumin, and add the hominy, if using. Continue to cook over low heat.

4. When the flavor has developed to your liking and the tripe is very tender, ladle the soup into warmed bowls and garnish with onion, cilantro, and additional chiles de árbol and oregano. Serve with warm tortillas and lime wedges.

Butternut Squash & Chorizo Bisque

YIELD: 4 SERVINGS / **ACTIVE TIME:** 15 MINUTES / **TOTAL TIME:** 1 HOUR AND 30 MINUTES

1 LARGE BUTTERNUT SQUASH, PEELED AND SLICED

1 ONION, SLICED

3 TABLESPOONS EXTRA-VIRGIN OLIVE OIL

SALT, TO TASTE

½ LB. MEXICAN CHORIZO, CASING REMOVED

2 BAY LEAVES

1 CUP HEAVY CREAM

1 CUP VEGETABLE STOCK (SEE PAGE 439)

1 CUP WHOLE MILK

4 TABLESPOONS UNSALTED BUTTER

1. Preheat the oven to 400°F. Place the squash, onion, 2 tablespoons of the olive oil, and a pinch of salt in a bowl and toss to combine. Place the mixture in a baking dish and roast until the onion is browned, 15 to 25 minutes. Transfer the onion to a bowl, return the squash to the oven, and roast for another 20 to 30 minutes, until the squash is fork-tender. Remove the squash from the oven and transfer it to the bowl containing the onion.

2. Place the remaining olive oil in a skillet and warm it over medium-high heat. Add the chorizo and cook, stirring occasionally, until it is browned all over, about 5 minutes. Transfer the chorizo to a paper towel–lined plate to drain.

3. Place the squash, onion, bay leaves, cream, stock, and milk in a large saucepan and bring to a boil over medium-high heat, stirring frequently. Reduce heat so that the soup simmers and cook until the flavor is to your liking, about 20 minutes.

4. Remove the bay leaves and discard them. Transfer the soup to a food processor or blender and puree until smooth. Return the soup to the saucepan, stir in the chorizo, and bring to a simmer. Add the butter, stir until it has melted, and ladle the soup into warmed bowls.

Baja Tortilla Soup

YIELD: 4 SERVINGS / **ACTIVE TIME:** 25 MINUTES / **TOTAL TIME:** 1 HOUR

6 TOMATILLOS, HUSKED AND RINSED WELL

3 MEDIUM HEIRLOOM TOMATOES

½ WHITE ONION, CHOPPED

2 GARLIC CLOVES, UNPEELED

1 JALAPEÑO CHILE PEPPER

2 TEASPOONS EXTRA-VIRGIN OLIVE OIL

1 TEASPOON SMOKED PAPRIKA

1 TEASPOON CHILI POWDER

1 TEASPOON CUMIN

SALT AND PEPPER, TO TASTE

6 CORN TORTILLAS (SEE PAGE 65)

4 CUPS VEGETABLE STOCK (SEE PAGE 439)

MARYLAND BLUE CRAB KNUCKLE MEAT, FOR GARNISH

LIME CREMA (SEE PAGE 437), FOR GARNISH

AVOCADO OIL, FOR GARNISH

FRESH CILANTRO, CHOPPED, FOR SERVING

FRIED TORTILLA STRIPS, FOR SERVING

1. Preheat the oven to 375°F. In a mixing bowl, combine the tomatillos, tomatoes, onion, garlic, and jalapeño. Add the olive oil, smoked paprika, chili powder, cumin, salt, and pepper and stir until the vegetables are coated.

2. Transfer the mixture to a baking sheet. Place the tortillas on a separate baking sheet. Place the pans in the oven and roast until the tomatillos and tomatoes are charred and starting to collapse and the tortillas are golden brown and crispy, about 20 minutes. Remove the pans from the oven and let the vegetables cool slightly. When cool enough to handle, chop the vegetables roughly, making sure to peel the garlic cloves and remove the stem and seeds from the jalapeño before chopping it.

3. Place the stock in a medium saucepan and bring it to a boil. Add the vegetables and any juices to the pan. Add the tortillas and simmer the soup until the flavors are combined, about 5 minutes.

4. Transfer the soup to a blender and puree until smooth. Ladle the soup into warm bowls and garnish each portion with some crabmeat, crema, and avocado oil. Serve with cilantro and fried tortilla strips.

SOUPS & STEWS

Baja Tortilla Soup
SEE PAGE 229

Carne Adobada

YIELD: 6 SERVINGS / **ACTIVE TIME:** 30 MINUTES / **TOTAL TIME:** 24 HOURS

2 TABLESPOONS EXTRA-VIRGIN OLIVE OIL

3 TABLESPOONS ALL-PURPOSE FLOUR

¼ CUP MEW MEXICO CHILE POWDER

6 CUPS HAM STOCK (SEE PAGE 440)

4 GARLIC CLOVES, MINCED

1 TABLESPOON CHOPPED FRESH MARJORAM

½ TEASPOON CUMIN

SALT AND PEPPER, TO TASTE

2½ LBS. BONELESS PORK SHOULDER, CUBED

CORN TORTILLAS (SEE PAGE 65), WARM, FOR SERVING

1. Place the olive oil in a large saucepan and warm it over medium heat. Add the flour and cook, stirring continually, until the mixture is a light golden brown, about 5 minutes.

2. Stir in the chile powder and then slowly add the stock, stirring to prevent any lumps from forming. Add the garlic, marjoram, cumin, salt, and pepper and cook for 2 minutes. Remove the pan from heat and let the broth cool.

3. Place the pork in a large casserole. Pour the broth over it and stir until combined. Place the casserole in the refrigerator and let the pork marinate overnight.

4. Preheat the oven to 300°F. Place the stew in the oven and cook for at least 4 hours, removing to stir occasionally.

5. When the sauce has thickened and the meat is very tender, ladle the stew into warmed bowls and serve with tortillas.

Sopa de Flor de Calabaza

YIELD: 4 SERVINGS / **ACTIVE TIME:** 30 MINUTES / **TOTAL TIME:** 30 MINUTES

2 TABLESPOONS EXTRA-VIRGIN OLIVE OIL, PLUS MORE FOR GARNISH

1 YELLOW ONION, BRUNOISED

7 GARLIC CLOVES, MINCED

2 OZ. GUERO OR MANZANO CHILE PEPPERS, STEMMED AND SEEDED

½ LB. SQUASH, PEELED AND SEEDED

1 LB. SQUASH BLOSSOMS, STAMENS REMOVED

SALT, TO TASTE

3 SPRIGS OF FRESH EPAZOTE

8 CUPS CHICKEN OR VEGETABLE STOCK (SEE PAGE 438 OR 439)

QUESO FRESCO (SEE PAGE 287), CRUMBLED, FOR SERVING

LIME WEDGES, FOR SERVING

1. Place the olive oil in a saucepan and warm it over medium heat. Add the onion, garlic, and chiles and cook until the onion is translucent, about 3 minutes, stirring frequently.

2. Add the squash and half of the squash blossoms and cook for 1 to 2 minutes, stirring frequently. Season the mixture with salt, add the epazote and stock, and bring to a simmer. Cook until the squash is tender, about 20 minutes.

3. Transfer the soup to a blender and puree until smooth, about 1 minute. Return the soup to the saucepan and stir in the remaining squash blossoms.

4. Ladle the soup into warm bowls, drizzle some olive oil over each portion, and serve with Queso Fresco and lime wedges.

Sopa de Frijol Colado

YIELD: 4 SERVINGS / **ACTIVE TIME:** 30 MINUTES / **TOTAL TIME:** 24 HOURS

1 LB. DRIED BLACK BEANS, SOAKED OVERNIGHT

½ TEASPOON CORIANDER SEEDS

½ TEASPOON CUMIN SEEDS

2 TABLESPOONS LARD

1 SMALL YELLOW ONION, BRUNOISED

7 GARLIC CLOVES, MINCED

1 BAY LEAF

½ TEASPOON GUAJILLO CHILE POWDER

½ TEASPOON CHIPOTLE CHILE POWDER

½ TEASPOON DRIED THYME

½ TEASPOON DRIED MEXICAN OREGANO

½ TEASPOON DRIED MARJORAM

1 SMALL BUNCH OF FRESH EPAZOTE, STEMMED, PLUS MORE FOR SERVING

8 CUPS CHICKEN OR VEGETABLE STOCK (SEE PAGE 438 OR 439)

SALT, TO TASTE

CORN TORTILLAS (SEE PAGE 65), WARM, FOR SERVING

LIME WEDGES, FOR SERVING

COTIJA CHEESE, CRUMBLED, FOR SERVING

1. Drain the beans and set them aside. Place the coriander and cumin seeds in a dry skillet and toast them over medium heat until fragrant, shaking the pan frequently. Use a mortar and pestle or a spice grinder to grind the mixture into a fine powder.

2. Place the lard in a large saucepan and warm it over medium heat. Add the onion, garlic, bay leaf, toasted spice powder, chile powders, thyme, oregano, and marjoram and cook, stirring frequently, until the onion is translucent, about 3 minutes.

3. Add the beans and cover with cold water by 4 inches. Add the epazote, bring to a simmer, and cook the beans until very tender, about 1 hour and 30 minutes. Drain the beans and reserve the cooking liquid for another preparation.

4. Remove the bay leaf and epazote from the mixture, place it in a blender, and puree until smooth.

5. Place the puree in a clean saucepan, add the stock, and simmer until the flavor has developed to your liking.

6. Season the soup with salt, ladle it into warmed bowls, and serve with the tortillas, lime wedges, and cotija.

Sopa de Chile Poblano

YIELD: 2 SERVINGS / **ACTIVE TIME:** 20 MINUTES / **TOTAL TIME:** 40 MINUTES

1 LB. POBLANO CHILE PEPPERS

3 TABLESPOONS UNSALTED BUTTER

1 SMALL WHITE ONION

7 GARLIC CLOVES, MINCED

2 SERRANO CHILE PEPPERS, STEMMED, SEEDED, AND DICED, PLUS MORE FOR GARNISH

1 JALAPEÑO CHILE PEPPER, STEMMED, SEEDED, AND DICED

3½ OZ. KALE OR SPINACH, STEMS REMOVED

4 CUPS CHICKEN OR VEGETABLE STOCK (SEE PAGE 438 OR 439)

½ CUP HEAVY CREAM

2 CORN TORTILLAS (SEE PAGE 65), TOASTED

½ CUP YOGURT

FRESH CILANTRO, CHOPPED, FOR GARNISH

LIME WEDGES, FOR SERVING

FRIED TORTILLA STRIPS, FOR SERVING

1. Place the poblanos in a comal or cast-iron skillet and toast them until they are charred all over. You can also do this under the broiler or over an open flame. Place the charred poblanos in a heatproof bowl and cover with plastic wrap. Let them steam for 10 minutes.

2. Remove the skins, stems, and seeds from the poblanos and discard. Roughly chop the remaining flesh and set it aside.

3. Place the butter in a large saucepan and melt it over medium-high heat. Add the onion and cook until it starts to soften, about 5 minutes, stirring occasionally. Add the garlic and cook for 1 minute.

4. Add the poblanos, serrano peppers, jalapeño, and kale and cook for 2 to 3 minutes, stirring occasionally. Add the stock and bring the soup to a boil. Reduce the heat to medium-low, add the cream, and simmer until the broth has reduced slightly, about 30 minutes.

5. Transfer the soup to a blender, add the tortillas, and puree until smooth, at least 1 minute.

6. Ladle the soup into warm bowls and top each one with a generous dollop of yogurt. Garnish with cilantro and additional serrano pepper and serve with lime wedges and tortilla strips.

Puchero de Tres Carnes

YIELD: 4 SERVINGS / **ACTIVE TIME:** 1 HOUR / **TOTAL TIME:** 1 HOUR AND 30 MINUTES

14 GARLIC CLOVES, UNPEELED

½ TEASPOON CORIANDER SEEDS

½ TEASPOON CUMIN SEEDS

½ TEASPOON BLACK PEPPERCORNS

1 STAR ANISE POD

2 WHOLE CLOVES

¼ CUP LARD

1 LB. BONELESS, SKINLESS CHICKEN THIGHS

1 LB. BEEF CHUCK, CUBED

1 LB. PORK SHOULDER, CUBED

1 MEDIUM WHITE ONION, HALVED AND CHARRED

¼ TEASPOON DRIED MEXICAN OREGANO

½ TEASPOON ACHIOTE POWDER

¼ TEASPOON CINNAMON

2 BAY LEAVES

4 CUPS CHICKEN STOCK (SEE PAGE 438) OR WATER

¾ CUP DICED SWEET POTATO (LARGE DICE)

¾ CUP DICED CARROTS

¾ CUP DICED POTATO

¾ CUP DICED SQUASH

½ LB. CABBAGE, QUARTERED

½ LB. RIPENED PLANTAIN, PEELED AND SLICED ½ INCH THICK

½ CUP COOKED CHICKPEAS

CORN TORTILLAS (SEE PAGE 65), WARM, FOR SERVING

SALPICON DE RABANO Y CHILE HABANERO (SEE PAGE 264), FOR SERVING

1. Place the garlic cloves in a dry skillet and toast over medium heat until they are lightly charred in spots, about 10 minutes, turning occasionally. Remove them from the pan and let the garlic cool slightly. When the garlic is cool enough to handle, peel and finely dice it.

2. Place the coriander seeds, cumin seeds, peppercorns, star anise, and cloves in the skillet and toast until they are fragrant, shaking the pan frequently. Use a mortar and pestle or a spice grinder to grind the mixture to a fine powder.

3. Place some of the lard in a large saucepan and melt it over medium heat. Working with one protein at a time, add them to the pan and sear until browned all over, turning them as necessary. Remove the browned meats and set them aside. Add some of the remaining lard to the pan if it starts to look dry while searing the meat. When the chicken is cool enough to handle, chop it into cubes.

4. Add the onion, garlic, toasted spice powder, oregano, achiote powder, cinnamon, and bay leaves to the pan and cook until the onion is translucent, about 3 minutes, stirring occasionally. Return the meats to the pan along with any juices. Cover the mixture with the stock and bring the soup to a simmer. Cook until the meats are very tender, about 1 hour.

5. Remove the proteins and strain the broth. Return the broth to the pan and bring it to a simmer. Working with one ingredient at a time, add the sweet potato, carrots, potato, squash, cabbage, and plantain to the pan and simmer until tender. Set the vegetables aside with the meats.

6. Add the chickpeas and cook until warmed through.

7. Divide the meats and vegetables between the serving bowls. Ladle some broth and chickpeas into each and serve with tortillas and Salpicon de Rabano y Chile Habanero.

Puchero de Tres Carnes
SEE PAGE 237

Sopa de Papa

YIELD: 4 SERVINGS / **ACTIVE TIME:** 10 MINUTES / **TOTAL TIME:** 35 MINUTES

4 LARGE TOMATOES

2 GARLIC CLOVES

¼ WHITE ONION

1 TABLESPOON EXTRA-VIRGIN OLIVE OIL

1 TEASPOON DRIED MEXICAN OREGANO

4 YUKON GOLD POTATOES, PEELED AND DICED

SALT, TO TASTE

1 CUP CRUMBLED QUESO FRESCO (SEE PAGE 287)

½ BUNCH OF FRESH CILANTRO

1. Bring water to a boil in a small saucepan. Add the tomatoes, garlic, and onion and cook until they have softened, about 10 minutes. Drain, place the vegetables in a blender, and puree until smooth.

2. Place the olive oil in a medium saucepan and warm it over medium heat. Strain the puree into the pan and add the oregano, potatoes, and 2 cups of water. Bring to a simmer and cook until the potatoes are tender but not falling apart, about 15 minutes.

3. Season the soup with salt, ladle it into warm bowls, and garnish each portion with Queso Fresco and sprigs of the cilantro.

Sopa de Fideo

YIELD: 6 SERVINGS / **ACTIVE TIME:** 10 MINUTES / **TOTAL TIME:** 25 MINUTES

4 LARGE TOMATOES

½ ONION

2 GARLIC CLOVES

1 TABLESPOON EXTRA-VIRGIN OLIVE OIL

½ LB. FIDEO OR ANGEL HAIR PASTA

SALT, TO TASTE

1. Place the tomatoes, onion, and garlic in a blender and puree until smooth.

2. Place the olive oil in a medium saucepan and warm it over medium-high heat. Add the pasta and cook until it is lightly browned, stirring occasionally.

3. Reduce the heat to low and carefully strain the puree into the pan. Cook for 2 minutes and then add 2 cups of water. Bring the soup to a simmer and cook until the pasta is tender, approximately 15 minutes.

4. Season the soup with salt and ladle it into warmed bowls.

Caldo de Espinazo de Puerco

YIELD: 4 SERVINGS / **ACTIVE TIME:** 15 MINUTES / **TOTAL TIME:** 24 HOURS

4 LBS. PORK NECK BONES

10 DRIED CALIFORNIA OR NEW MEXICO CHILE PEPPERS, STEMMED AND SEEDED

2 GARLIC CLOVES

½ WHITE ONION

½ CUP DRIED CHICKPEAS, SOAKED OVERNIGHT AND DRAINED

SALT, TO TASTE

1 BUNCH OF WATERCRESS, CHOPPED

1. Rinse the pork bones under cold water. Place them in a large saucepan and cover with water. Bring to a simmer.

2. Bring water to a boil in a small saucepan. Place the chiles in a bowl and cover them with the boiling water. Let them soak for 15 minutes. Drain the chiles and reserve the soaking liquid.

3. Place the chiles and garlic in a blender, add a little of the soaking liquid, and puree until smooth. Stir the puree into the simmering broth.

4. Add the onion and chickpeas to the pan and cook until the meat on the pork neck bones and the chickpeas are very tender, about 50 minutes.

5. Season the soup with salt. Remove the chickpeas from the soup and place them in a blender. Add 2 cups of the broth and puree until smooth. Stir the puree back into the soup and cook until it thickens slightly.

6. Stir in the watercress and ladle the soup into warmed bowls.

Caldo de Pescado

YIELD: 6 SERVINGS / **ACTIVE TIME:** 10 MINUTES / **TOTAL TIME:** 1 HOUR

2 LB. RED SNAPPER, FILLETED AND BONED, HEAD AND TAIL RESERVED

2 DRIED CALIFORNIA CHILE PEPPERS, STEMMED AND SEEDED

4 LARGE TOMATOES

¼ WHITE ONION

2 GARLIC CLOVES

2 TABLESPOONS EXTRA-VIRGIN OLIVE OIL

1 TEASPOON BLACK PEPPER

2 TABLESPOONS KOSHER SALT

2 BAY LEAVES

3 LARGE CARROTS, PEELED AND CUT ON A BIAS

4 CELERY STALKS, PEELED AND DICED

2 RUSSET POTATOES, PEELED AND DICED

1 TEASPOON DRIED MEXICAN OREGANO

1 LB. SHRIMP, SHELL ON, CLEANED AND DEVEINED

½ BUNCH OF FRESH CILANTRO

1. Cut the fillets into 3-inch pieces. Place the head and the tail of the fish in a saucepan, add 8 to 10 cups of water, and bring to a simmer over medium heat. Cook for 20 minutes and drain the stock into a large bowl. Reserve the fish head.

2. Place the chiles in a bowl of hot water and let them soak for 20 minutes.

3. Place the tomatoes in a small saucepan, add water, and simmer over medium heat until tender. Drain the tomatoes and place them in a blender. Add the onion, garlic, and chiles and puree until smooth.

4. Place the olive oil in a large saucepan and warm over medium heat. Strain the puree into the pan and cook for 5 minutes.

5. Add the pepper, salt, stock, bay leaves, carrots, celery, potatoes, and oregano and cook until the vegetables start to soften, about 20 minutes.

6. Add the fish and shrimp and simmer until they are cooked through, about 7 minutes.

7. Taste, adjust the seasoning, and add the fish head to the soup. Ladle into warmed bowls and garnish each portion with some of the cilantro.

Albondigas Soup

YIELD: 6 SERVINGS / **ACTIVE TIME:** 25 MINUTES / **TOTAL TIME:** 50 MINUTES

2 LBS. GROUND BEEF

1 EGG

2 TABLESPOONS COOKED RICE

3 SPRIGS OF FRESH HIERBABUENA, FINELY CHOPPED, PLUS MORE TO TASTE

2 SPRIGS OF FRESH OREGANO, FINELY CHOPPED

½ BUNCH OF FRESH PARSLEY, FINELY CHOPPED

SALT, TO TASTE

4 LARGE TOMATOES

¼ ONION

2 GARLIC CLOVES

1 TEASPOON CUMIN

½ TEASPOON TOMATO PASTE

2 TABLESPOONS EXTRA-VIRGIN OLIVE OIL

3 CARROTS, PEELED AND SLICED

3 ZUCCHINI, SLICED

CORN TORTILLAS (SEE PAGE 65), WARM, FOR SERVING

ROASTED SERRANO OR JALAPEÑO CHILE PEPPERS, FOR SERVING

1. In a large mixing bowl, combine the ground beef, egg, rice, hierbabuena, oregano, and parsley and season the mixture with salt. Form the mixture into meatballs that weigh about 1 oz. each.

2. Place the tomatoes, onion, and garlic in a small saucepan, cover them with water, and boil until the vegetables are tender. Drain, add the vegetables to a blender with the cumin and tomato paste, and puree until smooth.

3. Place the olive oil in a large saucepan and warm it over medium heat. Add the puree and cook for 2 minutes.

4. Add 4 cups of water and season with salt. If desired, add more sprigs of hierbabuena to the broth. Bring to a simmer.

5. Add the carrots and meatballs and cook over low heat until the meatballs are completely cooked through, about 20 minutes.

6. Add the zucchini and cook until tender, about 5 minutes.

7. Ladle the soup into warmed bowls and serve with warm tortillas and roasted chiles.

Caldo de Camarón Seco

YIELD: 4 SERVINGS / **ACTIVE TIME:** 30 MINUTES / **TOTAL TIME:** 1 HOUR

4 GUAJILLO CHILE PEPPERS, STEMMED AND SEEDED

2 TO 3 DRIED CHILES DE ÁRBOL, STEMMED AND SEEDED

½ LB. DRIED SHRIMP, WITH HEADS AND TAILS

2 TO 3 FRESH EPAZOTE LEAVES

2 TABLESPOONS LARD

1 SMALL WHITE ONION, JULIENNED

4 GARLIC CLOVES, SLICED THIN

⅛ TEASPOON DRIED MEXICAN OREGANO

1 BAY LEAF

1 CORN TORTILLA (SEE PAGE 65), TOASTED

SALT, TO TASTE

LIME WEDGES, FOR SERVING

1. Place the chiles in a dry skillet and toast until they are fragrant and pliable. Remove the chiles from the pan and chop them.

2. Place 4 cups water in a medium saucepan and bring it to a simmer. Add the dried shrimp and epazote and simmer for 10 minutes. Remove the pan from heat and let the mixture steep for 10 minutes. Strain and reserve the shrimp and broth.

3. Place the lard in a medium saucepan and warm it over medium heat. Add the onion, garlic, chiles, and half of the shrimp and cook, stirring continually, for 1 to 2 minutes. Add the oregano, shrimp broth, bay leaf, and tortilla and simmer for 5 to 10 minutes.

4. Remove the bay leaf and discard it. Place the soup in a blender and puree until smooth, 2 to 3 minutes. Return the mixture to the pan and simmer for 5 minutes.

5. Season the soup with salt. Divide the remaining shrimp between the serving bowls and ladle some soup into each one. Serve with lime wedges.

Caldo de Res

YIELD: 10 SERVINGS / **ACTIVE TIME:** 20 MINUTES / **TOTAL TIME:** 1 HOUR AND 10 MINUTES

5 LBS. BONELESS BEEF CHUCK, CUT INTO 4-INCH CUBES

SALT, TO TASTE

3 CARROTS

1 WHITE ONION, HALVED

1 GREEN CABBAGE, QUARTERED

5 YUKON GOLD POTATOES, QUARTERED

4 MEXICAN SQUASH, SLICED

LEMON WEDGES, FOR SERVING

SALSA, FOR SERVING

CORN TORTILLAS (SEE PAGE 65), WARM, FOR SERVING

1. Place the beef in a large saucepan and fill the pan with water. Bring to a boil, season with salt, reduce the heat to medium, and simmer until the meat is tender, approximately 1 hour.

2. Add the carrots, onion, and cabbage and cook for 20 minutes.

3. Add the potatoes and squash and cook until tender, about 20 minutes.

4. Ladle the soup into warmed bowls and serve with lemon wedges, salsa (a red salsa is recommended), and warm tortillas.

Caldo de Camarón Seco

SEE PAGE 244

Sopa de Lentejas

YIELD: 4 SERVINGS / **ACTIVE TIME:** 10 MINUTES / **TOTAL TIME:** 1 HOUR AND 30 MINUTES

1 CUP GREEN LENTILS

1 TABLESPOON EXTRA-VIRGIN OLIVE OIL

2 CARROTS, PEELED AND FINELY DICED

1 ONION, FINELY DICED

2 CELERY STALKS, PEELED AND FINELY DICED

2 GARLIC CLOVES, SLICED THIN

5 CUPS CHICKEN STOCK (SEE PAGE 438) OR WATER

1 CUP DICED CANNED TOMATOES

2 BAY LEAVES

1 CUP SPINACH (OPTIONAL)

SALT, TO TASTE

FRESH CILANTRO, CHOPPED, FOR GARNISH

1. Place the lentils in a bowl of cold water and soak for 1 hour. Drain the lentils, rinse them thoroughly, and discard any small pebbles or debris.

2. Place the olive oil in a medium saucepan and warm it over medium heat. Add the carrots, onion, celery, and garlic and cook until the onion is translucent, about 3 minutes, stirring frequently.

3. Add the lentils and cook for 2 minutes, stirring continually.

4. Add the stock, tomatoes, and bay leaves and bring the soup to a boil. Reduce the heat and simmer until the lentils are tender, about 25 minutes.

5. If desired, add the spinach and cook until wilted, about 2 minutes. Season the soup with salt, ladle it into warm bowls, and garnish with cilantro.

SAUCES & CONDIMENTS

Mole Negro

YIELD: 2 CUPS / **ACTIVE TIME:** 1 HOUR / **TOTAL TIME:** 4 HOURS

2 TO 3 DRIED CHILHUACLE NEGRO CHILE PEPPERS, STEMMED AND SEEDED, SEEDS RESERVED

1 CHIPOTLE MECO CHILE PEPPER, STEMMED AND SEEDED, SEEDS RESERVED

2 ANCHO CHILE PEPPERS, STEMMED AND SEEDED, SEEDS RESERVED

2 PASILLA CHILE PEPPERS, STEMMED AND SEEDED, SEEDS RESERVED

3 GUAJILLO CHILE PEPPERS, STEMMED AND SEEDED, SEEDS RESERVED

3 TABLESPOONS SESAME SEEDS

¼ CUP BLANCHED ALMONDS

3 TABLESPOONS PECANS

1½ SMALL WHITE ONIONS, CUT INTO 12 PIECES

10 GARLIC CLOVES, UNPEELED

5 ROMA TOMATOES, HALVED

4 OZ. TOMATILLOS, HUSKED AND RINSED

2 MEXICAN CINNAMON STICKS

¼ TEASPOON BLACK PEPPERCORNS

¼ TEASPOON WHOLE CLOVES

1 AVOCADO LEAF

1 HOJA SANTA LEAF

1 BAY LEAF

16 CUPS CHICKEN STOCK (SEE PAGE 438)

½ CUP LARD

1¾ OZ. BRIOCHE BREAD

½ CUP CHOPPED OVERRIPE PLANTAIN

2 TABLESPOONS RAISINS

½ TEASPOON DRIED THYME

½ TEASPOON DRIED MEXICAN OREGANO

5⅓ OZ. MEXICAN CHOCOLATE

SALT, TO TASTE

1. Place 2 quarts of water in a saucepan and bring it to a simmer. Turn off the heat.

2. Warm a comal or large cast-iron skillet over medium-high heat. Place all of the chiles in the pan and toast until they are charred all over. Using a spatula to press down on the chiles as they toast works nicely.

3. Place the chiles in the hot water and soak for 30 minutes. Preheat the oven to 350°F.

4. Drain the chiles and reserve the soaking liquid. Place the chiles in a blender and puree until smooth, adding the reserved liquid as needed. Strain the puree into a bowl, pressing down to extract as much liquid as possible, and discard the solids (or dehydrate them and use it as a spice powder).

5. Place the sesame seeds, almonds, and pecans on a parchment-lined baking sheet, place them in the oven, and and toast until they are dark brown, 10 to 12 minutes. Remove the pan from the oven and let the mixture cool.

6. Place the onions, garlic, tomatoes, and tomatillos in the comal or cast-iron skillet and toast until they are charred all over, turning them occasionally. Peel the garlic cloves, place the charred vegetables in a blender, and puree until smooth. Strain the puree into a bowl, pressing down to extract as much liquid as possible, and discard the solids.

7. Place the cinnamon sticks, peppercorns, cloves, avocado leaf, hoja santa leaf, and bay leaf in a dry skillet and toast until they are fragrant, shaking the pan frequently. Remove the mixture from the pan and let it cool. When the mixture has cooled, use a mortar and pestle or a spice grinder to grind it into a fine powder.

8. Place all of the chile seeds in a dry skillet and toast over medium-high heat until thoroughly blackened. Make sure to open windows, turn on the kitchen fan, and wear a mask, as the toasted chile seeds will produce noxious fumes.

9. Use a long match or a kitchen torch to light the seeds on fire. When they burn out, place them in a bowl of cold water. Soak the seeds in the cold water, and change the water every 10 minutes for a total of three changes. After the final soak, drain the seeds, place them in the blender with 1 cup of stock, and puree until smooth. Strain the liquid into a bowl through a fine-mesh sieve.

10. Place half of the lard in a skillet and warm it over medium heat. Add the bread and fry until it is dark brown, stirring occasionally. Remove the bread from the pan and set it aside.

11. Add the plantain and fry until it is dark brown and caramelized, about 4 minutes, stirring occasionally. Remove it from the pan and set it aside.

12. Add the raisins and fry them until plump and caramelized, about 3 minutes, stirring occasionally. Remove them from the pan and set them aside.

13. Add the toasted nuts and sesame seeds and fry for about 1 minute. Place the nuts and seeds in the blender with a small amount of stock and puree until the mixture is a smooth paste.

14. Add the vegetable puree, toasted chile puree, chile seed puree, fine powder made in Step 7, raisins, plantains, bread, and toasted nut-and-seed paste and puree until smooth. Strain the puree into a bowl through a fine-mesh sieve, again pressing down to get as much liquid as possible.

15. Place the remaining lard in a large saucepan and warm it over medium-high heat. Add the chile puree and cook until it bubbles vigorously, stirring with a whisk to prevent the mixture from scorching. Reduce the heat to low and cook for 30 minutes.

16. Add the thyme and oregano and cook for 1 to 2 hours, adding the stock as needed.

17. When the rawness of the ingredients has been completely cooked out, add the chocolate and stir to incorporate. Season with salt and let the mole cool, then taste and adjust the seasoning as necessary. As it sits, the mole will take on stronger, increasingly delicious flavors.

Mole Negro
SEE PAGE 252

Chile Colorado

YIELD: 4 CUPS / **ACTIVE TIME:** 30 MINUTES / **TOTAL TIME:** 1 HOUR AND 30 MINUTES

7 OZ. GUAJILLO CHILE PEPPERS, STEMMED AND SEEDED

1¾ OZ. ANCHO CHILE PEPPERS, STEMMED AND SEEDED

⅓ OZ. DRIED CHILES DE ÁRBOL, STEMMED AND SEEDED

1 TABLESPOON CORIANDER SEEDS

1½ TEASPOONS ALLSPICE BERRIES

1¼ TABLESPOONS CUMIN SEEDS

1 TABLESPOON EXTRA-VIRGIN OLIVE OIL

1 WHITE ONION, SLICED

10 GARLIC CLOVES

1 TABLESPOON DRIED MARJORAM

1 TABLESPOON DRIED MEXICAN OREGANO

1 TABLESPOON DRIED THYME

3 TABLESPOONS LARD

2 BAY LEAVES

CHICKEN OR VEGETABLE STOCK (SEE PAGE 438 OR 439), AS NEEDED

SALT, TO TASTE

1. Place the chiles in a dry skillet and toast until they are pliable and fragrant. Place them in a bowl of hot water and let them soak for 30 minutes.

2. Place the coriander seeds, allspice berries, and cumin seeds in the skillet and toast until fragrant, shaking the pan frequently. Grind the toasted seeds to a fine powder with a mortar and pestle or a spice grinder.

3. Place the olive oil in the skillet and warm it over medium heat. Add the onion, garlic, toasted spice powder, marjoram, oregano, and thyme and cook, stirring frequently, until the onion is translucent, about 3 minutes.

4. Drain the chiles and reserve the soaking liquid. Place the chiles and onion mixture in a blender and puree until smooth, adding the reserved liquid as necessary to get the desired texture.

5. Place the lard in a Dutch oven and warm it over high heat. Carefully add the puree (it will splatter) and the bay leaves, reduce the heat to low, and simmer for 1 hour, adding stock as necessary to get the flavor and texture to your liking. Season with salt before using or storing.

Mole Manchamanteles

YIELD: 4 TO 6 CUPS / **ACTIVE TIME:** 30 MINUTES / **TOTAL TIME:** 2 HOURS AND 30 MINUTES

½ LB. PILONCILLO

1 CUP WATER

1 APPLE, PEELED, CORED, AND SLICED

1 PEAR, PEELED, CORED, AND SLICED

1 PEACH, HALVED, PITTED, AND SLICED

¾ CUP SESAME SEEDS

½ MEXICAN CINNAMON STICK

1¼ TABLESPOONS CORIANDER SEEDS

1½ TEASPOONS ALLSPICE BERRIES

1 TABLESPOON CUMIN SEEDS

2 STAR ANISE PODS

1 WHITE ONION, QUARTERED

5 GARLIC CLOVES, UNPEELED

7 TABLESPOONS LARD

6 ANCHO CHILE PEPPERS, STEMMED AND SEEDED

5 GUAJILLO CHILE PEPPERS, STEMMED AND SEEDED

2 CHIPOTLE MECO CHILE PEPPERS, STEMMED AND SEEDED

½ CUP GOLDEN RAISINS

1 RIPE PLANTAIN, PEELED AND SLICED

10½ OZ. ROMA TOMATOES, HALVED

CHICKEN STOCK (SEE PAGE 438), AS NEEDED

SALT, TO TASTE

1. Preheat the oven to 400°F. Place the piloncillo and water in a saucepan and bring to a boil, stirring to dissolve the piloncillo. Toss the apple, pear, and peach into the syrup, transfer the mixture to a baking dish, and place it in the oven. Roast until the fruits are caramelized, about 20 minutes.

2. Place the sesame seeds in a dry skillet and toast until they are lightly browned, shaking the pan frequently. Add the cinnamon stick, coriander seeds, allspice berries, cumin seeds, and star anise to the skillet and toast until fragrant, shaking the pan frequently. Grind the mixture into a fine powder with a mortar and pestle or a spice grinder.

3. Place the onion and garlic in the skillet and cook over medium heat until they are charred, about 10 minutes, turning occasionally. Remove them from the pan and let them cool. When cool enough to handle, peel the garlic cloves.

4. Place the lard in a Dutch oven and warm it over medium heat. Add the chiles and fry until pliable and fragrant. Remove the chiles and soak them in hot water for 20 minutes.

5. Place the raisins and plantain in the lard and fry until the raisins are puffy and the plantain has caramelized. Add all of the ingredients to the Dutch oven and cook for 1 to 2 hours, adding stock as needed.

6. Place the mixture in a blender and puree until smooth. Strain, season with salt, and use as desired.

SAUCES & CONDIMENTS

Salsa de Chiltomate

YIELD: 1½ CUPS / **ACTIVE TIME:** 20 MINUTES / **TOTAL TIME:** 1 HOUR

8½ OZ. ROMA TOMATOES, HALVED

2 HABANERO CHILE PEPPERS

1 SMALL WHITE ONION, QUARTERED

4 GARLIC CLOVES, UNPEELED

2 TABLESPOONS EXTRA-VIRGIN OLIVE OIL

SALT, TO TASTE

JUICE OF 1 LIME

1. Preheat the oven to 450°F. Line a baking sheet with parchment paper, place the tomatoes, chiles, onion, and garlic on it, and place it in the oven.

2. Roast until the vegetables are charred all over, checking every 5 minutes or so and removing them as they become ready.

3. Peel the garlic cloves, remove the stems and seeds from the habaneros (gloves are strongly recommended while handling habaneros), and place the roasted vegetables in a blender. Puree until smooth.

4. Place the olive oil in a medium saucepan and warm it over medium-high heat. Carefully pour the puree into the pan, reduce the heat, and simmer until it has reduced slightly and the flavor is to your liking, 15 to 20 minutes.

5. Season with salt, stir in the lime juice, and let the salsa cool. Taste, adjust the seasoning if necessary, and use as desired.

Mole Blanco

YIELD: 4 CUPS / **ACTIVE TIME:** 30 MINUTES / **TOTAL TIME:** 1 HOUR

1 TABLESPOON PINE NUTS, LIGHTLY TOASTED

1 TABLESPOON SUNFLOWER SEEDS, LIGHTLY TOASTED

1 TABLESPOON SESAME SEEDS, LIGHTLY TOASTED

3½ TABLESPOONS CHICKEN STOCK (SEE PAGE 438), PLUS MORE AS NEEDED

2 TABLESPOONS EXTRA-VIRGIN OLIVE OIL

1½ TOMATILLOS, HUSKED AND RINSED

1 GARLIC CLOVE

¼ WHITE ONION

1 TABLESPOON CHOPPED HABANERO CHILE PEPPER

2 TABLESPOONS DICED TURNIP

1 TABLESPOON DICED FENNEL

1 TABLESPOON PEELED AND DICED GREEN APPLE

1 TABLESPOON SOURDOUGH BREAD CRUMBS

1 TABLESPOON GOLDEN RAISINS

1 TABLESPOON MINCED PLANTAIN

3 TABLESPOONS MASA HARINA

⅛ TEASPOON WHITE PEPPER

⅛ TEASPOON ALLSPICE

PINCH OF GROUND FENNEL

1 CORIANDER SEED, TOASTED AND GROUND

3½ TABLESPOONS WHOLE MILK

1 TEASPOON GRATED WHITE CHOCOLATE

SALT, TO TASTE

1. Use a mortar and pestle or a spice grinder to turn the pine nuts, sunflower seeds, and sesame seeds into a paste, adding stock as needed.

2. Place the olive oil in a Dutch oven and warm it over medium heat. Add the tomatillos, garlic, onion, habanero, turnip, fresh fennel, apple, bread crumbs, raisins, and plantain and cook until the onion is translucent, about 3 minutes, stirring continually so that the contents of the pan do not brown.

3. Add the seed paste, masa harina, white pepper, allspice, ground fennel, and coriander seed and stir to incorporate. Add the milk and stock and simmer until the fruits and vegetables are tender.

4. Stir in the white chocolate. Taste and adjust the seasoning as necessary. Place the mixture in a blender and puree until smooth. Strain before using or storing.

Preserved Limes with Chile de Árbol & Spices

YIELD: 8 SERVINGS / **ACTIVE TIME:** 15 MINUTES / **TOTAL TIME:** 2 TO 4 WEEKS

7 LIMES

2 TABLESPOONS GROUND CARDAMOM

2 TABLESPOONS SMOKED SPANISH PAPRIKA

2 TABLESPOONS TURMERIC

1½ TEASPOONS TOASTED AND GROUND CUMIN SEEDS

3 TABLESPOONS KOSHER SALT

5 CHILES DE ÁRBOL, STEMMED, SEEDED, AND GROUND

1. Squeeze the juice from the limes into a large bowl and save the spent halves. Add all of the remaining ingredients to the bowl and stir until the mixture is a paste.

2. Put on gloves, add the spent lime halves, and work the mixture until well combined.

3. Transfer the mixture to an airtight container and gently press down on it to make sure that the solids are completely submerged in the liquid and there are no pockets air can get into. Seal the container and store it at room temperature or chill in the refrigerator until the lime halves are tender. This will take about 2 weeks at room temperature, and a month in the refrigerator.

4. When the preserved limes are ready, mince them and use as desired.

Strawberry Hot Sauce

YIELD: 4 CUPS / **ACTIVE TIME:** 30 MINUTES / **TOTAL TIME:** 2 HOURS

1 LB. STRAWBERRIES, RINSED AND HULLED

2 TEASPOONS KOSHER SALT, PLUS MORE TO TASTE

3½ OZ. CHILES DE ÁRBOL

4 CUPS WATER

1½ TEASPOONS CUMIN

1 TABLESPOON CORIANDER SEEDS

1¼ CUPS PLUS 1 TABLESPOON APPLE CIDER VINEGAR

1¾ CUPS DISTILLED WHITE VINEGAR

1. Place the strawberries and salt in a blender and puree until smooth. Let the mixture sit at room temperature for 1 hour.

2. Place the chiles, strawberry puree, and water in a saucepan and bring to a boil, making sure to stir and scrape the bottom of the pan frequently to keep a skin from forming.

3. Add the cumin and coriander and cook for another 20 minutes, stirring and scraping the bottom of the pan frequently.

4. Working in batches, transfer the mixture to the blender and puree for about 3 minutes. The strawberry seeds should break down, as they have been cooking for a while.

5. Strain the mixture through a fine-mesh sieve into a clean saucepan. Add the vinegars and cook over medium-high heat until the sauce has reduced by half.

6. Season the sauce generously with salt. Use immediately or store in the refrigerator.

Salsa Verde Tatemada

YIELD: 1½ CUPS / **ACTIVE TIME:** 20 MINUTES / **TOTAL TIME:** 30 MINUTES

1 LB. TOMATILLOS, HUSKED AND RINSED WELL

5 GARLIC CLOVES, UNPEELED

1 SMALL WHITE ONION, QUARTERED

10 SERRANO CHILE PEPPERS

2 BUNCHES OF FRESH CILANTRO

SALT, TO TASTE

1. Warm a comal or large cast-iron skillet over high heat. Place the tomatillos, garlic, onion, and chiles in the pan and cook until they are charred all over, turning them occasionally.

2. Remove the charred vegetables from the pan and let them cool slightly.

3. Peel the garlic cloves and remove the stems and seeds from the chiles. Place the charred vegetables in a blender, add the cilantro, and puree until smooth.

4. Season the salsa with salt and use as desired.

Cumin & Cilantro Vinaigrette

YIELD: 2 CUPS / **ACTIVE TIME:** 10 MINUTES / **TOTAL TIME:** 10 MINUTES

¼ CUP CUMIN SEEDS

¼ CUP BROWN SUGAR

3 EGG YOLKS

⅓ CUP RED WINE VINEGAR

½ CUP WATER

2 CUPS FRESH CILANTRO, CHOPPED

SALT AND PEPPER, TO TASTE

1½ CUPS EXTRA-VIRGIN OLIVE OIL

1. Place the cumin seeds in a dry skillet and toast over low heat until fragrant, shaking the pan frequently. Remove the seeds from the pan and place them in a blender.

2. Place all of the remaining ingredients, except for the olive oil, in the blender and puree until smooth. With the blender running, slowly add the olive oil until it has been emulsified. Use immediately or store in the refrigerator.

Salpicon de Rabano y Chile Habanero

YIELD: 1½ CUPS / **ACTIVE TIME:** 20 MINUTES / **TOTAL TIME:** 1 HOUR AND 30 MINUTES

2 HABANERO CHILE PEPPERS

4 TO 5 RADISHES, TRIMMED AND JULIENNED

1 BAY LEAF

⅛ TEASPOON DRIED MEXICAN OREGANO

½ CUP FRESH LIME JUICE

½ CUP ORANGE JUICE

1 TABLESPOON EXTRA-VIRGIN OLIVE OIL

SALT, TO TASTE

1. Roast the habaneros over an open flame, in the oven, or on the grill until they are charred all over. Let them cool briefly, remove the stems and seeds (wearing gloves is strongly recommended when handling habaneros), and mince the remaining flesh.

2. Place the habaneros in a bowl, add the remaining ingredients, and let the mixture macerate for at least 1 hour before serving.

Barbacoa Adobo

YIELD: 1½ CUPS / **ACTIVE TIME:** 20 MINUTES / **TOTAL TIME:** 45 MINUTES

1 TABLESPOON CORIANDER SEEDS

1½ TEASPOONS WHOLE CLOVES

1½ TEASPOONS ALLSPICE BERRIES

1 TABLESPOON CUMIN SEEDS

1½ TABLESPOONS BLACK PEPPERCORNS

1 ANCHO CHILE PEPPER, STEMMED AND SEEDED

1 GUAJILLO CHILE PEPPER, STEMMED AND SEEDED

1 CHIPOTLE CHILE PEPPER, STEMMED AND SEEDED

1 PASILLA CHILE PEPPER, STEMMED AND SEEDED

14 TABLESPOONS ORANGE JUICE

14 TABLESPOONS FRESH LIME JUICE

2 SMALL ONIONS, SLICED

5 GARLIC CLOVES

2 AVOCADO LEAVES (OPTIONAL)

SALT, TO TASTE

1. Place the coriander, cloves, allspice, cumin, and peppercorns in a dry skillet and toast until fragrant, shaking the pan frequently. Using a mortar and pestle or a spice grinder, grind the mixture into a fine powder.

2. Place the chiles in the pan and toast until they are fragrant and pliable. Place the toasted chiles in a bowl of hot water and let them soak for 20 minutes.

3. Drain the chiles and reserve the soaking liquid. Place the chiles in a blender, add the juices, onions, garlic, and avocado leaves (if using), and puree until smooth, adding the reserved liquid as needed.

4. Stir in the spice powder, season the adobo with salt, and use as desired.

Epazote Oil

YIELD: 1 CUP / **ACTIVE TIME:** 5 MINUTES / **TOTAL TIME:** 5 MINUTES

3½ OZ. FRESH EPAZOTE

14 TABLESPOONS EXTRA-VIRGIN OLIVE OIL

1. Place the ingredients in a blender and puree until combined, making sure it takes no longer than 40 seconds.

2. Strain through a coffee filter. To preserve the oil for as long as possible, and to maintain the color, store it in the freezer.

Pipian Rojo

YIELD: 2 CUPS / **ACTIVE TIME:** 30 MINUTES / **TOTAL TIME:** 45 MINUTES

4 GUAJILLO CHILE PEPPERS, STEMMED AND SEEDED

1 ANCHO CHILE PEPPER, STEMMED AND SEEDED

2 DRIED CHILES DE ÁRBOL, STEMMED AND SEEDED

3½ OZ. PUMPKIN SEEDS, HULLED

⅔ CUP SESAME SEEDS

2½ ROMA TOMATOES

¾ SMALL WHITE ONION

4 GARLIC CLOVES

2 ALLSPICE BERRIES

1 WHOLE CLOVE

4 CINNAMON STICKS

2 CORN TORTILLAS (SEE PAGE 65), TOASTED

4 CUPS CHICKEN OR VEGETABLE STOCK (SEE PAGE 438 OR 439)

2 TABLESPOONS LARD

SALT, TO TASTE

1. Warm a comal or large cast-iron skillet over medium heat. Place the chiles in the pan and toast until they are fragrant and pliable. Place the toasted chiles in a bowl of hot water and let them soak for 20 minutes.

2. Drain the chiles and reserve the soaking liquid. Place the chiles in a blender and puree, adding the reserved liquid as needed. Strain into a bowl and reserve the pulp for another preparation.

3. Place the strained liquid in the blender, add all of the remaining ingredients, except for the lard and salt, and puree until smooth.

4. Place the lard in a medium saucepan and warm it over medium-high heat. Carefully add the puree and stir for 1 minute. Reduce the heat and simmer until the sauce is the desired texture. Season with salt and use as desired.

X'nipek

YIELD: 1 CUP / **ACTIVE TIME:** 10 MINUTES / **TOTAL TIME:** 20 MINUTES

4 ROMA TOMATOES, SEEDED AND DICED

2 TO 3 HABANERO PEPPERS, STEMMED, SEEDED, AND MINCED

1½ SMALL RED ONIONS, JULIENNED

1¼ CUPS FRESH CILANTRO, CHOPPED

1¾ OZ. FRESH LIME JUICE

10 TABLESPOONS ORANGE JUICE

1½ TEASPOONS DRIED MEXICAN OREGANO

SALT, TO TASTE

1. Place all of the ingredients, except for the salt, in a bowl and stir until combined. Let the mixture macerate for 10 minutes.
2. Season with salt and use as desired.

Salsa de Árbol

YIELD: ½ CUP / **ACTIVE TIME:** 10 MINUTES / **TOTAL TIME:** 35 MINUTES

¼ CUP LARD

3½ OZ. DRIED CHILES DE ÁRBOL, STEMMED AND SEEDED

1 OZ. GUAJILLO CHILE PEPPERS, STEMMED AND SEEDED

10 GARLIC CLOVES

SALT, TO TASTE

1. Place the lard in a cast-iron skillet and warm it over medium heat. Add the chiles and fry until they are fragrant and pliable. Place the chiles in a bowl of hot water and let them soak for 20 minutes.

2. Place the garlic in the skillet and fry until it is fragrant, about 1 minute. Place the garlic in a blender.

3. Drain the chiles and reserve the soaking liquid. Add the chiles to the blender and puree until the mixture is smooth, adding the reserved liquid as needed to get the desired texture.

4. Season the salsa with salt and use as desired.

YIELD: 1 CUP / **ACTIVE TIME:** 20 MINUTES / **TOTAL TIME:** 1 HOUR

8 TO 10 SERRANO OR JALAPEÑO CHILE PEPPERS

1 SMALL WHITE ONION, QUARTERED

2 TO 3 GARLIC CLOVES, UNPEELED

½ CUP SOY SAUCE

½ CUP FRESH LIME JUICE

2 TABLESPOONS MAGGI SEASONING SAUCE

1. Warm a comal or large cast-iron skillet over high heat. Place the chiles in the pan and toast until they are very charred all over, turning occasionally. Remove the chiles from the pan and let them cool.

2. Place the onion and garlic cloves in the pan and toast until they are lightly charred, turning occasionally. Remove them from the pan and let them cool.

3. Peel the garlic cloves and mince them. Julienne the onion and place it and the garlic in a mixing bowl.

4. Remove all but one-quarter of the charred skin from the chiles. Remove the stems and seeds and finely chop the remaining flesh. Add it to the garlic mixture along with the remaining ingredients and stir until combined.

5. Let the mixture macerate for at least 30 minutes before serving.

Recado Rojo

YIELD: 3 CUPS / **ACTIVE TIME:** 5 MINUTES / **TOTAL TIME:** 20 MINUTES

3½ OZ. ACHIOTE PASTE

14 TABLESPOONS FRESH LIME JUICE

14 TABLESPOONS ORANGE JUICE

7 TABLESPOONS GRAPEFRUIT JUICE

1 TEASPOON DRIED MEXICAN OREGANO

1 TEASPOON DRIED MARJORAM

1 HABANERO CHILE PEPPER, STEMMED AND SEEDED

5 GARLIC CLOVES

1 CINNAMON STICK, GRATED

SALT, TO TASTE

1. Place the achiote paste and juices in a bowl, gently stir to combine, and let the mixture sit for 15 minutes.

2. Place the mixture and the remaining ingredients in a blender and puree until smooth.

3. Taste, adjust the seasoning as needed, and use as desired.

Salsa de Aguacate

YIELD: 2 CUPS / **ACTIVE TIME:** 10 MINUTES / **TOTAL TIME:** 10 MINUTES

½ LB. TOMATILLOS, HUSKED AND RINSED WELL

½ WHITE ONION

4 GARLIC CLOVES

⅔ CUP DICED AVOCADO

4 CUPS FRESH CILANTRO LEAVES

FRESH LIME JUICE, TO TASTE

SALT, TO TASTE

1. Place the tomatillos, onion, garlic, and avocado in a blender and puree until smooth.

2. Add the cilantro and pulse to incorporate. Taste, season the salsa with lime juice and salt, and use as desired.

Fermented Chile Adobo

YIELD: 2 CUPS / **ACTIVE TIME:** 10 MINUTES / **TOTAL TIME:** 3 DAYS

13¼ CUPS WATER

⅓ CUP KOSHER SALT

2¼ LBS. CHIPOTLE MORITA CHILE PEPPERS, STEMMED AND SEEDED

2 BAY LEAVES

10 GARLIC CLOVES, SMASHED

1 CINNAMON STICK

⅛ TEASPOON WHOLE CLOVES

½ CUP APPLE CIDER VINEGAR

1 TEASPOON DRIED MEXICAN OREGANO

1. Place the water and salt in a saucepan and bring to a simmer, stirring to dissolve the salt. Turn off the heat and let the brine cool slightly.

2. Place the chiles, bay leaves, and garlic in a fermentation crock or large, food-grade storage container. Cover the mixture with the brine and place some plastic wrap on the surface. Let the mixture sit at room temperature for 3 to 5 days.

3. Place the cinnamon stick and cloves in a dry skillet and toast until they are fragrant, shaking the pan frequently. Use a mortar and pestle or a spice grinder to grind the mixture into a fine powder.

4. Strain the liquid from the fermented mixture and reserve it.

5. Place the chiles and garlic in a blender, add the toasted spice powder, vinegar, and oregano, and puree until the mixture is a smooth paste, adding the reserved liquid as needed to get the desired texture. Use immediately or store in the refrigerator.

Morita Salsa

YIELD: 2 CUPS / **ACTIVE TIME:** 15 MINUTES / **TOTAL TIME:** 45 MINUTES

3½ OZ. CHIPOTLE MORITA CHILE PEPPERS, STEMMED AND SEEDED

5 ROMA TOMATOES, HALVED

1 SMALL WHITE ONION, QUARTERED

5 GARLIC CLOVES

SALT, TO TASTE

1. Place the chiles in a skillet and gently toast until they are fragrant and pliable. Place the chiles in a bowl of hot water and let them soak for 30 minutes.

2. Drain the chiles, place them in a blender, and add the tomatoes, onion, and garlic. Puree until smooth.

3. Season the salsa with salt and use as desired.

Mole Verde

YIELD: 2 CUPS / **ACTIVE TIME:** 20 MINUTES / **TOTAL TIME:** 40 MINUTES

- ¼ TEASPOON WHOLE CLOVES
- ¼ TEASPOON ALLSPICE BERRIES
- ¼ TEASPOON CUMIN SEEDS
- ½ TEASPOON CORIANDER SEEDS
- ⅓ CUP SESAME SEEDS
- 3 TABLESPOONS PUMPKIN SEEDS, TOASTED
- SALT, TO TASTE
- 1½ CUPS FRESH EPAZOTE LEAVES
- ½ CUP FRESH MINT LEAVES
- ½ CUP FRESH PARSLEY LEAVES
- 1 CUP FRESH HOJA SANTA LEAVES
- 2 CUPS FRESH CILANTRO LEAVES
- 2 OZ. KALE, STEMS AND RIBS REMOVED
- ½ LB. TOMATILLOS, HUSKED AND RINSED WELL
- 3 SERRANO CHILE PEPPERS
- 10 GARLIC CLOVES
- 1 SMALL WHITE ONION, QUARTERED

1. Preheat the oven to 325°F. Place the cloves, allspice, cumin, and coriander in a dry skillet and toast until fragrant, shaking the pan frequently. Use a mortar and pestle or a spice grinder to grind the mixture into a fine powder.

2. Place the sesame and pumpkin seeds on a parchment-lined baking sheet, place it in the oven, and toast until the seeds are just golden brown, about 7 minutes. Remove them from the oven and let them cool.

3. Prepare an ice bath and bring generously salted water to a simmer in a large saucepan. Add the fresh herbs and kale and cook for 30 to 45 seconds. Drain and plunge them into the ice bath until they have cooled. Place the mixture in a linen towel and gently wring it to extract as much water as possible. Transfer the mixture to a blender.

4. Place the tomatillos, serrano peppers, garlic, and onion in a saucepan and cover with water by 1 inch. Season the water with salt and bring to a simmer. Cook until the vegetables are tender, about 15 minutes. Drain and add them to the blender.

5. Add the toasted seeds and the fine spice powder to the blender and puree until smooth. Season the mole with salt and gently warm it before serving.

SAUCES & CONDIMENTS

Mole Verde
SEE PAGE 277

Salsa Borracha

YIELD: 1½ CUPS / **ACTIVE TIME:** 20 MINUTES / **TOTAL TIME:** 30 MINUTES

½ LB. TOMATILLOS, HUSKED AND RINSED WELL

¾ SMALL WHITE ONION

5 GARLIC CLOVES, UNPEELED

2 TABLESPOONS LARD

3 PASILLA CHILE PEPPERS, STEMMED AND SEEDED

2 CHIPOTLE MORITA CHILE PEPPERS, STEMMED AND SEEDED

3½ OZ. MEXICAN LAGER

1 TEASPOON MEZCAL OR TEQUILA

1 TEASPOON MAGGI SEASONING SAUCE

SALT, TO TASTE

1. Preheat a comal or large cast-iron skillet over medium-high heat. Add the tomatillos, onion, and garlic and toast until they are charred all over, turning them as needed. Remove the vegetables from the pan and let them cool. When cool enough to handle, peel the garlic cloves and place the mixture in a blender.

2. Place half of the lard in the skillet and warm it over medium heat. Add the chiles and fry until they are fragrant and pliable. Place the chiles in the blender.

3. Add the beer, mezcal, and Maggi to the blender and puree until smooth.

4. Place the remaining lard in a saucepan and warm it over medium heat. Add the puree and fry it for 5 minutes. Season the salsa with salt and use immediately or store in the refrigerator.

Dzikil P'aak

YIELD: 1½ CUPS / **ACTIVE TIME:** 30 MINUTES / **TOTAL TIME:** 30 MINUTES

3 ROMA TOMATOES

4 OZ. TOMATILLOS, HUSKED AND RINSED WELL

¾ SMALL WHITE ONION

4 GARLIC CLOVES, UNPEELED

2 HABANERO CHILE PEPPERS

7 OZ. PUMPKIN SEEDS, HULLED AND ROASTED

7 TABLESPOONS FRESH LIME JUICE

7 TABLESPOONS ORANGE JUICE

1½ CUPS FRESH CILANTRO

1 TEASPOON MAGGI SEASONING SAUCE

SALT, TO TASTE

1. Warm a comal or large cast-iron skillet over medium-high heat. Add the tomatoes, tomatillos, onion, garlic, and habanero and cook until they are charred all over, turning them as needed.

2. Remove the vegetables from the pan and let them cool. When cool enough to handle, peel the garlic cloves, remove the stems and seeds from the habaneros (it is strongly recommended that you wear gloves while handling the habaneros), and place the mixture in a food processor.

3. Place the pumpkin seeds in the food processor and pulse until the mixture is a thick paste. Add the juices, cilantro, and Maggi and pulse until the mixture has a hummus-like consistency.

4. Season with salt and use immediately or store in the refrigerator.

Chileatole Verde

YIELD: 2 CUPS / **ACTIVE TIME:** 30 MINUTES / **TOTAL TIME:** 30 MINUTES

3 TABLESPOONS LARD

1 LB. FRESH CORN KERNELS

½ SMALL WHITE ONION, JULIENNED

3 GARLIC CLOVES, SLICED

SALT, TO TASTE

4 CUPS CHICKEN STOCK (SEE PAGE 438)

2½ OZ. MASA HARINA

2 TO 3 FRESH EPAZOTE LEAVES, PLUS MORE FOR GARNISH

1 FRESH HOJA SANTA LEAF (OPTIONAL)

1½ CUPS FRESH CILANTRO

3 SERRANO CHILE PEPPERS, STEMMED AND SEEDED

1 TABLESPOON HONEY

1 BAY LEAF

1. Place 2 tablespoons of the lard in a large skillet and warm it over medium heat. Add half of the corn, the onion, and the garlic and cook until the onion is translucent, about 3 minutes, stirring frequently. Remove the mixture from the pan, season it with salt, and let it cool.

2. Place half of the stock and the masa in a blender and puree until thoroughly combined. Place the masa mixture in a saucepan and warm it over low heat.

3. Place the vegetable mixture in the blender, add the epazote, hoja santa, cilantro, serrano peppers, honey, and bay leaf, and puree until smooth.

4. Stir the puree into the simmering masa. Simmer until the chileatole is the consistency of a thick stew, adding the remaining stock as needed.

5. Place the remaining lard in a skillet and warm it over medium heat. Add the remaining corn and cook until it is just tender, about 4 minutes, stirring occasionally. Remove the pan from heat and divide the corn between the serving bowls.

6. Season the chileatole with salt. Ladle the chileatole over the corn and use as desired.

SAUCES & CONDIMENTS

Dzikil P'aak

SEE PAGE 280

Salsa Cruda Verde

YIELD: 2 CUPS / **ACTIVE TIME:** 5 MINUTES / **TOTAL TIME:** 5 MINUTES

4 TOMATILLOS, HUSKED, RINSED WELL, AND QUARTERED

5 SERRANO CHILE PEPPERS, STEMMED AND SEEDED

1 GARLIC CLOVE

FLESH OF ½ AVOCADO

SALT, TO TASTE

1. Place the tomatillos, serrano peppers, and garlic in a blender and puree until the mixture is well combined but still chunky.
2. Add the avocado and pulse until incorporated.
3. Season the salsa with salt and use immediately or store in the refrigerator.

Salsa Macha

YIELD: 2 CUPS / **ACTIVE TIME:** 5 MINUTES / **TOTAL TIME:** 30 MINUTES

1 CUP RAW UNSALTED PEANUTS

2 CUPS EXTRA-VIRGIN OLIVE OIL

5 GARLIC CLOVES, SLICED

1 SHALLOT, SLICED

¼ CUP SUNFLOWER SEEDS

½ TEASPOON CUMIN SEEDS

½ TEASPOON FENNEL SEEDS

1 TABLESPOON WHITE SESAME SEEDS

1 TABLESPOON BLACK SESAME SEEDS

1 TABLESPOON CORIANDER SEEDS

2 ANCHO CHILE PEPPERS, STEMMED AND SEEDED

2 GUAJILLO CHILE PEPPERS, STEMMED AND SEEDED

5 CHILES DE ÁRBOL, STEMMED AND SEEDED

1 TEASPOON APPLE CIDER VINEGAR

SALT, TO TASTE

1. Place the peanuts and olive oil in a medium saucepan and cook over medium-low heat, stirring occasionally, until the peanuts start to brown, 10 to 15 minutes.

2. Add the remaining ingredients and cook, stirring occasionally, until the garlic and shallot have browned and all of the excess moisture has evaporated. Remove the pan from heat and let the mixture cool slightly.

3. Strain the mixture, reserving the oil. Using a mortar and pestle, grind the solids coarsely. Stir in the oil, season the salsa with salt, and use as desired.

Bay Leaf Oil

YIELD: ½ CUP / **ACTIVE TIME:** 20 MINUTES / **TOTAL TIME:** 24 HOURS

1 OZ. BAY LEAVES

10 TABLESPOONS EXTRA-VIRGIN OLIVE OIL

SALT, TO TASTE

1. Place the bay leaves and olive oil in a blender and puree until smooth, about 5 minutes.

2. Strain the oil into a bowl through a coffee filter and season it with salt.

3. Prepare an ice bath and place the bowl containing the oil in it. Transfer to the refrigerator and let it sit overnight.

4. Pour the oil through a cheesecloth-lined fine-mesh sieve and let it sit until the oil is free of any debris. Use immediately or store in the refrigerator, where it will keep for up to 2 weeks.

Habanero Honey

YIELD: 1 CUP / **ACTIVE TIME:** 10 MINUTES / **TOTAL TIME:** 2 HOURS

4 HABANERO CHILE PEPPERS, PIERCED

1 CUP HONEY

1. Place the chiles and honey in a saucepan and bring to a very gentle simmer over medium-low heat. Reduce the heat to the lowest possible setting and cook for 1 hour.

2. Remove the saucepan from heat and let the mixture infuse for another hour.

3. Remove the chiles. Transfer the honey to a container, cover, and store in the refrigerator.

Queso Fresco

YIELD: 3 CUPS / **ACTIVE TIME:** 30 MINUTES / **TOTAL TIME:** 24 HOURS

8 CUPS WHOLE MILK

2 TABLESPOONS KOSHER SALT

1⅓ CUPS WHITE VINEGAR

1. Place the milk and salt in a medium saucepan and bring to a gentle simmer over medium-low heat.

2. When the mixture reaches 180°F, remove the pan from heat, add the vinegar, and gently stir the mixture with a wooden spoon. You should see small curds begin to form. Cover the pan and let it rest for 45 minutes.

3. Strain the curds into a fine-mesh sieve lined with cheesecloth. Let the curds release all of their liquid, using a small plate to weigh down the curds.

4. Form the cheesecloth containing the curds into a bundle and let the cheese cool overnight in the refrigerator.

5. The cheese will be ready to crumble or break into chunks once fully cooled. Use immediately or store in the refrigerator for up to 1 week.

DESSERTS

Horchata Ice Cream

YIELD: 2 QUARTS / **ACTIVE TIME:** 45 MINUTES / **TOTAL TIME:** 5 HOURS

4 CUPS COOKED WHITE RICE

1 TABLESPOON CINNAMON

4 CUPS HEAVY CREAM

6 CUPS MILK

1½ CUPS EGG YOLKS

2 CUPS SUGAR

2 TEASPOONS MEXICAN VANILLA EXTRACT

⅛ TEASPOON FINE SEA SALT

BLUE CORN CRUNCHIES (SEE PAGE 444)

1. Prepare an ice bath. Place the rice, cinnamon, cream, and milk in a medium saucepan and bring to a simmer.

2. Place the egg yolks and sugar in the work bowl of a stand mixer fitted with the whisk attachment and whip until the mixture is pale and thick.

3. With the mixer running, add the milk mixture to the work bowl a little bit at a time. When all of the milk mixture has been incorporated, return the tempered mixture back to the pan and cook over low heat until the mixture is thick enough to coat the back of a wooden spoon.

4. Remove the pan from heat, stir in the vanilla and salt, and strain the mixture into a bowl, pressing down on the solids to extract as much liquid from them as possible.

5. Place the bowl in the ice bath until the custard is cool.

6. Churn the custard in an ice cream maker until it has the desired consistency. Transfer to an airtight container and freeze for 4 hours before topping with the Blue Corn Crunchies and serving.

Leche Quemada

YIELD: 36 SERVINGS / **ACTIVE TIME:** 40 MINUTES / **TOTAL TIME:** 1 HOUR AND 30 MINUTES

5½ CUPS SUGAR

2 (12 OZ.) CANS OF EVAPORATED MILK

5½ TABLESPOONS UNSALTED BUTTER

1 TEASPOON KOSHER SALT

1 TEASPOON MEXICAN VANILLA EXTRACT

½ CUP BROWN SUGAR

1. Coat a loaf pan with nonstick cooking spray. Place the sugar, evaporated milk, butter, salt, and vanilla in a large saucepan and bring to a boil. Add the brown sugar and stir until it has dissolved.
2. Cook over medium heat until the mixture comes together as a soft ball, stirring continually.
3. Remove the pan from heat and stir vigorously until the mixture thickens.
4. Pour the mixture into the loaf pan and let it cool completely. Cut the leche quemada into squares and enjoy.

Sweet Empanadas

YIELD: 12 EMPANADAS / **ACTIVE TIME:** 30 MINUTES / **TOTAL TIME:** 2 HOURS

FOR THE DOUGH

4 CUPS SIFTED ALL-PURPOSE FLOUR, PLUS MORE AS NEEDED

3 TABLESPOONS PLUS 1 TEASPOON SUGAR

1 TEASPOON FINE SEA SALT

¾ CUP SHORTENING

2 TABLESPOONS UNSALTED BUTTER, CHILLED

2 EGG YOLKS

1 CUP COLD WATER, PLUS MORE AS NEEDED

1 EGG WHITE, BEATEN

FOR THE FILLING

1 (14 OZ.) CAN OF PUMPKIN PUREE

½ CUP SUGAR

1 TEASPOON CINNAMON

1. To begin preparations for the dough, place the flour in a large mixing bowl and add the sugar, salt, shortening, and butter. Work the mixture with a pastry blender until it resembles coarse crumbs.

2. Combine the egg yolks and water in a separate mixing bowl and add the mixture to the flour mixture a little at a time until the resulting mixture comes together as a dough, whisking to incorporate. Knead the dough until it is smooth but slightly shaggy, adding more water or flour as needed. Cover the dough with plastic wrap and chill it in the refrigerator for about 1 hour.

3. Preheat the oven to 350°F and line a baking sheet with parchment paper. Roll out the dough on a flour-dusted work surface to about ¼ inch thick. Cut it into 5-inch circles.

4. To prepare the filling, place the pumpkin, sugar, and cinnamon in a mixing bowl and stir until combined.

5. Place about 2 tablespoons of the filling in the bottom-middle half of each circle, fold into a half-moon, and crimp the edges to seal.

6. Place the empanadas on the baking sheet, brush the tops with the egg white, and place them in the oven. Bake until they are golden brown, 20 to 25 minutes.

7. Remove the empanadas from the oven, transfer them to wire racks, and let them briefly cool before serving.

Sweet Empanadas
SEE PAGE 293

Orejas

YIELD: 12 OREJAS / **ACTIVE TIME:** 15 MINUTES / **TOTAL TIME:** 1 HOUR

1 SHEET OF FROZEN PUFF PASTRY, THAWED

1 EGG WHITE, BEATEN

1 TEASPOON CINNAMON

½ CUP SUGAR

1. Preheat the oven to 425°F and line a baking sheet with parchment paper. Brush the puff pastry with some of the egg white.

2. Combine the cinnamon and sugar in a bowl and then sprinkle the mixture all over the puff pastry. Fold the short edges of the pastry inward until they meet in the center of the sheet. Brush lightly with the egg white and fold in half again until sealed together. Chill the pastry in the refrigerator for 15 to 20 minutes.

3. Cut the pastry into ½-inch-thick slices. Place the slices on the baking sheet, cut side up so you can see the folds.

4. Place the orejas in the oven and bake until they are golden brown, 8 to 12 minutes. Remove them from the oven, transfer them to wire racks, and let them cool before enjoying.

Cornchata Hard Candies

YIELD: 30 TO 60 CANDIES / **ACTIVE TIME:** 30 MINUTES / **TOTAL TIME:** 1 HOUR

2 CUPS SUGAR

⅔ CUP CORN SYRUP

½ TEASPOON CREAM OF TARTAR

¾ CUP WATER

1 TEASPOON LORANN HORCHATA FLAVOR

½ TEASPOON CINNAMON

1. Coat a ⅛ silicone candy mold with nonstick cooking spray. Combine the sugar, corn syrup, cream of tartar, and water in a saucepan and bring to a boil. Cover the pan and let the mixture cook for 2 minutes.

2. Remove the cover and fit the pan with a candy thermometer. Cook until the mixture is 300°F. Remove the pan from heat and let it cool to 275°F.

3. Add the horchata flavor and cinnamon to the mixture and stir to incorporate. Pour the mixture into the molds with the help of a funnel.

4. Let the candies set for 20 minutes before serving.

Orejas
SEE PAGE 296

Abuelita's Chocolate Pots de Crème

YIELD: 8 SERVINGS / **ACTIVE TIME:** 30 MINUTES / **TOTAL TIME:** 1 HOUR AND 30 MINUTES

6 CUPS HEAVY CREAM

1½ CUPS HALF-AND-HALF

1 LB. ABUELITA CHOCOLATE, CHOPPED

18 EGG YOLKS

1 CUP SUGAR

1 TEASPOON PURE VANILLA EXTRACT

PINCH OF FINE SEA SALT

WHIPPED CREAM, FOR SERVING

1. Preheat the oven to 325°F. Place the heavy cream and half-and-half in a medium saucepan and bring to a simmer over medium heat.

2. Remove the pan from heat, add the chocolate, and whisk until the mixture is smooth.

3. Place the egg yolks, sugar, vanilla, and salt in a heatproof mixing bowl and slowly stream in the cream mixture, whisking continually to incorporate.

4. Strain the mixture through a fine-mesh sieve and then divide it among eight ramekins.

5. Place the ramekins in a large baking pan and fill the baking pan with hot water until it reaches halfway up the ramekins.

6. Place the baking pan in the oven and bake until the custards are set, about 40 minutes. Remove the pots de crème from the oven and let them cool before topping with whipped cream and serving.

Arroz con Leche

YIELD: 12 SERVINGS / **ACTIVE TIME:** 1 HOUR / **TOTAL TIME:** 1 HOUR AND 30 MINUTES

FOR THE BASE
7 CUPS MILK
SEEDS AND POD OF 1 VANILLA BEAN
4 CUPS COOKED WHITE RICE

FOR THE PASTRY CREAM
8 CUPS MILK
1 LB. SUGAR
2½ TEASPOONS PURE VANILLA EXTRACT
5½ OZ. CORNSTARCH
1½ CUPS EGG YOLKS
¼ CUP UNSALTED BUTTER

FOR THE MERINGUE
6½ OZ. POWDERED EGG WHITES
3⅓ OZ. WATER
1 TABLESPOON SUGAR

FOR THE TOPPING
PILONCILLO SYRUP (SEE PAGE 441)
CINNAMON, TO TASTE

1. Prepare an ice bath. To prepare the base, combine the milk and vanilla seeds and pod in a saucepan and bring to a boil. Add the rice and cook over low heat, stirring frequently until the mixture has the consistency of creamy oatmeal. Transfer the base to a mixing bowl and set the bowl in the ice bath to cool.

2. To begin preparations for the pastry cream, place the milk, half of the sugar, and the vanilla in a saucepan and warm the mixture over medium-low heat until it starts to steam, stirring to dissolve the sugar.

3. Place the remaining sugar, cornstarch, and egg yolks in a mixing bowl and whip until the mixture is pale and fluffy. Incorporate the warm milk mixture a little bit at a time, whipping continually.

4. Add the tempered egg yolks to the saucepan and cook over medium-low heat until the mixture has thickened and is just about to come to a simmer.

5. Place the butter in the work bowl of a stand mixer fitted with the paddle attachment. Strain the warm mixture into the work bowl and beat until it has cooled. Transfer the pastry cream into a container and place plastic wrap directly on the surface to prevent a skin from forming. Chill the pastry cream in the refrigerator.

6. To prepare the meringue, place the powdered egg whites, water, and sugar in the work bowl of a stand mixer fitted with the whisk attachment. Whip until the mixture is voluminous and can hold stiff peaks. Chill the mixture in the refrigerator.

7. Combine the base and the pastry cream in a bowl. Add the meringue and fold to incorporate. Scoop into bowls, drizzle a little syrup over each portion, and sprinkle cinnamon on top.

Conchas Pudding

YIELD: 12 SERVINGS / **ACTIVE TIME:** 15 MINUTES / **TOTAL TIME:** 1 HOUR

4 EGGS

4 EGG YOLKS

4 CUPS HALF-AND-HALF

¼ CUP SUGAR

1 TABLESPOON PURE VANILLA EXTRACT

½ TEASPOON FINE SEA SALT

2 LBS. STALE CONCHAS (SEE PAGE 324), CHOPPED

1. Preheat the oven to 325°F. Line an 18 x 13–inch baking sheet with parchment paper and coat it with nonstick cooking spray.

2. Place all of the ingredients, except for the Conchas, in a large bowl and whisk until well combined.

3. Add the Conchas, gently toss to combine, and push them down so they are covered in the custard. Let the mixture sit for 15 minutes, tossing and pressing down on the bread a few times.

4. Spread the bread pudding into the pan in an even layer.

5. Place the bread pudding in the oven and bake until it is golden brown and bubbling along the edges, about 30 minutes, making sure to rotate the pan halfway through.

6. Remove the bread pudding from the oven and let it cool slightly before enjoying.

Bonbonaise

YIELD: 30 TO 40 MARSHMALLOWS / **ACTIVE TIME:** 45 MINUTES / **TOTAL TIME:** 9 HOURS

CONFECTIONERS' SUGAR, AS NEEDED

1 CUP COLD WATER

3 TABLESPOONS GELATIN

1¼ CUPS SUGAR

1¼ CUPS CORN SYRUP

¼ TEASPOON FINE SEA SALT

2 TEASPOONS MEXICAN VANILLA EXTRACT

1 CUP SHREDDED COCONUT

1. Coat an 18 x 13-inch baking sheet with nonstick cooking spray, dust it with confectioners' sugar, and knock out any excess.

2. In the work bowl of a stand mixer fitted with the whisk attachment, add ½ cup of the cold water and sprinkle the gelatin over it.

3. Place the remaining water, the sugar, corn syrup, and salt in a saucepan and cook the mixture over medium heat until it is 240°F, 12 to 15 minutes.

4. Pour the hot syrup into the work bowl and whip on high until the bowl is just warm to the touch.

5. Stir in the vanilla and spread the mixture in the pan, working quickly. Dust the mixture generously with confectioners' sugar.

6. Let the mixture sit at room temperature, uncovered, for at least 8 hours, and up to 24.

7. Cut the bonbonaise into the desired shapes. Place the coconut in a shallow bowl and toss the bonbonaise in the coconut until coated.

Coffee Flan with Buñuelos

YIELD: 12 SERVINGS / **ACTIVE TIME:** 45 MINUTES / **TOTAL TIME:** 4 HOURS

1 CUP SUGAR

½ CUP WATER

1½ CUPS CREAM CHEESE, SOFTENED

6 EGGS

1 (14 OZ.) CAN OF SWEETENED CONDENSED MILK

1 (12 OZ.) CAN OF EVAPORATED MILK

¼ TEASPOON PURE VANILLA EXTRACT

1 TABLESPOON FINELY GROUND ESPRESSO

¼ TEASPOON KOSHER SALT

PERFECT CARAMEL (SEE PAGE 444), FOR SERVING

BUÑUELOS (SEE PAGE 312), FOR SERVING

1. Preheat the oven to 350°F. Place the sugar and water in a saucepan and warm over medium heat until the mixture is caramelized. Do not stir the mixture, but gently swirl the pan once or twice. Pour the caramel into a square 9-inch cake pan and let it cool completely.

2. In the work bowl of a stand mixer fitted with the paddle attachment, beat the cream cheese until light and fluffy. Incorporate the eggs one at a time, scraping down the work bowl as needed. Add the condensed milk and beat to incorporate.

3. Add the evaporated milk, vanilla, espresso, and salt and beat until the mixture is well combined. Strain it through a fine-mesh sieve to remove excess liquid.

4. Spread the strained mixture evenly over the caramel. Cover the pan with aluminum foil and place it in a roasting pan. Fill the roasting pan with water until it comes halfway up the side of the cake pan.

5. Place the flan in the oven and bake until it is set, about 45 minutes. Remove it from the oven and let it cool.

6. Chill the flan in the refrigerator for 2 hours.

7. Remove it from the pan, cut into 12 pieces, and place them on a plate. Drizzle some caramel over the each portion, top it with a buñuelo, and serve.

Chocolate Mole Profiteroles

YIELD: 50 PROFITEROLES / **ACTIVE TIME:** 20 MINUTES / **TOTAL TIME:** 1 HOUR

2 CUPS WATER

½ LB. UNSALTED BUTTER

PINCH OF FINE SEA SALT

PINCH OF SUGAR

11 OZ. ALL-PURPOSE FLOUR

8 EGGS

2 CUPS CHOCOLATE ICE CREAM

CHOCOLATE MOLE (SEE PAGE 441), FOR TOPPING

1. Preheat the oven to 375°F and line two baking sheets with parchment paper. Place the water, butter, salt, and sugar in a saucepan and bring it to a boil.

2. Add the flour and cook, stirring constantly, until the mixture pulls away from the side of the pan.

3. Place the mixture in the work bowl of a stand mixer fitted with the paddle attachment and beat until the dough is almost cool. Incorporate the eggs one at a time, scraping down the work bowl as needed.

4. Place the dough in a piping bag fitted with a round tip and pipe mounds of dough onto the baking sheets, making sure to leave enough space between them.

5. Place the profiteroles in the oven and bake until they are set and golden brown, 8 to 12 minutes. Remove from the oven and let the profiteroles cool completely.

6. Cut the profiteroles in half and fill each one with a scoop of ice cream. Drizzle the Chocolate Mole over the top and enjoy.

Chocolate Mole Profiteroles
SEE PAGE 307

Chocoflan

YIELD: 8 SERVINGS / **ACTIVE TIME:** 1 HOUR / **TOTAL TIME:** 3 HOURS

1. To begin preparations for the caramel, place the sugar in a small saucepan and warm it over medium heat, stirring constantly.

2. When all of the sugar has melted and turned amber, remove the pan from heat and pour it into a greased Bundt pan, making sure the entire bottom of the pan is covered. Let the caramel cool for 10 minutes.

3. To prepare the flan, place all of the ingredients in a blender and puree until smooth. Set the mixture aside.

4. To begin preparations for the cake, preheat the oven to 350°F. In the work bowl of a stand mixer fitted with the paddle attachment, combine the butter and brown sugar and cream on medium speed until the mixture is light and fluffy, about 5 minutes. Add the egg and vanilla and beat until incorporated.

5. Sift the flour, cocoa powder, baking soda, and baking powder together in a separate mixing bowl.

6. Place the instant coffee in a small bowl and add some of the milk. Heat the mixture in the microwave for a few seconds, until the instant coffee has dissolved. Stir the remaining milk into the coffee milk.

7. Alternating between the flour mixture and the milk mixture, add each one to the work bowl in three increments and beat until both mixtures have been incorporated and the overall mixture is a smooth batter.

8. Pour the batter into the Bundt pan, on top of the hardened caramel. Smooth the surface and gently tap the pan on the counter a couple of times to remove any air bubbles and ensure the top is level.

9. Slowly pour the flan over the back of a spoon so that it sits on top of the cake batter in an even layer.

10. Place the Bundt pan in a roasting pan. Pour hot water into the roasting pan until it goes at least 2 inches up the side of the Bundt pan. Place the roasting pan in the oven and bake until the flan is set, about 1 hour.

11. Remove it from the oven and let the flan cool for at least 1 hour before turning it out onto a serving dish.

FOR THE CARAMEL

1½ CUPS SUGAR

FOR THE FLAN

4 EGGS

1 (14 OZ.) CAN OF SWEETENED CONDENSED MILK

2½ CUPS EVAPORATED MILK

PINCH OF KOSHER SALT

1 TEASPOON MEXICAN VANILLA EXTRACT

FOR THE CAKE

5⅓ OZ. UNSALTED BUTTER

6⅔ OZ. BROWN SUGAR

1 EGG

1 TABLESPOON MEXICAN VANILLA EXTRACT

7 OZ. ALL-PURPOSE FLOUR

1 OZ. COCOA POWDER

1 TEASPOON BAKING SODA

1 TEASPOON BAKING POWDER

¼ CUP INSTANT COFFEE

1 CUP MILK

Chocolate-Covered Chicharron

YIELD: 12 SERVINGS / **ACTIVE TIME:** 20 MINUTES / **TOTAL TIME:** 45 MINUTES

2 CUPS CHOPPED DARK CHOCOLATE, PLUS MORE FOR SERVING

3½ OZ. CHICHARRON

1. Fill a small saucepan halfway with water and bring it to a simmer. Place the chocolate in a heatproof bowl, place it over the simmering water, and stir until it is melted and smooth. Remove the bowl from heat and let it cool to 90°F.

2. Dip each chicharron into the melted chocolate, covering as much of it as desired.

3. Place the dipped chicharron on a parchment-lined baking sheet and let the chocolate set for 10 to 20 minutes before enjoying.

Buñuelos

YIELD: 12 PASTRIES / **ACTIVE TIME:** 20 MINUTES / **TOTAL TIME:** 1 HOUR

2 CUPS ALL-PURPOSE FLOUR, PLUS MORE AS NEEDED

1 TEASPOON BAKING POWDER

1 TABLESPOON SUGAR

½ TEASPOON KOSHER SALT

1 EGG

1 TABLESPOON UNSALTED BUTTER, MELTED AND COOLED

1 TEASPOON MEXICAN VANILLA EXTRACT

WATER, AS NEEDED

CANOLA OIL, AS NEEDED

1. In a large mixing bowl, combine the flour, baking powder, sugar, and salt. Add the egg, melted butter, and vanilla and work the mixture until it resembles coarse bread crumbs.

2. Incorporate water 1 tablespoon at a time until the mixture comes together as a soft, smooth dough. Cover the mixing bowl with plastic wrap and let the dough rest for 30 minutes.

3. Divide the dough into 12 pieces and roll them out as thin as possible, without breaking them, on a flour-dusted work surface.

4. Add canola oil to a Dutch oven until it is about 2 inches deep and warm it to 350°F. Working in batches to avoid overcrowding the pot, gently slip the buñuelos into the oil and fry until they are crispy and golden brown, about 2 minutes. Transfer the fried buñuelos to a paper towel–lined plate and let them drain before serving.

Chocolate Tamarind Truffles

YIELD: 40 TRUFFLES / **ACTIVE TIME:** 40 MINUTES / **TOTAL TIME:** 2 HOURS

2 CUPS HEAVY CREAM

1 LB. DARK CHOCOLATE, CHOPPED, PLUS MORE AS NEEDED

3 OZ. MILK CHOCOLATE, CHOPPED

5 OZ. TAMARIND PASTE

¼ CUP MEXICAN VANILLA EXTRACT

COCOA POWDER, FOR DUSTING

1. Fill a small saucepan halfway with water and bring it to a simmer.
2. Place the cream, chocolates, and tamarind in a heatproof mixing bowl and place it over the simmering water. Stir until the mixture is smooth.
3. Remove the bowl from heat, stir in the vanilla, and strain the mixture into a large baking dish. Place it in the refrigerator and let the mixture cool completely.
4. Scoop the desired size for your truffles onto parchment-lined baking sheets. Place the truffles in the refrigerator and chill for 10 to 15 minutes.
5. Roll the scoops into balls using your hands. Place them back on the baking sheets and chill them in the refrigerator.
6. Fill a small saucepan halfway with water and bring it to a simmer. Place additional dark chocolate in a heatproof bowl, place it over the simmering water, and stir until it is melted and smooth. Let cool for 5 minutes.
7. Dip the balls into the melted chocolate twice, so that they are completely coated. Place them back on the baking sheets and chill them in the refrigerator until they are set.
8. Roll the truffles in cocoa powder until they are completely coated and serve.

Chocolate-Covered Chicharron

SEE PAGE 312

Spicy Chocolate Truffles

YIELD: 40 TRUFFLES / **ACTIVE TIME:** 40 MINUTES / **TOTAL TIME:** 1 HOUR AND 30 MINUTES

2 CUPS HEAVY CREAM

1 LB. DARK CHOCOLATE, CHOPPED, PLUS MORE AS NEEDED

3 OZ. MILK CHOCOLATE, CHOPPED

5 OZ. GUAJILLO CHILE PEPPERS, STEMMED, SEEDED, AND GROUND

½ CUP MEXICAN VANILLA EXTRACT

¼ CUP COCOA POWDER, FOR DUSTING

1. Fill a small saucepan halfway with water and bring it to a simmer.
2. Place the cream, chocolates, and chiles in a heatproof mixing bowl and place it over the simmering water. Stir until the mixture is smooth.
3. Remove the pan from heat, stir in the vanilla, and strain the mixture into a large baking dish. Place it in the refrigerator and let the mixture cool completely.
4. Scoop the desired size for your truffles onto parchment-lined baking sheets. Place the truffles in the refrigerator and chill them for 10 to 15 minutes.
5. Roll the scoops into balls using your hands. Place them back on the baking sheets and chill them in the refrigerator.
6. Fill a small saucepan halfway with water and bring it to a simmer. Place additional dark chocolate in a heatproof bowl, place it over the simmering water, and stir until it is melted and smooth. Let the chocolate cool for 5 minutes.
7. Dip the balls into the melted chocolate twice, so that they are completely coated. Place them back on the baking sheets and chill them in the refrigerator until set.
8. Roll the truffles in the cocoa powder until completely coated and serve.

Cinnamon & Chocolate Cake

YIELD: 1 CAKE / **ACTIVE TIME:** 1 HOUR / **TOTAL TIME:** 6 HOURS

14 OZ. DARK CHOCOLATE (64 PERCENT)

6½ OZ. UNSALTED BUTTER

2 TABLESPOONS CINNAMON

7 EGGS, SEPARATED

6 OZ. SUGAR

¼ TEASPOON FINE SEA SALT

DARK CHOCOLATE GANACHE (SEE PAGE 443)

1. Preheat the oven to 300°F. Line two round 9-inch cake pans with parchment paper and coat them with nonstick cooking spray.

2. Fill a small saucepan halfway with water and bring it to a simmer. Place the chocolate and butter in a heatproof bowl, place it over the simmering water, and stir until the mixture is melted and smooth. Remove from heat and let cool.

3. Stir the cinnamon into the cooled chocolate mixture.

4. Place the egg yolks, half of the sugar, and the salt in the work bowl of a stand mixer fitted with the whisk attachment and whip until the mixture has tripled in volume.

5. Place the egg whites and remaining sugar in a separate mixing bowl and whip until the mixture holds medium peaks.

6. Fold the whipped egg yolk mixture into the chocolate mixture. Fold the whipped egg whites in.

7. Pour 10 oz. of batter into each cake pan, place them in the oven, and bake until a knife inserted into their centers comes out clean, about 15 minutes.

8. Remove from the oven, set the pans on wire racks, and let the cakes cool completely.

9. Refrigerate the cakes for 4 hours.

10. Cut the top ½ inch off of one of the cakes and spread some of the ganache over it. Place the other cake on top, spread the ganache over the entire cake, and serve.

Mango con Chile Pate de Fruit

YIELD: 60 CANDIES / **ACTIVE TIME:** 25 MINUTES / **TOTAL TIME:** 3 HOURS AND 30 MINUTES

3 TABLESPOONS APPLE PECTIN

20 OZ. SUGAR, PLUS MORE TO TASTE

1½ TEASPOONS CITRIC ACID

1½ TEASPOONS WATER

17½ OZ. MANGO PUREE

3½ OZ. CORN SYRUP

PINCH OF LIME ZEST

TAJÍN, TO TASTE

SALT, TO TASTE

1. Line a baking sheet with a Silpat mat and place a silicone candy mold on it. Place the pectin and a little bit of the sugar in a mixing bowl and stir to combine. In a separate bowl, add the citric acid to the water and let it dissolve.

2. Place the mango puree in a saucepan and warm it to 120°F. Add the pectin-and-sugar mixture and whisk to prevent any clumps from forming. Bring the mixture to a boil and let it cook for 1 minute.

3. Stir in the corn syrup and remaining sugar and cook the mixture until it is 223°F. The mixture should have thickened and should cool quickly and hold its shape when a small portion of it is dropped from a rubber spatula.

4. Stir in the lime zest and citric acid-and-water mixture and cook for another minute or so. Remove the pan from heat, strain the mixture, and pour it into the candy mold.

5. Let the candy set for at least 3 hours before cutting it into the desired shapes. Toss in Tajín, sugar, and salt and enjoy.

Churros

YIELD: 36 CHURROS / **ACTIVE TIME:** 25 MINUTES / **TOTAL TIME:** 30 MINUTES

CANOLA OIL, AS NEEDED

17.1 OZ. MILK

40.6 OZ. WATER

1.4 OZ. SUGAR, PLUS MORE TO TASTE

0.7 OZ. SALT

19.4 OZ. "00" FLOUR

19.4 OZ. ALL-PURPOSE FLOUR

16 EGGS

CINNAMON, TO TASTE

DARK CHOCOLATE GANACHE (SEE PAGE 443), WARM, FOR SERVING

PERFECT CARAMEL (SEE PAGE 444), FOR SERVING

1. Add canola oil to a Dutch oven until it is about 2 inches deep and warm it to 350°F. Place the milk, water, sugar, and salt in a large saucepan and bring it to a boil.

2. Gradually add the flours and cook, stirring constantly, until the mixture pulls away from the side of the pan.

3. Place the mixture in the work bowl of a stand mixer fitted with the paddle attachment and beat until the dough is almost cool. Incorporate the eggs one at a time, scraping down the work bowl as needed.

4. Combine some cinnamon and sugar in a baking dish and set the mixture aside.

5. Place the dough in a piping bag fitted with a star tip. Pipe 6-inch lengths of dough into the oil and fry until they are golden brown. Place them on paper towel–lined plates to drain and cool slightly. Toss in cinnamon sugar and enjoy, or store the churros in the freezer.

6. To serve frozen churros, preheat the oven to 450°F. Remove the churros from the freezer and toss them in cinnamon sugar until they are coated. Place them in the oven and bake for 5 minutes. Remove them from the oven, toss them in cinnamon sugar again, and serve with the ganache and caramel.

Strawberry Shortcake con Conchas

YIELD: 4 SERVINGS / **ACTIVE TIME:** 10 MINUTES / **TOTAL TIME:** 50 MINUTES

2 LBS. STRAWBERRIES, HULLED AND HALVED

¼ CUP PLUS 2 TABLESPOONS SUGAR

¼ TEASPOON CINNAMON

1½ CUPS HEAVY CREAM

4 CONCHAS (SEE PAGE 324)

1. Place the strawberries and ¼ cup of sugar in a large bowl and cover it with plastic wrap. Let the mixture sit until the strawberries start to release their juice, about 45 minutes.

2. Place the remaining sugar, the cinnamon, and heavy cream in a mixing bowl and whip until it holds medium peaks. Set the whipped cream aside.

3. Starting at the equator, cut each of the Conchas in half. Place a dollop of the whipped cream on top of one of the halves, followed by a few scoops of the strawberries and their juices. Top with the other half and serve.

Mezcal Ice Cream

YIELD: 1 QUART / **ACTIVE TIME:** 45 MINUTES / **TOTAL TIME:** 5 HOURS

4 CUPS HALF-AND-HALF

1⅓ CUPS SUGAR

¼ CUP HEAVY CREAM

⅓ CUP CORN SYRUP

⅓ CUP EGG YOLKS

¼ CUP MEZCAL

PINCH OF KOSHER SALT

1. Prepare an ice bath. Place the half-and-half, sugar, cream, and corn syrup in a medium saucepan and bring to a simmer.

2. Place the yolks in the work bowl of a stand mixer fitted with the whisk attachment and whip until they are pale and thick.

3. With the mixer running, add the half-and-half mixture to the whipped yolks a little bit at a time. When all of the half-and-half mixture has been incorporated, return the tempered mixture back to the pan and cook over low heat until the mixture is thick enough to coat the back of a wooden spoon.

4. Remove the pan from heat, stir in the mezcal and salt, and strain the custard into a bowl.

5. Place the bowl in the ice bath and let it sit until the custard is cool.

6. Churn the custard in an ice cream maker until it reaches the desired consistency. Transfer it to an airtight container and freeze for 4 hours before serving.

DESSERTS

Churros
SEE PAGE 320

Conchas

YIELD: 42 CONCHAS / **ACTIVE TIME:** 1 HOUR AND 30 MINUTES / **TOTAL TIME:** 13 HOURS

1. To begin preparations for the dough, place the milk, sugar, and yeast in the work bowl of a stand mixer fitted with the dough hook and stir gently to combine. Let the mixture sit until it starts to foam, about 10 minutes.

2. Add the eggs and stir gently to incorporate. Add the vanilla, flour, salt, and cardamom and work the mixture until it comes together as a shaggy dough.

3. Knead the dough on medium speed for about 3 minutes.

4. Add the butter in four increments and work the mixture for 2 minutes after each addition, scraping down the work bowl as needed.

5. Increase the mixer's speed and knead the dough until it can be lifted cleanly out of the bowl, about 10 minutes.

6. Place the dough on a flour-dusted work surface and lightly flour your hands and the top of the dough. Fold the edges of the dough toward the middle and gently press them into the dough.

7. Carefully turn the dough over and use your palms to shape the dough into a tight ball. Carefully pick up the dough and place it in a mixing bowl. Let it rise in a naturally warm place until it has doubled in size, about 1 hour.

8. Place the dough on a flour-dusted work surface and gently press it down to deflate the dough. Fold the edges in toward the middle and press down on them.

9. Carefully flip the dough over and tighten the dough into a ball with a smooth, taut surface.

10. Place the dough back in the mixing bowl, cover it with plastic wrap, and chill it in the refrigerator for 8 hours.

11. Divide the dough into 2.6 oz. portions and form them into balls. Place the balls on parchment-lined baking sheets, cover them with kitchen towels, and let them rest at room temperature for 2 hours.

12. To begin preparations for the topping, place all of the ingredients in the work bowl of a stand mixer fitted with the paddle attachment and beat until the mixture comes together as a smooth dough.

13. Divide the topping into ⅓ oz. portions. Line a tortilla press with plastic, place a piece of the topping mixture on top, and top with another piece of plastic. Preheat the oven to 350°F.

14. Flatten the mixture, place it on one of the proofed conchas, and make small cuts in the topping that resemble the ridges on top of an oyster shell. Repeat with the remaining topping mixture and let the conchas rest for 10 minutes.

15. Place in the oven and bake for 10 minutes. Rotate the pans, lower the oven's temperature to 300°F, and bake for an additional 2 minutes.

16. Remove the conchas from the oven and let them cool before enjoying.

FOR THE DOUGH

2 CUPS MILK, WARMED TO 90°F

2 CUPS SUGAR

2 OZ. ACTIVE DRY YEAST

18 OZ. EGGS

SEEDS FROM 1 VANILLA BEAN

45 OZ. ALL-PURPOSE FLOUR, PLUS MORE AS NEEDED

½ OZ. FINE SEA SALT

⅛ (SCANT) TEASPOON CARDAMOM

1 LB. UNSALTED BUTTER, SOFTENED

FOR THE TOPPING

6 OZ. ALL-PURPOSE FLOUR

6 OZ. CONFECTIONERS' SUGAR

5 OZ. UNSALTED BUTTER, SOFTENED

Mayan Chocolate & Bourbon Truffles

YIELD: 40 TRUFFLES / **ACTIVE TIME:** 40 MINUTES / **TOTAL TIME:** 1 HOUR AND 30 MINUTES

2 CUPS HEAVY CREAM

1 LB. DARK CHOCOLATE, CHOPPED, PLUS MORE AS NEEDED

3 OZ. MILK CHOCOLATE, CHOPPED

1 TEASPOON CINNAMON

½ CUP BOURBON

¼ CUP COCOA POWDER, FOR DUSTING

1. Fill a small saucepan halfway with water and bring it to a simmer.

2. Place the cream, chocolates, and cinnamon in a heatproof mixing bowl and place it over the simmering water. Stir until the mixture is smooth.

3. Remove the bowl from heat, stir in the bourbon, and strain the mixture into a large baking dish. Place in the refrigerator and let it cool completely.

4. Scoop the desired size for your truffles onto parchment-lined baking sheets. Return the truffles to the refrigerator and chill them for 10 to 15 minutes.

5. Roll the scoops into balls using your hands. Place them back on the baking sheets and chill them in the refrigerator.

6. Fill a small saucepan halfway with water and bring it to a simmer. Place additional dark chocolate in a heatproof bowl, place it over the simmering water, and stir until it is melted and smooth. Let the chocolate cool for 5 minutes.

7. Dip the balls into the melted chocolate twice, so that they are completely coated. Place them back on the baking sheets and chill them in the refrigerator until set.

8. Roll the truffles in the cocoa powder until completely coated and enjoy.

Mole Brownies

YIELD: 30 BROWNIES / **ACTIVE TIME:** 15 MINUTES / **TOTAL TIME:** 1 HOUR AND 45 MINUTES

47½ OZ. UNSALTED BUTTER

79½ OZ. SUGAR

ZEST OF ½ ORANGE ZEST

1 ANCHO CHILE PEPPER, STEMMED, SEEDED, AND CHOPPED

½ CUP SESAME SEEDS, TOASTED

¼ CUP CREAMY PEANUT BUTTER

⅓ TEASPOON PLUS 1 PINCH CINNAMON

20½ OZ. COCOA POWDER

2½ TEASPOONS FINE SEA SALT

22 OZ. ALL-PURPOSE FLOUR

½ TEASPOON CAYENNE PEPPER

3 TABLESPOONS PURE VANILLA EXTRACT

18 EGGS

CHOCOLATE & MEXICAN VANILLA FROSTING (SEE PAGE 445)

1. Preheat the oven to 350°F. Coat two 9 x 13-inch baking pans with nonstick cooking spray. In the work bowl of a stand mixer fitted with the paddle attachment, cream the butter, sugar, orange zest, ancho chile, sesame seeds, peanut butter, and cinnamon on medium until the mixture is light and fluffy.

2. Combine the cocoa powder, salt, flour, and cayenne in a separate mixing bowl. Add half of the dry mixture to the work bowl and beat until incorporated.

3. Add the vanilla and then incorporate the eggs one at a time, scraping down the work bowl as needed. Add the remaining dry mixture and beat until the resulting mixture comes together as a smooth batter.

4. Pour the batter into the pans, place them in the oven, and bake until a knife inserted into their centers comes out clean, 30 to 40 minutes.

5. Remove the pans from the oven, place them on wire racks, and let the brownies cool completely.

6. Run a paring knife along the sides of the pans. Spread the frosting over the brownies, cut them into squares, and enjoy.

Coconut Tres Leches

YIELD: 1 CAKE / **ACTIVE TIME:** 1 HOUR / **TOTAL TIME:** 4 HOURS

FOR THE SPONGE CAKE

16 EGGS, SEPARATED

28 OZ. SUGAR

29 OZ. ALL-PURPOSE FLOUR, SIFTED

⅔ TEASPOON FINE SEA SALT

¼ CUP BAKING POWDER

4½ OZ. WATER

5 TEASPOONS MEXICAN VANILLA EXTRACT

RAICILLA-SOAKED BERRIES (SEE PAGE 443)

FOR THE SOAKING LIQUID

2 (14 OZ.) CANS OF SWEETENED CONDENSED MILK

2 (12 OZ.) CANS OF EVAPORATED MILK

½ CUP HEAVY CREAM

1¾ CUPS COCONUT MILK

½ CUP SUGAR

1. Preheat the oven to 325°F. Coat a baking pan with nonstick cooking spray. To begin preparations for the sponge cake, place the egg whites and sugar in the work bowl of a stand mixer fitted with the whisk attachment and whip until the mixture has tripled in volume.

2. Combine the flour, sea salt, and baking powder in a separate bowl.

3. Incorporate the egg yolks into the meringue one at a time. Add one-third of the meringue to the dry mixture along with the water and vanilla and beat until incorporated. Add another one-third of the meringue and fold to combine. Add the remaining one-third and carefully fold until incorporated.

4. Transfer the batter into the baking pan and gently spread with a rubber spatula until it is even. Place the cake in the oven and bake until a knife inserted into the center comes out clean, about 40 minutes.

5. While the cake is in the oven, prepare the soaking liquid. Place all of the ingredients in a saucepan and warm the mixture over medium heat, stirring to combine. When the mixture starts to steam and all of the sugar has dissolved, remove the pan from heat.

6. Remove the cake from the oven. Pour the soaking liquid over the cake and chill it in the refrigerator for 2 hours.

7. To serve, top slices with the berries, drizzle some of the liquid from the berries over the top, and enjoy.

Mixed Nut Marzipan

YIELD: 36 BARS / **ACTIVE TIME:** 10 MINUTES / **TOTAL TIME:** 20 MINUTES

1¼ CUPS ROASTED, UNSALTED PEANUTS

½ CUP SLICED ALMONDS

¼ CUP PECANS

1 CUP CONFECTIONERS' SUGAR

1 TEASPOON CREAMY PEANUT BUTTER

1. Line two baking sheets with parchment paper and coat them with nonstick cooking spray.

2. Place the nuts in a food processor and pulse until they are coarsely ground. Add the confectioners' sugar and peanut butter and pulse until the mixture is a thick paste.

3. Place the mixture on a flat surface and roll it out to ¾ inch thick. Use cookie cutters to cut the marzipan into the desired shapes and place them on the baking sheets. Enjoy immediately or store in the refrigerator.

Gluten-Free Spicy Chocolate Cookies

YIELD: 12 COOKIES / **ACTIVE TIME:** 15 MINUTES / **TOTAL TIME:** 2 HOURS

⅔ CUP GLUTEN-FREE ALL-PURPOSE FLOUR

¾ CUP PLUS 2 TABLESPOONS COCOA POWDER

½ TEASPOON XANTHAN GUM (IF MISSING FROM FLOUR)

1 TEASPOON BAKING SODA

2 TEASPOONS CINNAMON

½ TEASPOON CAYENNE PEPPER

2 LARGE EGGS

1 CUP SUGAR

½ CUP CANOLA OIL

1 TABLESPOON PURE VANILLA EXTRACT

1 CUP CHOCOLATE CHIPS

1. Combine the flour, cocoa powder, xanthan gum, baking soda, cinnamon, and cayenne pepper in a mixing bowl and set the mixture aside.

2. In the work bowl of a stand mixer fitted with the paddle attachment, beat the eggs, sugar, canola oil, and vanilla extract until well combined. Add the dry mixture, set the speed to low, and beat until the resulting mixture comes together as a smooth dough. Fold in the chocolate chips, cover the bowl with plastic wrap, and chill the dough in the refrigerator for 1 hour.

3. Preheat the oven to 325°F. Line a baking sheet with parchment paper. Form the dough into 12 balls and arrange them on the baking sheet, making sure to leave enough space between them.

4. Place the cookies in the oven and bake until the edges are set, about 12 minutes.

5. Remove the cookies from the oven and let them cool completely on the baking sheet before serving.

Mexican Wedding Cookies

YIELD: 36 COOKIES / **ACTIVE TIME:** 20 MINUTES / **TOTAL TIME:** 1 HOUR

- 1 CUP UNSALTED BUTTER, SOFTENED
- ½ CUP CONFECTIONERS' SUGAR, PLUS MORE AS NEEDED
- 1 TEASPOON MEXICAN VANILLA EXTRACT
- ¼ TEASPOON KOSHER SALT
- 2¼ CUPS SIFTED ALL-PURPOSE FLOUR
- ¾ CUP PECANS, CHOPPED

1. Preheat the oven to 325°F. Line two baking sheets with parchment paper.

2. In the work bowl of a stand mixer fitted with the paddle attachment, cream the butter and confectioners' sugar on medium until light and fluffy, about 5 minutes.

3. Add the vanilla and salt and beat until incorporated. Add the flour and pecans and beat the mixture until it comes together as a dough, scraping down the work bowl as needed.

4. Form the dough into 1¼-inch balls, place them on the baking sheets, place them in the oven, and bake until they are golden brown, 10 to 12 minutes. Remove the cookies from the oven and let them cool slightly.

5. Roll the cookies in confectioners' sugar until evenly coated. Let them cool completely before serving.

Pan de Hoja Santa

YIELD: 24 ROLLS / **ACTIVE TIME:** 1 HOUR AND 30 MINUTES / **TOTAL TIME:** 24 HOURS

FOR THE DOUGH

35¼ OZ. ALL-PURPOSE FLOUR

3½ OZ. SUGAR

1½ TABLESPOONS KOSHER SALT

9 OZ. WHOLE MILK

4 TEASPOONS ACTIVE DRY YEAST

8 EGGS

17½ OZ. UNSALTED BUTTER, SOFTENED

FOR THE TOPPING

1 LB. UNSALTED BUTTER

2 TABLESPOONS PLUS 1 TEASPOON CINNAMON

1 TABLESPOON FINELY CHOPPED FRESH HOJA SANTA, PLUS MORE TO TASTE

1. To begin preparations for the dough, combine the flour, sugar, and salt in a mixing bowl.
2. Warm the milk to 95°F. Place it in the work bowl of a stand mixer fitted with the dough hook, stir in the yeast, and let the mixture sit until it starts to foam, about 10 minutes.
3. Place the dry mixture in the work bowl, followed by the eggs. Beat until the mixture is combined and let rest for 20 minutes.
4. Incorporate the butter in three increments, folding the mixture three times and then letting it rest for 30 minutes with each addition.
5. Cover the bowl with plastic wrap and let the dough rest in the refrigerator overnight.
6. To prepare the topping, place the butter in a saucepan and melt it over medium heat. Prepare an ice bath and cool the butter in it briefly. Stir in the cinnamon and hoja santa.
7. Place the pot containing the topping over another pot of hot water to keep the butter from setting up too quickly.
8. Drop small balls of the dough into the butter mixture and toss to coat.
9. Place the balls two-thirds of the way into greased square molds that are on top of a greased and parchment-lined baking sheet. Spread the squares out so they have space to breathe.
10. Sprinkle additional hoja santa over each ball and cover them with plastic wrap.
11. Let the balls rest until they have doubled in size, about 2 hours.
12. Preheat the oven to 325°F. Place the rolls in the oven and bake until they are golden brown, about 8 minutes.
13. Remove the rolls from the oven and let them cool slightly before enjoying.

No-Fry Fried Ice Cream

YIELD: 4 SERVINGS / **ACTIVE TIME:** 30 MINUTES / **TOTAL TIME:** 1 HOUR AND 45 MINUTES

8 SCOOPS OF ICE CREAM

2 CUPS CORNFLAKES

½ CUP UNSALTED BUTTER

2 TEASPOONS CINNAMON

3 TABLESPOONS SUGAR

1. Place the ice cream on a parchment-lined baking sheet and place it in the freezer for 1 hour.

2. Roll the scoops into balls and place them back in the freezer.

3. Place the cornflakes in a food processor and pulse until they are finely ground.

4. Place the butter in a medium saucepan and melt it over medium heat.

5. Stir in the cornflake crumbs and cinnamon and cook until golden brown. Remove the pan from heat and stir in the sugar.

6. Pour the mixture into a shallow pan and let it cool.

7. Roll the ice cream balls in the cornflake mixture until they are completely coated. Place the coated ice cream balls in the freezer until ready to serve.

The Perfect Flan

YIELD: 6 SERVINGS / **ACTIVE TIME:** 30 MINUTES / **TOTAL TIME:** 6 HOURS AND 30 MINUTES

2 CUPS SUGAR

¼ CUP WATER

5 EGG YOLKS

5 EGGS

5 OZ. CREAM CHEESE, SOFTENED

1 (14 OZ.) CAN OF SWEETENED CONDENSED MILK

1 (12 OZ.) CAN OF EVAPORATED MILK

1½ CUPS HEAVY CREAM

½ TEASPOON ALMOND EXTRACT

½ TEASPOON PURE VANILLA EXTRACT

1. Preheat the oven to 350°F. Bring 2 quarts of water to a boil and set aside.

2. Place 1 cup of the sugar and the water in a small saucepan and bring to a boil over high heat, swirling the pan instead of stirring. Cook until the caramel is a deep golden brown, taking care not to burn it. Remove the pan from heat and pour the caramel into a round 8-inch cake pan. Place the cake pan on a cooling rack and let the caramel sit until it has set.

3. Place the egg yolks, eggs, cream cheese, remaining sugar, condensed milk, evaporated milk, heavy cream, almond extract, and vanilla in a blender and puree until the mixture has emulsified.

4. Pour the mixture over the caramel and place the cake pan in a roasting pan. Pour the boiling water into the roasting pan until it reaches halfway up the side of the cake pan.

5. Place the flan in the oven and bake until it is just set, 60 to 70 minutes. The flan should still be jiggly without being runny. Remove the flan from the oven, place the pan on a wire rack, and let it cool for 1 hour.

6. Place the flan in the refrigerator and chill it for 4 hours.

7. Run a knife along the edge of the pan and invert the flan onto a plate so that the caramel layer is on top. Slice the flan and serve.

Sweet Corn Pudding Pops

YIELD: 12 POPS / **ACTIVE TIME:** 30 MINUTES / **TOTAL TIME:** 24 HOURS

8 EARS OF CORN

4 CUPS HEAVY CREAM

6 CUPS MILK

1½ CUPS EGG YOLKS

2 CUPS SUGAR

2 TEASPOONS MEXICAN VANILLA EXTRACT

⅛ TEASPOON FINE SEA SALT

1. Prepare an ice bath. Grate the corn kernels into a saucepan and discard the cobs. Add the cream and milk and bring the mixture to a simmer.

2. Place the yolks and sugar in the work bowl of a stand mixer fitted with the whisk attachment and whip until the mixture is pale and thick.

3. With the mixer running, add the milk mixture to the whipped yolks a little bit at a time. When all of the milk mixture has been incorporated, return the tempered mixture back to the pan and cook over low heat until the mixture is thick enough to coat the back of a wooden spoon.

4. Remove the pan from heat, stir in the vanilla and salt, and strain the mixture into a bowl.

5. Place the bowl in the ice bath and let it sit until the custard is cool.

6. Pour the custard into popsicle molds and freeze them overnight before serving.

Mexican Chocolate Crinkle Cookies

YIELD: 20 COOKIES / **ACTIVE TIME:** 30 MINUTES / **TOTAL TIME:** 2 HOURS

9 OZ. MEXICAN CHOCOLATE

4½ OZ. UNSALTED BUTTER, SOFTENED

7 OZ. DARK BROWN SUGAR

¾ TEASPOON PURE VANILLA EXTRACT

2 EGGS

7 OZ. ALL-PURPOSE FLOUR

2½ OZ. COCOA POWDER

2 TEASPOONS BAKING POWDER

½ TEASPOON CINNAMON

¼ TEASPOON ANCHO CHILE POWDER

1 TEASPOON KOSHER SALT

2 CUPS CONFECTIONERS' SUGAR, FOR COATING

1. Line two baking sheets with parchment paper. Fill a small saucepan halfway with water and bring it to a simmer. Place the chocolate in a heatproof bowl, place it over the simmering water, and stir until the chocolate has melted. Remove the bowl from heat and set the chocolate aside.

2. In the work bowl of a stand mixer fitted with the paddle attachment, cream the butter, brown sugar, and vanilla on medium speed until the mixture is very light and fluffy, about 5 minutes. Scrape down the work bowl and then beat the mixture for another 5 minutes.

3. Reduce the speed to low, add the melted chocolate, and beat to incorporate.

4. Add the eggs one at a time and beat to incorporate, again scraping the work bowl as needed. When both eggs have been incorporated, scrape down the work bowl. Set the speed to medium and beat for 1 minute.

5. Add the flour, cocoa powder, baking powder, cinnamon, ancho chile powder, and salt, reduce the speed to low, and beat until the mixture comes together as a dough.

6. Drop 2 oz. portions of the dough on the baking sheets, making sure to leave enough space between them. Place the baking sheets in the refrigerator and let the dough firm up for 1 hour.

7. Preheat the oven to 350°F. Place the confectioners' sugar in a mixing bowl, toss the dough balls in the sugar until completely coated, and then place them back on the baking sheets.

8. Place the cookies in the oven and bake until a cake tester comes out clean after being inserted, 12 to 14 minutes.

9. Remove the cookies from the oven, transfer them to a cooling rack, and let them cool for 20 to 30 minutes before enjoying.

Sopaipillas

YIELD: 24 SOPAIPILLAS / **ACTIVE TIME:** 35 MINUTES / **TOTAL TIME:** 1 HOUR

3 CUPS SELF-RISING FLOUR

1½ TEASPOONS BAKING POWDER

1 TEASPOON FINE SEA SALT

1 TEASPOON SUGAR

1 CUP WARM WATER (105°F)

4 CUPS CANOLA OIL

CONFECTIONERS' SUGAR, FOR DUSTING

CINNAMON, FOR DUSTING

HONEY, FOR SERVING

1. In the work bowl of a stand mixer fitted with the whisk attachment, combine the flour, baking powder, salt, and sugar. Turn the mixer on low and slowly drizzle in the warm water. Beat until the mixture comes together as a soft, smooth dough. Cover the bowl with a kitchen towel and let the dough rest for 20 minutes.

2. Place the canola oil in a Dutch oven and warm it over medium heat until it is 325°F. Line a baking sheet with paper towels and place it beside the stove.

3. Divide the dough in half and pat each piece into a rectangle. Cut each rectangle into 12 squares and roll each square to ¼ inch thick.

4. Working in batches of three, gently slip the sopaipillas into the hot oil and use a pair of tongs to gently submerge them until they are puffy and golden brown, about 1 minute.

5. Transfer the fried pastries to the baking sheet to drain and cool. When all of the sopaipillas have been fried, dust them with confectioners' sugar and cinnamon and serve with honey.

Mexican Vanilla Ice Cream

YIELD: 1 QUART / **ACTIVE TIME:** 30 MINUTES / **TOTAL TIME:** 5 HOURS

2 CUPS HEAVY CREAM

1 CUP WHOLE MILK

¼ CUP SUGAR

¼ TEASPOON FINE SEA SALT

SEEDS AND PODS FROM 2 MEXICAN VANILLA BEANS

6 LARGE EGG YOLKS

1. In a small saucepan, combine the heavy cream, milk, sugar, salt, and vanilla seeds and pods and bring to a simmer over medium-low heat, stirring until the sugar completely dissolves, about 5 minutes.

2. Remove the saucepan from heat. Place the egg yolks in a heatproof mixing bowl and whisk them until combined. While whisking constantly, slowly whisk about a third of the hot cream mixture into the yolks. Whisk the tempered egg yolks into the saucepan.

3. Warm the mixture over medium-low heat, stirring constantly, until the mixture is thick enough to coat the back of a wooden spoon (about 170°F on an instant-read thermometer).

4. Strain the custard through a fine-mesh sieve into a bowl and let it cool to room temperature. Cover the bowl, place the custard in the refrigerator, and let it chill for at least 4 hours.

5. Churn the custard in an ice cream maker until it has the desired consistency. Transfer to an airtight container and freeze for 4 hours before serving.

BEVERAGES

Margarita

YIELD: 1 SERVING / **ACTIVE TIME:** 2 MINUTES / **TOTAL TIME:** 2 MINUTES

SALT, FOR THE RIM

2 OZ. SILVER TEQUILA

½ OZ. COINTREAU

1 OZ. FRESH LIME JUICE

½ OZ. SIMPLE SYRUP (SEE PAGE 447)

3 DASHES OF SALINE SOLUTION (SEE PAGE 446)

1 LIME WEDGE, FOR GARNISH

1. Wet the rim of a rocks glass and rim it with salt.

2. Place all of the remaining ingredients, except for the garnish, in a cocktail shaker, fill it two-thirds of the way with ice, and shake until chilled.

3. Pour the cocktail into the rimmed glass, add more ice if desired, garnish with the lime wedge, and enjoy.

Mezcal & Mango Float

YIELD: 1 SERVING / **ACTIVE TIME:** 2 MINUTES / **TOTAL TIME:** 2 MINUTES

1 CUP MANGO PUREE

1 CUP GINGER BEER

3 TO 4 SCOOPS MEZCAL ICE CREAM (SEE PAGE 321)

1. Place the puree and ginger beer in a large mason jar and stir to combine.

2. Place the ice cream in a fountain glass and pour the mango soda over the top. Enjoy immediately.

Playa Rosita

YIELD: 1 SERVING / **ACTIVE TIME:** 2 MINUTES / **TOTAL TIME:** 2 MINUTES

¾ OZ. REPOSADO TEQUILA

¾ OZ. JOVEN MEZCAL

½ OZ. PINEAPPLE-INFUSED CAMPARI

½ OZ. SWEET VERMOUTH

½ OZ. DRY VERMOUTH

DASH OF BITTERMENS 'ELEMAKULE TIKI BITTERS

1 ORANGE TWIST, FOR GARNISH

1. Combine all of the ingredients, except for the garnish, in a mixing glass, fill it two-thirds of the way with ice, and stir until chilled.

2. Strain into a cocktail glass, garnish with the orange twist, and enjoy.

Vampiro

YIELD: 1 SERVING / **ACTIVE TIME:** 2 MINUTES / **TOTAL TIME:** 2 MINUTES

TAJÍN, FOR THE RIM

2 OZ. MEZCAL

2 OZ. VAMPIRO MIX (SEE PAGE 447)

½ OZ. FRESH LIME JUICE

2 OZ. FRESH GRAPEFRUIT JUICE

¾ OZ. SIMPLE SYRUP (SEE PAGE 447)

PINCH OF KOSHER SALT

2 OZ. SELTZER WATER

1 DEHYDRATED BLOOD ORANGE WHEEL, FOR GARNISH

1. Wet the rim of a Collins glass and rim half of it with Tajín.

2. Place the mezcal, Vampiro Mix, juices, and syrup in a cocktail shaker, add 1 ice cube, and whip shake until chilled.

3. Pour the cocktail into the rimmed glass, add the salt and seltzer, garnish with the dehydrated blood orange wheel, and serve.

Michelada

YIELD: 2 SERVINGS / **ACTIVE TIME:** 10 MINUTES / **TOTAL TIME:** 24 HOURS

2 CUPS CLAMATO

¼ CUP GREEN OLIVE BRINE

1 TABLESPOON TAJÍN, PLUS MORE FOR GARNISH

1 TABLESPOON SOY SAUCE

1 TABLESPOON MAGGI SEASONING SAUCE

1 TABLESPOON CELERY SALT

¼ CUP FRESH LIME JUICE, PLUS MORE FOR GARNISH

1 TEASPOON TABASCO

2 TEASPOONS WORCESTERSHIRE SAUCE

SALT AND PEPPER, TO TASTE

12 OZ. MEXICAN LAGER

1 OZ. CHAMOY, FOR GARNISH

1. Place all of the ingredients, except for the lager and chamoy, in a mixing bowl and stir to combine. Refrigerate the mixture overnight.

2. If desired, rim pint glasses with salt. Fill them halfway with the michelada mix, pour the beer on top, and gently stir to combine. Garnish with chamoy and additional lime juice and Tajín and enjoy.

East LA

YIELD: 1 SERVING / **ACTIVE TIME:** 2 MINUTES / **TOTAL TIME:** 2 MINUTES

TAJÍN, FOR THE RIM

4 TO 5 CUCUMBER SLICES, PLUS MORE FOR GARNISH

1 OZ. FRESH KEY LIME JUICE

2 OZ. SILVER TEQUILA

¾ OZ. SIMPLE SYRUP (SEE PAGE 447)

8 FRESH MINT LEAVES

3 DASHES OF SALINE SOLUTION (SEE PAGE 446)

1. Wet the rim of a double rocks glass and rim half of it with Tajín. Add ice to the glass.

2. Place the cucumber and key lime juice in a cocktail shaker and muddle.

3. Add the tequila and syrup, give the mint leaves a smack, and drop them into the shaker. Fill it two-thirds of the way with ice, add the Saline Solution, and shake until chilled.

4. Double-strain into the rimmed glass, garnish with an additional slice of cucumber, and enjoy.

Última Palabra

YIELD: 1 SERVING / **ACTIVE TIME:** 2 MINUTES / **TOTAL TIME:** 2 MINUTES

¾ OZ. MEZCAL

¾ OZ. GREEN CHARTREUSE

¾ OZ. LUXARDO MARASCHINO LIQUEUR

¾ OZ. FRESH LIME JUICE

1. Place the mezcal, liqueurs, and lime juice in a cocktail shaker, fill it two-thirds of the way with ice, and shake until chilled.

2. Double-strain into a coupe and enjoy.

Batanga

YIELD: 1 SERVING / **ACTIVE TIME:** 2 MINUTES / **TOTAL TIME:** 2 MINUTES

2 PINCHES OF KOSHER SALT, PLUS MORE FOR THE RIM

½ OZ. FRESH LIME JUICE

2 OZ. SILVER TEQUILA

3½ OZ. MEXICAN COCA-COLA

1 LIME WEDGE, FOR GARNISH

1. Wet the rim of a highball glass and rim it with salt.
2. Place the lime juice and salt in the glass and stir until the salt has dissolved.
3. Add the tequila and ice, top with the cola, and gently stir to combine.
4. Garnish with the lime wedge and enjoy.

Paloma

YIELD: 1 SERVING / **ACTIVE TIME:** 2 MINUTES / **TOTAL TIME:** 2 MINUTES

SALT, FOR THE RIM

2 OZ. EL TESORO BLANCO TEQUILA

1 OZ. FRESH GRAPEFRUIT JUICE

½ OZ. FRESH LIME JUICE

½ OZ. SIMPLE SYRUP (SEE PAGE 447)

2 OZ. SELTZER WATER

1 GRAPEFRUIT SLICE, FOR GARNISH

1. Wet the rim of a Collins glass and rim half of it with salt.

2. Place the tequila, juices, and syrup in a cocktail shaker, add 1 to 2 ice cubes, and whip shake until chilled.

3. Pour the cocktail into the rimmed glass, top with the seltzer, and add more ice. Garnish with the grapefruit slice and enjoy.

Ranch Water

YIELD: 1 SERVING / **ACTIVE TIME:** 2 MINUTES / **TOTAL TIME:** 2 MINUTES

SALT, FOR THE RIM, PLUS MORE TO TASTE

2 OZ. SILVER TEQUILA

½ OZ. FRESH LIME JUICE

4 OZ. TOPO CHICO

1 LIME WEDGE, FOR GARNISH

1. Wet the rim of a highball glass and rim it with salt. Add ice to the glass along with the tequila and lime juice.

2. Top with the Top Chico, add a pinch of salt, and gently stir.

3. Garnish with the lime wedge and enjoy.

Spicy Margarita

YIELD: 1 SERVING / **ACTIVE TIME:** 2 MINUTES / **TOTAL TIME:** 2 MINUTES

TAJÍN, FOR THE RIM

2 OZ. SILVER TEQUILA

½ OZ. COINTREAU

1 OZ. FRESH LIME JUICE

½ OZ. BLISTERED JALAPEÑO SYRUP (SEE PAGE 448)

3 DASHES OF SALINE SOLUTION (SEE PAGE 446)

1 LIME WEDGE, FOR GARNISH

1. Wet the rim of a double rocks glass and rim half of it with Tajín.

2. Place all of the ingredients, except for the garnish, in a cocktail shaker, fill it two-thirds of the way with ice, and shake until chilled.

3. Pour the cocktail into the rimmed glass and add more ice if desired. Garnish with the lime wedge and enjoy.

Oaxaca Old Fashioned

YIELD: 1 SERVING / **ACTIVE TIME:** 2 MINUTES / **TOTAL TIME:** 2 MINUTES

1½ OZ. EL TESORO REPOSADO TEQUILA

½ OZ. DEL MAGUEY MEZCAL

2 DASHES OF ANGOSTURA BITTERS

1 BAR SPOON AGAVE NECTAR

1 STRIP OF ORANGE PEEL, TORCHED, FOR GARNISH

1. Place all of the ingredients, except for the garnish, in a mixing glass, fill it two-thirds of the way with ice, and stir until chilled.

2. Strain into a rocks glass, garnish with the torched orange peel, and enjoy.

Cooper's Café

YIELD: 1 SERVING / **ACTIVE TIME:** 2 MINUTES / **TOTAL TIME:** 2 MINUTES

1 OZ. FRESHLY BREWED ESPRESSO

2 OZ. MEZCAL

½ OZ. CINNAMON SYRUP (SEE PAGE 452)

1 STRIP OF ORANGE PEEL, FOR GARNISH

1. Place the espresso, mezcal, and syrup in a cocktail shaker, fill it two-thirds of the way with ice, and shake until chilled.

2. Strain into a Nick & Nora glass, garnish with the strip of orange peel, and enjoy.

Oaxacarajillo

YIELD: 1 SERVING / **ACTIVE TIME:** 2 MINUTES / **TOTAL TIME:** 2 MINUTES

1½ OZ. LICOR 43

1 OZ. MEZCAL

1 BAR SPOON AGAVE NECTAR

1 OZ. FRESHLY BREWED ESPRESSO, COOLED SLIGHTLY

1. Add the Licor 43, mezcal, and agave nectar to a double rocks glass.
2. Add 1 large ice cube. Slowly pour the espresso over the back of a bar spoon positioned as close to the cube as possible so that it floats atop the cocktail. Enjoy immediately.

Ramon Bravo

YIELD: 1 SERVING / **ACTIVE TIME:** 2 MINUTES / **TOTAL TIME:** 2 MINUTES

SALT, FOR THE RIM

1½ OZ. CHORIZO-WASHED MEZCAL (SEE PAGE 448)

½ OZ. ANCHO REYES LIQUEUR

1 OZ. CHARRED PINEAPPLE PUREE (SEE PAGE 449)

1 OZ. FRESH LIME JUICE

¾ OZ. SIMPLE SYRUP (SEE PAGE 447)

4 SPRIGS OF FRESH CILANTRO

1. Wet the rim of a highball glass and rim it with salt.
2. Place all of the remaining ingredients in a cocktail shaker, fill it two-thirds of the way with ice, and shake until chilled.
3. Strain into the rimmed glass and enjoy.

Oaxaca Old Fashioned
SEE PAGE 364

Lavagave

YIELD: 1 SERVING / **ACTIVE TIME:** 2 MINUTES / **TOTAL TIME:** 2 MINUTES

1½ OZ. TEQUILA

½ OZ. MEZCAL

¾ OZ. LAVENDER AGAVE (SEE PAGE 452)

½ OZ. GRAPEFRUIT JUICE

½ OZ. FRESH LIME JUICE

¾ OZ. EGG WHITES

DASH OF BITTERCUBE CHERRY BARK VANILLA BITTERS

DRIED LAVENDER BUDS, GRATED, FOR GARNISH

1. Place all of the ingredients, except for the garnish, in a cocktail shaker, fill it two-thirds of the way with ice, and shake until chilled.
2. Strain, discard the ice in the shaker, return the cocktail to the shaker, and dry shake for 15 seconds.
3. Pour the drink into a coupe and garnish with grated lavender buds.

Jamaica Collins

YIELD: 1 SERVING / **ACTIVE TIME:** 2 MINUTES / **TOTAL TIME:** 2 MINUTES

¾ OZ. JAMAICA SYRUP (SEE PAGE 449)

1 OZ. FRESH LIME JUICE

1½ OZ. BOMBAY SAPPHIRE GIN

3 DROPS OF ROSEWATER

2 OZ. TOPO CHICO

1 LIME WEDGE, FOR GARNISH

1. Place all of the ingredients, except for the Topo Chico and garnish, in a cocktail shaker, add 2 ice cubes, and shake until the cubes have dissolved.

2. Add the Topo Chico to the shaker and pour the cocktail over ice into a double rocks glass.

3. Garnish with the lime wedge and enjoy.

El Chavo del Ocho

YIELD: 1 SERVING / **ACTIVE TIME:** 2 MINUTES / **TOTAL TIME:** 2 MINUTES

2 OZ. TEQUILA OCHO BLANCO

½ OZ. LICOR 43

½ OZ. FRESH LIME JUICE

¾ OZ. PASSION FRUIT PUREE

½ OZ. THYME SYRUP (SEE PAGE 450)

1 EGG WHITE

1 SPRIG OF FRESH THYME, FOR GARNISH

1. Place all of the ingredients, except for the garnish, in a cocktail shaker, add 1 ice cube, and whip shake until chilled.

2. Strain into a large coupe or a wineglass, garnish with the thyme, and enjoy.

Canoe Club

YIELD: 1 SERVING / **ACTIVE TIME:** 2 MINUTES / **TOTAL TIME:** 2 MINUTES

1½ OZ. MEZCAL

½ OZ. CRÈME DE MURE

¾ OZ. GINGER & SERRANO SYRUP (SEE PAGE 451)

½ OZ. FRESH LIME JUICE

3 DASHES OF PEYCHAUD'S BITTERS

1. Place all of the ingredients in a cocktail shaker and stir to combine. Fill the shaker two-thirds of the way with ice and shake until chilled.
2. Strain over ice into a rocks glass and enjoy.

Flor de Jalisco

YIELD: 1 SERVING / **ACTIVE TIME:** 2 MINUTES / **TOTAL TIME:** 2 MINUTES

1½ OZ. REPOSADO TEQUILA

½ OZ. MEZCAL

½ OZ. STRAWBERRY JAM

½ OZ. AGAVE NECTAR

½ OZ. FRESH LIME JUICE

DASH OF BLACK LAVA SOLUTION (SEE PAGE 451)

3 DASHES OF BITTERMENS HELLFIRE HABANERO SHRUB

2 PINEAPPLE LEAVES, FOR GARNISH

1 LIME WHEEL, FOR GARNISH

1 MARIGOLD BLOSSOM, FOR GARNISH

1. Place all of the ingredients, except for the garnishes, in a cocktail shaker, fill it two-thirds of the way with ice, and shake until chilled.

2. Strain over ice into a rocks glass and garnish with pineapple leaves, a lime wheel, and a marigold blossom.

Blacker the Berry, the Sweeter the Juice

YIELD: 1 SERVING / **ACTIVE TIME:** 2 MINUTES / **TOTAL TIME:** 2 MINUTES

- 5 BLACKBERRIES
- 1½ OZ. MEZCAL
- ¾ OZ. ST-GERMAIN
- ½ OZ. GINGER SYRUP (SEE PAGE 461)
- 2 DASHES BITTERMENS HELLFIRE HABANERO SHRUB
- ¾ OZ. FRESH LIME JUICE
- ½ OZ. AGAVE NECTAR
- 1 LIME WHEEL, FOR GARNISH
- 2 FRESH SAGE LEAVES, FOR GARNISH

1. Place blackberries in a highball glass and muddle them. Add crushed ice to the glass.
2. Place the mezcal, St-Germain, syrup, lime juice, and agave in a cocktail shaker, fill it two-thirds of the way with ice, and shake until chilled.
3. Strain into the highball glass, garnish with a lime wheel and sage leaves, and enjoy.

Maya Gold

YIELD: 1 SERVING / **ACTIVE TIME:** 2 MINUTES / **TOTAL TIME:** 2 MINUTES

1½ OZ. CHAMOMILE MEZCAL (SEE PAGE 450)

¾ OZ. FINO SHERRY

½ OZ. APEROL

½ OZ. YELLOW CHARTREUSE

1 LEMON TWIST, FOR GARNISH

1. Place all of the ingredients, except for the garnish, in a mixing glass, fill it two-thirds of the way with ice, and stir until chilled.
2. Strain into a coupe, garnish with the lemon twist, and enjoy.

Drunken Rabbit

YIELD: 1 SERVING / **ACTIVE TIME:** 2 MINUTES / **TOTAL TIME:** 2 MINUTES

2 OZ. MEZCAL

1 OZ. ANCHO REYES LIQUEUR

1½ OZ. PINEAPPLE JUICE

1½ OZ. GUAVA JUICE

1 OZ. CINNAMON SYRUP (SEE PAGE 452)

PINEAPPLE LEAVES, FOR GARNISH

1 ORANGE SLICE, FOR GARNISH

FRESH MINT, FOR GARNISH

TAJÍN, FOR GARNISH

1. Place all of the ingredients, except for the garnishes, in a blender with 1 cup of crushed ice and puree until smooth.
2. Pour the cocktail into a pineapple shell, tumbler, or rocks glass, garnish with pineapple leaves, an orange slice, mint, and Tajín, and enjoy.

Shake Your Tamarind

YIELD: 1 SERVING / **ACTIVE TIME:** 2 MINUTES / **TOTAL TIME:** 2 MINUTES

1½ OZ. RESPOSADO TEQUILA

¼ OZ. MEZCAL

¼ OZ. CAMPARI

¾ OZ. TAMARIND CONCENTRATE

¾ OZ. CINNAMON SYRUP (SEE PAGE 452)

¼ OZ. FRESH LIME JUICE

FRESH MINT, FOR GARNISH

1 CINNAMON STICK, FOR GARNISH

1. Place all of the ingredients, except for the garnishes, in a mixing glass, fill it two-thirds of the way with ice, and stir until chilled.
2. Double-strain into a coupe, garnish with mint and the cinnamon stick, and enjoy.

Brujera

YIELD: 1 SERVING / **ACTIVE TIME:** 2 MINUTES / **TOTAL TIME:** 2 MINUTES

1½ OZ. REPOSADO TEQUILA

½ OZ. RUM

2 DASHES OF ANGOSTURA BITTERS

¼ OZ. AGAVE NECTAR

DASH OF ACTIVATED CHARCOAL

1 STRIP OF ORANGE PEEL, FOR GARNISH

1. Place all of the ingredients, except for the garnish, in a mixing glass, fill it two-thirds of the way with ice, and stir until chilled.
2. Strain over a large ice cube into a rocks glass. Express the strip of orange peel over the cocktail, use it as a garnish, and enjoy.

Pineapple Express

YIELD: 1 SERVING / **ACTIVE TIME:** 2 MINUTES / **TOTAL TIME:** 2 MINUTES

2 OZ. TEQUILA

1 OZ. THAI CHILE AGAVE (SEE PAGE 453)

1 OZ. FRESH LIME JUICE

2 OZ. PINEAPPLE JUICE

MEZCAL, TO MIST

PINCH OF KOSHER SALT, FOR GARNISH

1 PINEAPPLE RING, FOR GARNISH

1. Place the tequila, agave, lime juice, and pineapple juice in a cocktail shaker, fill it two-thirds of the way with ice, and shake until chilled.

2. Double-strain over ice into a rocks glass.

3. Using a spray bottle filled with mezcal, mist the cocktail. Garnish with the salt and pineapple and enjoy.

El Vato Swizzle

YIELD: 1 SERVING / **ACTIVE TIME:** 2 MINUTES / **TOTAL TIME:** 2 MINUTES

1½ OZ. TEQUILA

1 OZ. FRESH LIME JUICE

¾ OZ. FRESH WATERMELON JUICE

¾ OZ. MEXICAN PEPPER REDUCTION (SEE PAGE 453)

LARGE PINCH OF FRESH CILANTRO, PLUS MORE FOR GARNISH

DASH OF PEYCHAUD'S BITTERS

1 SLICE OF WATERMELON, FOR GARNISH

1. Place the tequila, juices, reduction, and cilantro in a pilsner glass, add some crushed ice, and use the swizzle method to combine. To use the swizzle method, place a swizzle stick between your palms and rub them together to rotate the stick, while also moving it up and down in the cocktail to aerate it.

2. Top with the bitters and more crushed ice. Garnish with a slice of watermelon and additional cilantro and enjoy.

Rising Sun

YIELD: 1 SERVING / **ACTIVE TIME:** 2 MINUTES / **TOTAL TIME:** 2 MINUTES

SALT, FOR THE RIM

1 MARASCHINO CHERRY

1½ OZ. TEQUILA

⅓ OZ. YELLOW CHARTREUSE

½ OZ. LIME CORDIAL

1 BAR SPOON SLOE GIN

1. Wet the rim of a coupe and rim it with salt. Place the cherry in the bottom of the glass.

2. Place the tequila, Chartreuse, and lime cordial in a cocktail shaker, fill it two-thirds of the way with ice, shake until chilled, and strain into the rimmed coupe.

3. Top with the sloe gin, allowing it to slowly filter through the cocktail, and enjoy.

Desert Daisy

YIELD: 1 SERVING / **ACTIVE TIME:** 2 MINUTES / **TOTAL TIME:** 2 MINUTES

1½ OZ. TEQUILA

½ OZ. AMARO AVERNA

¾ OZ. FRESH LIME JUICE

¾ OZ. ORANGE BELL PEPPER & BEET SYRUP (SEE PAGE 455)

4 DROPS OF SALINE SOLUTION (SEE PAGE 446)

10 DASHES OF BITTERMENS HELLFIRE HABANERO SHRUB

1 EDIBLE FLOWER, FOR GARNISH

1. Place all of the ingredients, except for the garnish, in a cocktail shaker, fill it two-thirds of the way with ice, and shake until chilled.

2. Strain over ice into a glass and garnish with an edible flower.

Hay Zeus

YIELD: 1 SERVING / **ACTIVE TIME:** 2 MINUTES / **TOTAL TIME:** 2 MINUTES

½ OZ. TEQUILA

½ OZ. FRESH LIME JUICE

1¾ OZ. ZEUS JUICE CORDIAL (SEE PAGE 456)

CORNFLOWER LEAVES, FOR GARNISH

1. Place all of the ingredients, except for the garnish, in a cocktail shaker, fill it two-thirds of the way with ice, and shake until chilled.

2. Strain over a block of ice into a ceramic bowl or cup, garnish with the cornflower leaves, and enjoy.

The Fifth Element

YIELD: 1 SERVING / **ACTIVE TIME:** 2 MINUTES / **TOTAL TIME:** 2 MINUTES

CITRUS SALT (SEE PAGE 454), FOR THE RIM

2 OZ. TEQUILA

2 OZ. AVOCADO MIX (SEE PAGE 454)

¾ OZ. FRESH LIME JUICE

½ OZ. AGAVE NECTAR

1 EGG WHITE

1 DEHYDRATED LEMON SLICE, FOR GARNISH

1. Wet the rim of a coupe and rim it with the Citrus Salt.
2. Place all of the remaining ingredients, except for the garnish, in a cocktail shaker, fill it two-thirds of the way with ice, and shake until chilled.
3. Strain into the coupe, garnish with the dehydrated lemon slice, and enjoy.

Sunday Morning Coming Down

YIELD: 1 SERVING / **ACTIVE TIME:** 2 MINUTES / **TOTAL TIME:** 2 MINUTES

1½ OZ. TEQUILA

½ OZ. DRY VERMOUTH

⅓ OZ. APEROL

1 TEASPOON AGAVE NECTAR

5 DROPS OF CHILE PEPPER EXTRACT

1 STRIP OF ORANGE PEEL, FOR GARNISH

1. Place all of the ingredients, except for the garnish, in a mixing glass and fill it two-thirds of the way with ice. Using another, empty mixing glass, pour the cocktail back and forth between the glasses until combined.

2. Strain over two ice cubes into a cocktail glass. Express the strip of orange peel over the cocktail and use it as a garnish.

Peach Tea

YIELD: 1 SERVING / **ACTIVE TIME:** 2 MINUTES / **TOTAL TIME:** 2 MINUTES

½ OZ. SILVER NEEDLE-INFUSED TEQUILA (SEE PAGE 456)

½ OZ. TEQUILA

¾ OZ. PEACH CORDIAL (SEE PAGE 457)

DROP OF CLARY SAGE TINCTURE

DASH OF MERLET CRÈME DE PÊCHE

CLUB SODA, TO TOP

1 LEMON WEDGE, FOR GARNISH

1. Add the ingredients, except for the club soda and garnish, to a highball glass filled with ice and stir until chilled.

2. Top with club soda, garnish with the lemon wedge, and enjoy.

Champagne Paloma

YIELD: 1 SERVING / **ACTIVE TIME:** 2 MINUTES / **TOTAL TIME:** 2 MINUTES

¾ OZ. TEQUILA

2½ OZ. PINK-AND-WHITE GRAPEFRUIT JUICE BLEND (1:1 RATIO)

DASH OF CINNAMON SYRUP (SEE PAGE 452)

CHAMPAGNE, TO TOP

1 GRAPEFRUIT TWIST, FOR GARNISH

1. Place the tequila, juice blend, and syrup in a mixing glass, fill it two-thirds of the way with ice, and stir until chilled.
2. Strain into a Champagne flute, top with Champagne, garnish with the grapefruit twist, and enjoy.

Lost in the Rain in Juárez

YIELD: 1 SERVING / **ACTIVE TIME:** 2 MINUTES / **TOTAL TIME:** 2 MINUTES

1 OZ. MEZCAL

¾ OZ. APEROL

⅞ OZ. FRESH LIME JUICE

½ OZ. DEMERARA SYRUP (SEE PAGE 458)

1¼ OZ. PINEAPPLE JUICE

3 DASHES OF ABSINTHE

1 EGG WHITE

1 DEHYDRATED PINEAPPLE CHUNK, FOR GARNISH

1. Place all of the ingredients, except for the garnish, in a cocktail shaker and dry shake for 15 seconds.
2. Add ice and shake until chilled.
3. Double-strain into a coupe, garnish with the chunk of dehydrated pineapple, and enjoy.

La Diosa

YIELD: 1 SERVING / **ACTIVE TIME:** 2 MINUTES / **TOTAL TIME:** 2 MINUTES

1½ OZ. TEQUILA

¾ OZ. TRIPLE SEC

½ OZ. FRESH LIME JUICE

1 TABLESPOON PINEAPPLE MARMALADE (SEE PAGE 455)

½ BAR SPOON CHILI POWDER

1 SMALL BUNCH OF FRESH CILANTRO

1 EGG WHITE

TAJÍN, FOR GARNISH

EDIBLE FLOWERS, FOR GARNISH

1. Place all of the ingredients, except for the egg white and garnishes, in a cocktail shaker, fill it two-thirds of the way with ice, and shake until chilled.

2. Strain, discard the ice, and return the mixture to the shaker. Add the egg white and dry shake for 15 seconds.

3. Strain into a coupe and garnish with the Tajín and flowers.

Diablo Otoño

YIELD: 1 SERVING / **ACTIVE TIME:** 2 MINUTES / **TOTAL TIME:** 2 MINUTES

1 OZ. TEQUILA

1 OZ. FIG CORDIAL (SEE PAGE 457)

1 TEASPOON FIG LIQUEUR

TONIC WATER, TO TOP

1. Add all of the ingredients, except for the tonic water, to a highball glass containing three ice spheres and stir until chilled.
2. Top with tonic water and enjoy.

Unscalpe

YIELD: 1 SERVING / **ACTIVE TIME:** 2 MINUTES / **TOTAL TIME:** 2 MINUTES

1½ OZ. MEZCAL

1 OZ. KAMM & SONS ISLAY CASK BITTERS

1 OZ. APEROL

1 STRIP OF ORANGE PEEL, FOR GARNISH

1. Place the mezcal, bitters, and Aperol in a mixing glass, fill it two-thirds of the way with ice, and stir until chilled.
2. Strain into a goblet, garnish with the strip of orange peel, and enjoy.

Piña Fumada

YIELD: 1 SERVING / **ACTIVE TIME:** 2 MINUTES / **TOTAL TIME:** 2 MINUTES

1¼ OZ. MEZCAL

¾ OZ. FRESH LEMON JUICE

2 TEASPOONS VELVET FALERNUM

½ OZ. HONEY

CLUB SODA, TO TOP

1 PINEAPPLE LEAF, FOR GARNISH

1 LEMON WEDGE, FOR GARNISH

1. Place all of the ingredients, except for the club soda and garnishes, in a cocktail shaker, fill it two-thirds of the way with ice, and shake until chilled.
2. Strain over crushed ice into a highball glass and top with club soda.
3. Add more crushed ice, garnish with the pineapple leaf and lemon wedge, and enjoy.

Mezcal Survivor

YIELD: 1 SERVING / **ACTIVE TIME:** 2 MINUTES / **TOTAL TIME:** 2 MINUTES

1¾ OZ. MEZCAL

⅞ OZ. COCCHI AMERICANO

¾ OZ. LIME SYRUP (SEE PAGE 459)

⅞ OZ. FRESH LEMON JUICE

ABSINTHE, TO MIST

3 MARASCHINO CHERRIES, FOR GARNISH

1. Place the mezcal, Cocchi Americano, syrup, and lemon juice in a cocktail shaker, fill it two-thirds of the way with ice, and shake until chilled.
2. Strain into a cocktail glass and mist the cocktail with absinthe. If desired, light the absinthe on fire. Garnish with the maraschino cherries, skewered on a toothpick, and enjoy.

Dons of Soul

YIELD: 1 SERVING / **ACTIVE TIME:** 2 MINUTES / **TOTAL TIME:** 2 MINUTES

- 1⅔ OZ. TEQUILA
- 1 OZ. FRESH TOMATO, CHOPPED
- ⅔ OZ. PAPRIKA
- 2 BAR SPOONS FRESH LIME JUICE
- 2 BAR SPOONS FRESH LEMON JUICE
- 1 BAR SPOON AGAVE NECTAR
- ¼ TEASPOON CHILI POWDER
- PINCH OF PINK PEPPER
- DASH OF BOB'S CORIANDER BITTERS
- 1 STRIP OF LIME PEEL, FOR GARNISH

1. Place all of the ingredients, except for the garnish, in a blender and pulse until combined.
2. Strain the mixture into a cocktail shaker, fill it two-thirds of the way with ice, and shake until chilled.
3. Strain into a cocktail glass, garnish with the strip of lime peel, and enjoy.

Cantaritos

YIELD: 1 SERVING / **ACTIVE TIME:** 2 MINUTES / **TOTAL TIME:** 2 MINUTES

2 OZ. REPOSADO TEQUILA

1½ OZ. FRESH ORANGE JUICE

¾ OZ. FRESH PINK GRAPEFRUIT JUICE

½ OZ. FRESH LIME JUICE

2 PINCHES OF KOSHER SALT

2 OZ. PINK GRAPEFRUIT SODA

1 LIME WEDGE, FOR GARNISH

1. Add the ingredients, except for the garnish, to a Collins glass filled with ice.
2. Gently stir to combine, garnish with the lime wedge, and enjoy.

Kinda Knew Anna

YIELD: 1 SERVING / **ACTIVE TIME:** 2 MINUTES / **TOTAL TIME:** 2 MINUTES

1 OZ. TEQUILA

1 OZ. CRÈME DE MURE

1 OZ. FRESH LIME JUICE

2 OZ. GINGER BEER

1 FRESH SAGE LEAF, FOR GARNISH

1. Place the tequila, liqueur, and lime juice in a cocktail shaker, fill it two-thirds of the way with ice, and shake until chilled.
2. Strain over ice into a double rocks glass, top with the ginger beer, and garnish with the sage leaf.

Naked & Famous

YIELD: 1 SERVING / **ACTIVE TIME:** 2 MINUTES / **TOTAL TIME:** 2 MINUTES

¾ OZ. MEZCAL

¾ OZ. YELLOW CHARTREUSE

¾ OZ. APEROL

¾ OZ. FRESH LIME JUICE

1. Chill a coupe in the freezer.
2. Place all of the ingredients in a cocktail shaker, fill the shaker two-thirds of the way with ice, and shake until chilled.
3. Strain into the chilled coupe and enjoy.

Jalisco Sour

YIELD: 1 SERVING / **ACTIVE TIME:** 2 MINUTES / **TOTAL TIME:** 2 MINUTES

1 OZ. TEQUILA

1 OZ. PISCO

¾ OZ. FRESH LIME JUICE

¾ OZ. SIMPLE SYRUP (SEE PAGE 447)

3 DASHES OF ANGOSTURA BITTERS, FOR GARNISH

1. Place the tequila, pisco, lime juice, and syrup in a cocktail shaker, fill it two-thirds of the way with crushed ice, and shake until chilled.
2. Strain into a coupe, garnish with the bitters, and enjoy.

She's a Rainbow

YIELD: 1 SERVING / **ACTIVE TIME:** 2 MINUTES / **TOTAL TIME:** 2 MINUTES

2 OZ. TEQUILA

1 OZ. MIDORI

5 OZ. WHITE GRAPEFRUIT JUICE

1 GRAPEFRUIT SLICE, FOR GARNISH

1. Place the ingredients in a cocktail shaker, fill it two-thirds of the way with ice, and shake until chilled.

2. Strain over ice into a highball glass and garnish with the slice of grapefruit.

True Romance

YIELD: 1 SERVING / **ACTIVE TIME:** 2 MINUTES / **TOTAL TIME:** 2 MINUTES

1½ OZ. MEZCAL

1 OZ. YELLOW CHARTREUSE

¾ OZ. AMARO AVERNA

1 LIME TWIST, FOR GARNISH

PINCH OF SEA SALT, FOR GARNISH

1. Place the mezcal, Chartreuse, and amaro in a rocks glass containing one large ice cube and stir until chilled.
2. Garnish with the lime twist and pinch of sea salt and enjoy.

Fire Walk with Me

YIELD: 1 SERVING / **ACTIVE TIME:** 2 MINUTES / **TOTAL TIME:** 2 MINUTES

½ OZ. FRESH LIME JUICE

½ OZ. ORGEAT

2 SLICES OF JALAPEÑO CHILE PEPPER

2 OZ. REPOSADO TEQUILA

½ OZ. VELVET FALERNUM

1 STRIP OF ORANGE PEEL, FOR GARNISH

1. Place the lime juice, orgeat, and jalapeño in a cocktail shaker and muddle.
2. Add ice, the tequila, and falernum and shake until chilled.
3. Strain into a coupe, garnish with the strip of orange peel, and enjoy.

Mámù Vida

YIELD: 1 SERVING / **ACTIVE TIME:** 2 MINUTES / **TOTAL TIME:** 2 MINUTES

¾ OZ. SZECHUAN & CHIPOTLE HONEY (SEE PAGE 460)

¾ OZ. FRESH LEMON JUICE

2 OZ. MEZCAL

1 SZECHUAN FLOWER, FOR GARNISH

PINCH OF FLAKY SEA SALT, FOR GARNISH

1. Place the honey, lemon juice, and mezcal in a cocktail shaker, fill it two-thirds of the way with ice, and shake until chilled.

2. Strain over ice into a double rocks glass, garnish with the Szechuan flower and pinch of salt, and enjoy.

L & N

YIELD: 1 SERVING / **ACTIVE TIME:** 2 MINUTES / **TOTAL TIME:** 2 MINUTES

1½ OZ. CINCORO TEQUILA REPOSADO

¾ OZ. HONEY & BASIL SYRUP (SEE PAGE 462)

2 DASHES OF ANGOSTURA BITTERS

BITTERMENS XOCOLATL MOLE BITTERS, TO TASTE

1 STRIP OF ORANGE PEEL, FOR GARNISH

1. Place all of the ingredients, except for the garnish, in a cocktail shaker, fill it two-thirds of the way with ice, and shake until chilled.

2. Strain the cocktail into a coupe, garnish with the strip of orange peel, and enjoy.

Pan

YIELD: 1 SERVING / **ACTIVE TIME:** 2 MINUTES / **TOTAL TIME:** 2 MINUTES

- 1 OZ. TEQUILA
- ⅓ OZ. DRY VERMOUTH
- ⅓ OZ. LEMONGRASS SYRUP (SEE PAGE 459)
- ⅔ OZ. PEAR PUREE
- 1 SPRIG OF FRESH DILL, FOR GARNISH
- 1 PIECE OF FRESH GINGER, FOR GARNISH

1. Place the tequila, vermouth, syrup, and puree in a cocktail shaker, fill it two-thirds of the way with ice, and shake until chilled.
2. Strain into a goblet, garnish with the dill and ginger, and enjoy.

Ghost in the Shell

YIELD: 1 SERVING / **ACTIVE TIME:** 2 MINUTES / **TOTAL TIME:** 2 MINUTES

1 OZ. DEL MAGUEY VIDA MEZCAL

1 OZ. AMONTILLADO SHERRY

¾ OZ. FRESH LIME JUICE

½ OZ. ORGEAT

½ OZ. GINGER SYRUP (SEE PAGE 461)

FRESH MINT, FOR GARNISH

1. Place all of the ingredients, except for the garnish, in a cocktail shaker, fill it two-thirds of the way with ice, and shake until chilled.

2. Fill a Collins glass with crushed ice and double-strain the cocktail over it.

3. Top with more crushed ice, garnish with fresh mint, and enjoy.

La Mula

YIELD: 1 SERVING / **ACTIVE TIME:** 2 MINUTES / **TOTAL TIME:** 2 MINUTES

1½ OZ. OLMECA ALTOS PLATA TEQUILA

½ OZ. DOMAINE DE CANTON

1 OZ. FRESH LIME JUICE

4 SLICES OF JALAPEÑO CHILE PEPPER, PLUS MORE FOR GARNISH

4 OZ. GINGER BEER, TO TOP

1. Place all of the ingredients, except for the ginger beer, in a cocktail shaker, fill it two-thirds of the way with ice, and shake until chilled.

2. Double-strain over ice into a rocks glass and top with the ginger beer.

3. Garnish with additional jalapeño and enjoy.

Guera

YIELD: 1 SERVING / **ACTIVE TIME:** 2 MINUTES / **TOTAL TIME:** 2 MINUTES

1½ OZ. TEQUILA

1 OZ. GRAPEFRUIT JUICE

¾ OZ. FRESH LIME JUICE

¼ OZ. APEROL

¼ OZ. ST-GERMAIN

¼ OZ. THAI PEPPER SHRUB (SEE PAGE 463)

FEVER-TREE BITTER LEMON SODA, TO TOP

1 GRAPEFRUIT WHEEL, FOR GARNISH

1 LIME WHEEL, FOR GARNISH

1. Place all of the ingredients, except for the soda and garnishes, in a Collins glass, add ice, and stir until chilled.

2. Top with soda, garnish with the grapefruit wheel and lime wheel, and enjoy.

Mr. Kotter

YIELD: 1 SERVING / **ACTIVE TIME:** 2 MINUTES / **TOTAL TIME:** 2 MINUTES

2 OZ. TAPATIO TEQUILA

½ OZ. PIERRE FERRAND DRY CURAÇAO

1 OZ. FRESH LIME JUICE

¼ OZ. AGAVE NECTAR

1 ORANGE WEDGE, FOR GARNISH

1. Place all of the ingredients, except for the garnish, in a cocktail shaker, fill it two-thirds of the way with ice, and shake until chilled.

2. Double-strain over a Hibiscus Ice Cube (see page 463) into a rocks glass, garnish with the orange wedge, and enjoy.

Oaxacan Bottle Rocket

YIELD: 1 SERVING / **ACTIVE TIME:** 2 MINUTES / **TOTAL TIME:** 2 MINUTES

- HANDFUL OF FRESH MINT, PLUS MORE FOR GARNISH
- ¾ OZ. DEL MAGUEY VIDA MEZCAL
- ¾ OZ. SMITH & CROSS RUM
- 1 OZ. FRESH LIME JUICE
- ¾ OZ. THAI CHILE & BASIL SYRUP (SEE PAGE 464)
- ½ OZ. VELVET FALERNUM
- ½ OZ. ORANGE JUICE
- PEYCHAUD'S BITTERS, TO TOP

1. Place the fresh mint at the bottom of a Collins glass and fill the glass with pebble ice.
2. Fill the glass with the remaining ingredients, except for the bitters, and top with more pebble ice.
3. Top with bitters until you see a nice red layer on the top of the drink. Garnish with additional fresh mint and enjoy.

Violet Skies

YIELD: 1 SERVING / **ACTIVE TIME:** 2 MINUTES / **TOTAL TIME:** 2 MINUTES

¾ OZ. BUTTERFLY PEA FLOWER–INFUSED MEZCAL (SEE PAGE 465)

½ OZ. HOOD RIVER DISTILLERS LEWIS AND CLARK LOOKOUT GIN

½ OZ. VENTURA SPIRITS STRAWBERRY BRANDY

¼ OZ. KALANI COCONUT LIQUEUR

¼ OZ. ROTHMAN & WINTER CRÈME DE VIOLETTE

½ OZ. FRESH LEMON JUICE

2 DASHES OF SCRAPPY'S GRAPEFRUIT BITTERS

1 EDIBLE FLOWER, FOR GARNISH

1. Chill a coupe in the freezer.
2. Place all of the ingredients, except for the garnish, in a cocktail shaker and dry shake for 10 seconds. Add ice and shake vigorously until chilled.
3. Double-strain into the chilled coupe, garnish with an edible flower, and enjoy.

El Nacional

YIELD: 1 SERVING / **ACTIVE TIME:** 2 MINUTES / **TOTAL TIME:** 2 MINUTES

1 OZ. DEL MAGUEY VIDA MEZCAL

1 OZ. CAMPARI

½ OZ. LUXARDO AMARO ABANO

½ OZ. DRY VERMOUTH

3 DASHES OF BITTERMENS XOCOLATL MOLE BITTERS

SPRITZ OF ARDBEG 5-YEAR ISLAY SCOTCH WHISKY, TO TOP

1 LEMON TWIST, FOR GARNISH

1. Place all of the ingredients, except for the Scotch and garnish, in a mixing glass, fill it two-thirds of the way with ice, and stir until chilled.
2. Strain the cocktail into a coupe and spritz it with the Ardbeg.
3. Garnish with the lemon twist and enjoy.

La Santa

YIELD: 1 SERVING / **ACTIVE TIME:** 2 MINUTES / **TOTAL TIME:** 2 MINUTES

4 CUCUMBER SLICES, PLUS MORE FOR GARNISH

2 OZ. FRESH LIME JUICE

4 OZ. GREEN APPLE JUICE

1¼ OZ. SNAP PEA SYRUP (SEE PAGE 460)

½ OZ. SIMPLE SYRUP (SEE PAGE 447)

4 SMALL PIECES OF HOJA SANTA

1. Place the cucumber and lime juice in a cocktail shaker and muddle.
2. Add the remaining ingredients and 2 to 3 ice cubes and shake until chilled.
3. Strain over ice into a Collins glass, garnish with an additional slice of cucumber, and enjoy.

La Cura

YIELD: 1 SERVING / **ACTIVE TIME:** 2 MINUTES / **TOTAL TIME:** 2 MINUTES

4 OZ. MINT ICED TEA

½ OZ. GINGER SYRUP (SEE PAGE 461)

½ OZ. SIMPLE SYRUP (SEE PAGE 447), MADE WITH HONEY

1 OZ. FRESH LEMON JUICE

6 SPRIGS OF FRESH MINT, PLUS MORE FOR GARNISH

1. Place all of the ingredients, except for the garnish, in a cocktail shaker, add 1 ice cube, and whip shake until chilled.
2. Pour the cocktail into a Collins glass, add more ice, garnish with additional mint, and enjoy.

Home Is Where the Heat Is

YIELD: 1 SERVING / **ACTIVE TIME:** 2 MINUTES / **TOTAL TIME:** 2 MINUTES

- BLACK LAVA SALT, FOR THE RIM
- CUMIN, FOR THE RIM
- 1½ OZ. SPICY MEZCAL (SEE PAGE 464)
- ¼ OZ. GIFFARD BANANE DU BRÉSIL
- ½ OZ. FRESH LIME JUICE
- ½ OZ. MANZANILLA SHERRY
- ¾ OZ. TAMARIND SYRUP (SEE PAGE 465)
- 1 SLICE OF DEHYDRATED JALAPEÑO CHILE PEPPER, FOR GARNISH

1. Place lava salt and cumin in a dish and stir to combine. Wet the rim of a double rocks glass and rim it with the mixture.
2. Place the remaining ingredients, except for the garnish, in a cocktail shaker, fill it two-thirds of the way with ice, and shake until chilled.
3. Strain over ice into the rimmed glass, garnish with the dehydrated slice of jalapeño, and enjoy.

Cornchata

YIELD: 6 SERVINGS / **ACTIVE TIME:** 10 MINUTES / **TOTAL TIME:** 45 MINUTES

4 CUPS CORN

1½ CUPS WATER

2 TABLESPOONS SUGAR

3 PINCHES OF CINNAMON

1. Place all of the ingredients in a blender and puree until smooth.
2. Strain the mixture into a container, pressing down on the solids to extract as much liquid as possible. Chill in the refrigerator for 30 minutes and serve over ice.

Horchata con Rum

YIELD: 1 SERVING / **ACTIVE TIME:** 2 MINUTES / **TOTAL TIME:** 2 MINUTES

¾ OZ. HORCHATA (SEE OPPOSITE PAGE)

2 OZ. RUM

1 CINNAMON STICK, FOR GARNISH

ZEST OF 1 LIME, FOR GARNISH

1. Place the Horchata and rum in a cocktail shaker, add ice, and shake until chilled.
2. Strain over crushed ice into a Collins glass, grate some of the cinnamon stick over the top, and garnish the cocktail with it and the lime zest.

Horchata

YIELD: 6 SERVINGS / **ACTIVE TIME:** 1 HOUR / **TOTAL TIME:** 24 HOURS

4¼ CUPS LONG-GRAIN RICE

8½ CUPS WATER

6 CINNAMON STICKS

1 (14 OZ.) CAN OF SWEETENED CONDENSED MILK

1 (14 OZ.) CAN OF COCONUT MILK

1 TEASPOON CINNAMON

SIMPLE SYRUP (SEE PAGE 447), TO TASTE

1. Place the rice in a large skillet and toast over medium heat until it is fragrant and lightly browned, about 15 minutes, stirring frequently. Remove the pan from heat and let the rice cool completely; if immersed in water while hot, the rice will cook and become too mushy.

2. Transfer the rice to a large container and cover it with the water. Add the cinnamon sticks, cover the container with a kitchen towel, and let the mixture sit at room temperature overnight.

3. Add the mixture to a blender in batches and pulse each batch 10 times. You want to break the rice down, not completely pulverize it. Strain the mixture through a fine-mesh sieve, pressing down on the solids to extract as much liquid and flavor as possible.

4. Add the condensed milk, coconut milk, and cinnamon and stir until incorporated. Add Simple Syrup to taste and chill the horchata in the refrigerator before serving.

Horchata con Espresso

YIELD: 1 SERVING / **ACTIVE TIME:** 2 MINUTES / **TOTAL TIME:** 2 MINUTES

1 CUP HORCHATA (SEE ABOVE)

VANILLA SYRUP (SEE PAGE 461), TO TASTE

2 OZ. FRESHLY BREWED ESPRESSO

1. Pour the Horchata over ice into a glass. Add the syrup and stir until combined.

2. Pour the espresso over the back of a spoon to float it on top.

Horchata
SEE PAGE 419

Xocolatl

YIELD: 4 SERVINGS / **ACTIVE TIME:** 10 MINUTES / **TOTAL TIME:** 10 MINUTES

4 CUPS MILK

6 OZ. MEXICAN CHOCOLATE, CHOPPED

1. Place the milk in a small saucepan and warm it over medium heat.
2. When the milk starts to simmer, add the chocolate. Stir until the chocolate has melted, making sure the mixture does not come to a boil.
3. Pour the mixture into a blender and puree until frothy. Pour into mugs and enjoy.

Agua de Melon

YIELD: 4 TO 6 SERVINGS / **ACTIVE TIME:** 10 MINUTES / **TOTAL TIME:** 10 MINUTES

1 WHOLE CANTALOUPE OR HONEYDEW MELON, HALVED AND SEEDED

6 CUPS WATER

1 TABLESPOON HONEY

1. Cut the melon into quarters and remove the rind.
2. Place half of the melon, water, and honey in a blender and puree until smooth.
3. Strain the mixture through a fine-mesh sieve into a pitcher.
4. Place the remaining melon, water, and honey in the blender, puree until smooth, and strain it into the pitcher.
5. Stir until thoroughly combined and serve over ice.

Agua de Tamarindo

YIELD: 4 TO 6 SERVINGS / **ACTIVE TIME:** 1 HOUR / **TOTAL TIME:** 4 HOURS

8 CUPS WATER

15 TAMARIND PODS

¾ CUP SUGAR

¼ CUP BROWN SUGAR

1. Place half of the water in a medium saucepan and bring it to a boil.
2. Remove the tamarind from its shells, remove the strings, and discard the strings.
3. Add the tamarind, sugar, and brown sugar to the boiling water. Reduce the heat and simmer for 20 minutes.
4. Turn off the heat and let the mixture steep for 2 hours.
5. Once the mixture has cooled, use your hands to remove the tamarind seeds, and squeeze the pulp back into the mixture.
6. Place the mixture in a blender and puree until smooth.
7. Strain the puree through a fine-mesh sieve. Add the remaining water and stir to combine.
8. Chill in the refrigerator for 1 hour and serve over ice.

Agua de Jamaica

YIELD: 4 TO 6 SERVINGS / **ACTIVE TIME:** 15 MINUTES / **TOTAL TIME:** 2 HOURS

2 CUPS HIBISCUS BLOSSOMS

½ OZ. CINNAMON STICKS, CRUSHED

PINCH OF CARDAMOM

2 WHOLE CLOVES

4 ALLSPICE BERRIES

½ CUP SUGAR

12 CUPS WATER

1. Place all of the ingredients in a saucepan and bring to a boil, stirring to dissolve the sugar.
2. Reduce the heat and simmer for 20 minutes.
3. Remove the pan from heat and let the mixture cool completely.
4. Strain through a fine-mesh sieve and refrigerate for at least 1 hour before serving over ice.

Agua de Jamaica

SEE PAGE 423

Atole

YIELD: 6 SERVINGS / **ACTIVE TIME:** 30 MINUTES / **TOTAL TIME:** 30 MINUTES

4 CUPS WHOLE MILK

4 OZ. PILONCILLO

1 CINNAMON STICK

1½ CUPS WARM WATER (105°F)

½ CUP MASA HARINA

2 TEASPOONS MEXICAN VANILLA EXTRACT

PINCH OF KOSHER SALT

CINNAMON, FOR GARNISH

1. Place the milk, piloncillo, and cinnamon stick in a medium saucepan and cook over medium-low heat, stirring until the piloncillo has dissolved. Remove the pan from heat, strain the mixture, and set it aside.

2. Combine the warm water and masa in a bowl and whisk until smooth. Place the mixture in the saucepan and stir in the milk mixture, vanilla, and salt.

3. Bring the mixture to a simmer, stirring continually. Reduce the heat and cook until the mixture has thickened and is smooth and velvety. Pour the atole into mugs, sprinkle a little cinnamon on top, and enjoy.

Mexican Hot Chocolate

YIELD: 4 SERVINGS / **ACTIVE TIME:** 15 MINUTES / **TOTAL TIME:** 15 MINUTES

3 CUPS WHOLE MILK

1 CUP HALF-AND-HALF

3 CINNAMON STICKS

1 RED CHILE PEPPER, STEMMED AND SEEDED

¼ CUP SWEETENED CONDENSED MILK

1½ LBS. SEMISWEET CHOCOLATE CHIPS

½ TEASPOON PURE VANILLA EXTRACT

1 TEASPOON FRESHLY GRATED NUTMEG

½ TEASPOON FINE SEA SALT

WHIPPED CREAM, FOR GARNISH

1. Place the milk, half-and-half, cinnamon sticks, and chile in a saucepan and warm it over medium-low heat for 5 to 6 minutes, making sure the mixture does not come to a boil. When the mixture starts to steam, remove the cinnamon sticks and chile.

2. Add the sweetened condensed milk and whisk to incorporate. Add the chocolate chips and cook, stirring occasionally, until they have melted. Stir in the vanilla, nutmeg, and salt.

3. Ladle the hot chocolate into warmed mugs, top with whipped cream, and enjoy.

Champurrado

YIELD: 6 SERVINGS / **ACTIVE TIME:** 30 MINUTES / **TOTAL TIME:** 30 MINUTES

4 CUPS WHOLE MILK

4 OZ. PILONCILLO

1 CINNAMON STICK

6 OZ. MEXICAN CHOCOLATE

1½ CUPS WARM WATER (105°F)

½ CUP MASA HARINA

2 TEASPOONS MEXICAN VANILLA EXTRACT

PINCH OF KOSHER SALT

CINNAMON, FOR GARNISH

1. Place the milk, piloncillo, cinnamon stick, and chocolate in a medium saucepan and cook over medium-low heat, stirring until the piloncillo has dissolved. Remove the pan from heat, strain the mixture, and set it aside.

2. Combine the warm water and masa in a bowl and whisk until smooth. Place the mixture in the saucepan and stir in the milk mixture, vanilla, and salt.

3. Bring the mixture to a simmer, stirring continually. Reduce the heat and cook until the mixture has thickened and is smooth and velvety. Pour the champurrado into mugs, sprinkle a little cinnamon on top, and enjoy.

Tejuino

YIELD: 32 SERVINGS / **ACTIVE TIME:** 10 MINUTES / **TOTAL TIME:** 4 TO 7 DAYS

32 CUPS WATER

10 OZ. PILONCILLO

1 CINNAMON STICK

1 LB. PREPARED MASA (SEE PAGE 65)

SIMPLE SYRUP (SEE PAGE 447), TO TASTE

1 CUP FRESH LIME JUICE

SALT, FOR SERVING

LIME WEDGES, FOR SERVING

1. Place the water, piloncillo, and cinnamon stick in a large saucepan and bring to a simmer, whisking to dissolve the piloncillo.

2. Whisk in the masa and remove the pan from heat.

3. Pour the mixture into a large glass container, cover it with cheesecloth, and secure the cheesecloth with a rubber band. Let the mixture ferment at room temperature for 4 days.

4. Taste the tejuino. The flavor should be slightly sour and sweet, with an aroma similar to a sourdough starter. Add Simple Syrup to taste. If you want a more robust fermented taste, let the tejuino ferment for another 3 days.

5. Add the lime juice and ice and stir to incorporate. Serve over crushed ice with salt (a pinch per glass should be the right amount) and lime wedges. The tejuino will keep in the refrigerator for up to 2 weeks.

Pineapple Tepache Kombucha

YIELD: 6 SERVINGS / **ACTIVE TIME:** 10 MINUTES / **TOTAL TIME:** 5 TO 10 DAYS

12 CUPS WATER

13½ OZ. TEPACHE SYRUP (SEE PAGE 462)

21 OZ. SCOBY LIQUID (STARTER KOMBUCHA)

5- TO 7-INCH SCOBY

1. While wearing gloves, combine the water and syrup in a large mason jar. Add the SCOBY liquid and make sure that the pH level of the mixture is under 4.2. Add more SCOBY liquid if needed.

2. Add the SCOBY, cover the container with a paper towel, and secure it with a rubber band. Let the mixture ferment for 5 to 10 days, tasting the kombucha every day to see if the flavor has developed to your liking.

3. Bottle the kombucha once you are happy with the flavor.

Tepache de Piña

YIELD: 6 TO 8 SERVINGS / **ACTIVE TIME:** 15 MINUTES / **TOTAL TIME:** 4 TO 7 DAYS

32 CUPS WATER

4 OZ. PILONCILLO

1 LARGE MEXICAN CINNAMON STICK

3 WHOLE CLOVES

1 PINEAPPLE

1. Place half of the water, the piloncillo, cinnamon, and cloves in a large saucepan and warm over medium heat, stirring to dissolve the piloncillo.

2. Cut the top and bottom off of the pineapple and rinse the pineapple well. Cut it into 4-inch pieces, leaving the skin on. Place the chopped pineapple in the warm liquid and turn off the heat.

3. Strain the liquid into a bowl. Place the pineapple in a large, 3- to 4-gallon glass jar or vessel and add the remaining water along with the warm syrup and spices. Use a plate to keep the pineapple submerged in the liquid and cover the container with cheesecloth. Secure the cheesecloth with a rubber band or tie.

4. Let the pineapple ferment at room temperature for anywhere from 4 to 7 days, depending on the time of the year. Hotter months will result in a faster ferment and therefore less time is necessary. Colder months may require 7 days to fully ferment. While wearing a pair of gloves, gently stir the contents of the jar with your hands each day.

5. Fermenting should begin the second day, and bubbling or foaming inside the container is perfectly normal. You will begin to sense a sweet-and-sour smell emanating from the mixture.

6. As the fourth day approaches, taste the beverage. It should taste similar to a pineapple mineral water, and should have developed tiny bubbles. If mold begins to form on the side of the jar at any point, do not drink any of the liquid and discard it.

7. When the tepache is fully fermented and it has the desired taste, strain the liquid and store it in the refrigerator. Serve over ice on its own, or with your favorite tequila or mezcal.

Pineapple Tepache Kombucha
SEE PAGE 428

APPENDIX

Masa for Tamales

YIELD: 3 LBS. / **ACTIVE TIME:** 30 MINUTES / **TOTAL TIME:** 1 HOUR AND 30 MINUTES

1 CUP LARD, CHILLED

2 TABLESPOONS BAKING POWDER

1½ TABLESPOONS KOSHER SALT

2 LBS. PREPARED MASA (SEE PAGE 65)

2 CUPS CHICKEN OR VEGETABLE STOCK (SEE PAGE 438 OR 439), CHILLED, PLUS MORE AS NEEDED

1. Place the lard in the work bowl of a stand mixer fitted with the paddle attachment. Add the baking powder and salt and beat until the mixture is light and fluffy, about 3 minutes.

2. Slowly add the masa and beat until it is thoroughly incorporated. Beat for another 2 to 3 minutes, adding the stock a little at a time until the mixture is the consistency of a very thick pancake batter. Cover the work bowl with plastic wrap and chill the masa mixture in the refrigerator for 1 hour.

3. Remove the masa mixture from the refrigerator and check its consistency. If the masa is too thick, incorporate additional stock until the masa is the correct consistency.

4. Form a teaspoon of the masa into a ball and drop it into a cup of cold water. The ball should float. If it doesn't float, beat the masa for another 5 to 10 minutes. Do not allow the masa to get warm, as the lard will melt and make the tamales too dense. Cover with plastic wrap and chill in the refrigerator until ready to use.

Cilantro Pesto

YIELD: 1¾ CUPS / **ACTIVE TIME:** 5 MINUTES / **TOTAL TIME:** 5 MINUTES

1 CUP FRESH CILANTRO

1 GARLIC CLOVE, CHOPPED

¼ CUP SUNFLOWER SEEDS

¼ CUP SHREDDED QUESO ENCHILADO

¼ CUP EXTRA-VIRGIN OLIVE OIL

1 TEASPOON FRESH LEMON JUICE

SALT AND PEPPER, TO TASTE

1. Place all of the ingredients in a food processor, blitz until the mixture has emulsified, and use as desired.

Avocado Panna Cotta

YIELD: 4 SERVINGS / **ACTIVE TIME:** 25 MINUTES / **TOTAL TIME:** 24 HOURS

2 SHEETS OF SILVER GELATIN

1 CUP WHOLE MILK

1 CUP HEAVY CREAM

ZEST OF ½ LEMON

FLESH OF 1 AVOCADO

SALT, TO TASTE

1. Place the sheets of gelatin in a bowl of ice water and let them sit until they have softened, about 20 minutes.

2. Combine the milk, heavy cream, and lemon zest in a medium saucepan and bring to a simmer. Remove the pan from heat and let the mixture steep for 10 minutes.

3. Remove the gelatin from the ice water and squeeze to remove excess water. Add it to the milk mixture and stir until the mixture is smooth.

4. Place the avocado in a blender and add half of the milk mixture. Puree until smooth.

5. Stir the puree back into the saucepan. Pour the mixture into the wells of a muffin tin and refrigerate overnight before serving.

Coconut Dressing

YIELD: 4 CUPS / **ACTIVE TIME:** 10 MINUTES / **TOTAL TIME:** 40 MINUTES

1 (14 OZ.) CAN OF COCONUT MILK

3½ OZ. GINGER, PEELED AND GRATED

14 TABLESPOONS FRESH LEMON JUICE

1⅓ TEASPOONS KOSHER SALT

5 TEASPOONS SUGAR

1½ CUPS FRESH CILANTRO, CHOPPED

1½ TABLESPOONS CORIANDER SEEDS

1. Combine all of the ingredients in a mixing bowl and chill the mixture in the refrigerator for 30 minutes.

2. Place the mixture in a blender and puree until it has emulsified, making sure the mixture does not get hot at all.

3. Strain the dressing through a fine-mesh sieve and use as desired.

APPENDIX

Mole Spice

YIELD: ¼ CUP / **ACTIVE TIME:** 5 MINUTES / **TOTAL TIME:** 5 MINUTES

- 2 TABLESPOONS ALLSPICE
- 2 TEASPOONS GROUND CLOVES
- 2 TEASPOONS CINNAMON
- 2 TEASPOONS CUMIN
- 2 TABLESPOONS CORIANDER
- 2 TABLESPOONS GROUND GINGER

1. Place all of the ingredients in a mixing bowl and stir to combine. Use as desired.

Habanero Agave

YIELD: 1 CUP / **ACTIVE TIME:** 5 MINUTES / **TOTAL TIME:** 25 MINUTES

- 1 CUP AGAVE NECTAR
- 2 TEASPOONS FRESH LIME JUICE
- 1 TEASPOON HABANERO POWDER

1. Place all of the ingredients in a small saucepan and cook over medium heat until the mixture has reduced by half, 15 to 20 minutes.
2. Remove the pan from heat, strain the agave through a coffee filter, and use as desired.

Roasted Bone Marrow

YIELD: 4 SERVINGS / **ACTIVE TIME:** 5 MINUTES / **TOTAL TIME:** 20 MINUTES

4 MARROW BONES

1. Preheat the oven to 450°F.
2. Place the marrow bones upright on a baking sheet, carefully place them in the oven, and roast for 15 minutes.
3. Remove the marrow bones from the oven, scrape the roasted marrow out of the bones, and use immediately.

Lime Crema

YIELD: ½ CUP / **ACTIVE TIME:** 5 MINUTES / **TOTAL TIME:** 5 MINUTES

½ CUP CREMA

1 TABLESPOON FRESH LIME JUICE

SALT, TO TASTE

1. Place all of the ingredients in a small bowl, stir to combine, and use as desired.

Chicken Stock

YIELD: 16 CUPS / **ACTIVE TIME:** 1 HOUR / **TOTAL TIME:** 10 HOURS

4 LBS. LEFTOVER CHICKEN BONES

32 CUPS COLD WATER

¼ CUP WHITE WINE

1 ONION, CHOPPED

1 CELERY STALK, CHOPPED

1 CARROT, CHOPPED

2 BAY LEAVES

10 SPRIGS OF FRESH PARSLEY

10 SPRIGS OF FRESH THYME

1 TEASPOON BLACK PEPPERCORNS

SALT, TO TASTE

1. Preheat the oven to 400°F. Place the chicken bones on a baking sheet, place them in the oven, and roast them until they are caramelized, about 1 hour.

2. Remove the chicken bones from the oven and place them in a stockpot. Cover them with the water and bring to a boil, skimming to remove any impurities that rise to the surface.

3. Deglaze the baking sheet with the white wine, scraping up any browned bits from the bottom. Stir the liquid into the stock, add the remaining ingredients, and reduce the heat so that the stock simmers. Simmer the stock until it has reduced by three-quarters and the flavor is to your liking, about 6 hours, skimming the surface as needed.

4. Strain the stock and either use immediately or let it cool completely and store it in the refrigerator.

Toasted Rice Powder

YIELD: ½ CUP / **ACTIVE TIME:** 5 MINUTES / **TOTAL TIME:** 5 MINUTES

½ CUP JASMINE RICE

1. Warm a large cast-iron skillet over medium-high heat. Add the rice and toast until it is browned, shaking the pan occasionally.

2. Remove the rice from the pan and use a mortar and pestle to grind it into a fine powder. Use immediately or store in an airtight container.

Chile Toreado Mayonnaise

YIELD: 1½ CUPS / **ACTIVE TIME:** 20 MINUTES / **TOTAL TIME:** 20 MINUTES

2 SERRANO CHILE PEPPERS

2 TABLESPOONS SOY SAUCE

2 TABLESPOONS FRESH LIME JUICE

1 CUP MAYONNAISE

1. Warm a large cast-iron skillet over high heat. Add the serrano peppers and cook until charred all over, turning as necessary. Transfer the charred peppers to a bowl and add the soy sauce and lime juice. Let the mixture steep for 15 minutes.

2. Remove the peppers from the liquid, place them in a bowl, and mash until smooth. Add the mayonnaise and stir to combine. Incorporate the soy-and-lime mixture a little bit at a time until the taste of the mayo is to your liking. Use immediately or store in the refrigerator.

Vegetable Stock

YIELD: 6 CUPS / **ACTIVE TIME:** 20 MINUTES / **TOTAL TIME:** 3 HOURS

2 TABLESPOONS EXTRA-VIRGIN OLIVE OIL

2 LARGE LEEKS, TRIMMED AND RINSED WELL

2 LARGE CARROTS, PEELED AND SLICED

2 CELERY STALKS, SLICED

2 LARGE YELLOW ONIONS, SLICED

3 GARLIC CLOVES, UNPEELED BUT SMASHED

2 SPRIGS OF FRESH PARSLEY

2 SPRIGS OF FRESH THYME

1 BAY LEAF

8 CUPS WATER

½ TEASPOON BLACK PEPPERCORNS

SALT, TO TASTE

1. Place the olive oil and vegetables in a large stockpot and cook over low heat until the liquid they release has evaporated. This will allow the flavor of the vegetables to become concentrated.

2. Add the garlic, parsley, thyme, bay leaf, water, peppercorns, and salt. Raise the heat to high and bring to a boil. Reduce the heat so that the stock simmers and cook for 2 hours, while skimming to remove any impurities that float to the surface.

3. Strain through a fine-mesh sieve, let the stock cool slightly, and place in the refrigerator, uncovered, to chill. Remove the fat layer and cover the stock. The stock will keep in the refrigerator for 3 to 5 days, and in the freezer for up to 3 months.

Beef Stock

YIELD: 8 CUPS / **ACTIVE TIME:** 1 HOUR / **TOTAL TIME:** 10 HOURS

2 LBS. YELLOW ONIONS, CHOPPED

1 LB. CARROTS, CHOPPED

1 LB. CELERY, CHOPPED

5 LBS. BEEF BONES

2 TABLESPOONS TOMATO PASTE

16 CUPS WATER

1 CUP RED WINE

1 TABLESPOON BLACK PEPPERCORNS

2 BAY LEAVES

3 SPRIGS OF FRESH THYME

3 SPRIGS OF FRESH PARSLEY

1. Preheat the oven to 375°F. Divide the onions, carrots, and celery between two baking sheets in even layers. Place the beef bones on top, place the pans in the oven, and roast the vegetables and beef bones for 45 minutes.

2. Spread the tomato paste over the beef bones and then roast for another 5 minutes.

3. Remove the pans from the oven, transfer the vegetables and beef bones to a stockpot, and cover with the water. Bring to a boil.

4. Reduce the heat so that the stock simmers. Deglaze the pans with the red wine, scraping up any browned bits from the bottom. Stir the liquid into the stock, add the remaining ingredients, and cook, skimming any impurities that rise to the surface, until the stock has reduced by half and the flavor is to your liking, about 6 hours.

5. Strain the stock and either use immediately or let it cool completely before storing in the refrigerator.

Ham Stock

YIELD: 6 CUPS / **ACTIVE TIME:** 25 MINUTES / **TOTAL TIME:** 2 HOURS

¾ LB. HAM

8 CUPS WATER

2 GARLIC CLOVES

1 ONION, CHOPPED

1 BAY LEAF

1 SPRIG OF FRESH THYME

1. Place all of the ingredients in a stockpot and bring to a boil. Reduce the heat so that the stock simmers and cook for 1 hour, skimming any impurities that rise to the surface.

2. Strain the stock through a fine-mesh sieve and chill it in the refrigerator.

3. When the stock has cooled completely, remove the fat layer and use as desired.

Piloncillo Syrup

YIELD: 3 CUPS / **ACTIVE TIME:** 10 MINUTES / **TOTAL TIME:** 1 HOUR

½ LB. PILONCILLO

2 CUPS WATER

2 TABLESPOONS ANCHO CHILE POWDER

½ CUP SUGAR

SEEDS FROM ¼ VANILLA BEAN

1. Place all of the ingredients in a saucepan and bring to a boil, stirring to dissolve the piloncillo and sugar.
2. Remove the pan from heat and let the syrup cool completely. Strain before using.

Chocolate Mole

YIELD: 8 CUPS / **ACTIVE TIME:** 30 MINUTES / **TOTAL TIME:** 1 HOUR

6 CUPS WATER

1 LB. UNSALTED BUTTER

1½ LBS. SUGAR

1⅔ LBS. BROWN SUGAR

66⅓ OZ. HEAVY CREAM

½ TEASPOON FINE SEA SALT

2¼ LBS. COCOA POWDER

1 CUP SESAME SEEDS, TOASTED

¼ CUP PEANUT BUTTER

1 TABLESPOON MEXICAN VANILLA EXTRACT

2 TEASPOONS CAYENNE PEPPER

1 TEASPOON CINNAMON

1 TEASPOON ORANGE ZEST

1. Prepare an ice bath. Place the water, butter, and sugars in a large saucepan and bring to a boil.
2. Add the cream, salt, and cocoa powder and whisk until the mixture is smooth.
3. Strain the mixture into a heatproof bowl. Add the remaining ingredients and stir until thoroughly incorporated. Place the bowl in the ice bath and stir until the mole is completely cool. Puree and strain before using.

Mexican Chocolate Sauce

YIELD: 6 QUARTS / **ACTIVE TIME:** 40 MINUTES / **TOTAL TIME:** 40 MINUTES

1 CUP SESAME SEEDS

4¾ CUPS WATER

1 LB. UNSALTED BUTTER

25 OZ. SUGAR

56 OZ. BROWN SUGAR

8 CUPS HEAVY CREAM

1½ TEASPOONS FINE SEA SALT

SEEDS AND POD OF ½ VANILLA BEAN

1½ TEASPOONS CINNAMON

1 TEASPOON CAYENNE PEPPER

2 TABLESPOONS PEANUT BUTTER

2¼ LBS. COCOA POWDER

¾ CUP ALMONDS

1. Prepare an ice bath. Place the sesame seeds in a dry skillet and toast over low heat until they are just browned, shaking the pan occasionally. Remove the sesame seeds from the pan and set them aside.

2. Place the water, butter, sugars, cream, salt, vanilla, cinnamon, cayenne, sesame seeds, and peanut butter in a large saucepan and bring to a simmer, stirring frequently.

3. Remove the pan from heat, add the cocoa powder, and whisk until combined.

4. Place the almonds in a dry skillet and toast over low heat until they are just browned, shaking the pan occasionally. Remove them from the pan and set them aside.

5. Strain the chocolate-and-cream mixture and reserve ¾ cup of the sesame seeds. Add these, 2 cups of the strained chocolate sauce, and the almonds to a blender and pulse until the almonds are finely ground.

6. Add the blended mixture to the strained chocolate sauce and cool the mixture in the ice bath. Use as desired.

Dark Chocolate Ganache

YIELD: 1½ CUPS / **ACTIVE TIME:** 10 MINUTES / **TOTAL TIME:** 15 MINUTES

½ LB. DARK CHOCOLATE

1 CUP HEAVY CREAM

1. Place the chocolate in a heatproof mixing bowl and set aside.
2. Place the heavy cream in a small saucepan and bring to a simmer over medium heat.
3. Pour the cream over the chocolate and let the mixture rest for 1 minute.
4. Gently whisk the mixture until thoroughly combined. Use immediately if drizzling over a cake or serving with fruit. Let the ganache cool for 2 hours if piping.

Raicilla-Soaked Berries

YIELD: 6 SERVINGS / **ACTIVE TIME:** 5 MINUTES / **TOTAL TIME:** 1 HOUR

2 CUPS FRESH BERRIES

½ CUP POWDERED SUGAR

¼ CUP RAICILLA

1. Place all of the ingredients in a mixing bowl and stir gently to combine.
2. Let the berries macerate for 1 hour. Use as desired.

APPENDIX

Perfect Caramel

YIELD: 3 CUPS / **ACTIVE TIME:** 15 MINUTES / **TOTAL TIME:** 30 MINUTES

3 CUPS SUGAR

3¾ CUPS WATER

1. Prepare an ice bath. Place the sugar and 1½ cups of the water in a saucepan and bring to a boil. Cook until the mixture is amber.

2. Remove the pan from heat and carefully deglaze the mixture with the remaining water. The mixture will splatter, so use a good deal of caution here.

3. Return the pan to the stove and melt any residual caramelized sugar over low heat.

4. Place the caramel in the ice bath and let it cool completely. Use as desired.

Blue Corn Crunchies

YIELD: 1 CUP / **ACTIVE TIME:** 30 MINUTES / **TOTAL TIME:** 1 HOUR

1 LB. PILONCILLO, CHOPPED

2½ CUPS WATER

¼ TEASPOON CINNAMON

⅛ TEASPOON GROUND CLOVES

5 BLUE CORN TORTILLAS

CANOLA OIL, AS NEEDED

1. Place a piece of parchment paper beneath a wire rack. Place the piloncillo, water, cinnamon, and cloves in a small saucepan and warm over medium heat, stirring to dissolve the piloncillo.

2. Strain the syrup into a shallow bowl. Place a single tortilla in the liquid and let it absorb the syrup for a few minutes. Flip the tortilla over and soak the other side in the syrup. Place the tortilla on the cooling rack to drain. Repeat with the remaining tortillas.

3. Add canola oil to a Dutch oven until it is about 2 inches deep and warm it to 350°F. Gently slip the tortillas into the hot oil and fry until they are crispy, 1 to 2 minutes. Transfer the fried tortillas to paper towel–lined plates to drain and cool.

4. Break the tortillas up and place them in a food processor. Pulse until they are the texture of coarse bread crumbs and use as desired.

Chocolate & Mexican Vanilla Frosting

YIELD: 4 CUPS / **ACTIVE TIME:** 10 MINUTES / **TOTAL TIME:** 30 MINUTES

2 CUPS HEAVY CREAM

1 LB. DARK CHOCOLATE, CHOPPED

3 OZ. MILK CHOCOLATE, CHOPPED

½ CUP MEXICAN VANILLA EXTRACT

1. Place the cream in a saucepan and warm it over medium heat. Place the chocolates in a heatproof bowl.

2. When the cream starts to steam, pour it over the chocolates and stir until the mixture is melted and smooth. Stir in the vanilla and let the frosting cool before using.

Cajeta

YIELD: 1½ CUPS / **ACTIVE TIME:** 1 HOUR / **TOTAL TIME:** 5 HOURS

4 CUPS GOAT MILK

1 CUP SUGAR

1 CINNAMON STICK

⅛ TEASPOON KOSHER SALT

¼ TEASPOON BAKING SODA

1½ TEASPOONS WATER

1. Place the goat milk, sugar, cinnamon stick, and salt in a medium saucepan and bring to a simmer over medium-low heat.

2. In a small bowl, combine the baking soda and water. Whisk the mixture into the saucepan.

3. Continue to simmer for 1 to 2 hours, stirring frequently.

4. When the mixture turns a caramel color and is thick enough to coat the back of a wooden spoon, remove the pan from heat and let the cajeta cool for 1 hour.

5. Transfer to mason jars and chill in the refrigerator until it has set before using.

Saline Solution

YIELD: ½ CUP / **ACTIVE TIME:** 5 MINUTES / **TOTAL TIME:** 5 MINUTES

⅓ OZ. KOSHER SALT

3½ OZ. WARM WATER (105°F)

1. Place the ingredients in a mason jar, cover it, and shake until the salt has dissolved. Use as desired.

Pineapple-Infused Campari

YIELD: 1½ CUPS / **ACTIVE TIME:** 5 MINUTES / **TOTAL TIME:** 24 TO 48 HOURS

¾ LB. PINEAPPLE, FINELY DICED

1½ CUPS CAMPARI

1. Place the ingredients in a large container and let the mixture steep for 24 to 48 hours.
2. Strain and use as desired.

Vampiro Mix

YIELD: 2 CUPS / **ACTIVE TIME:** 5 MINUTES / **TOTAL TIME:** 5 MINUTES

1¼ CUPS CLAMATO

2 TABLESPOONS APPLE CIDER VINEGAR

6 TABLESPOONS FRESH LIME JUICE

¼ CUP AGAVE NECTAR

1 TABLESPOON SRIRACHA

2 TEASPOONS BLOOD ORANGE JUICE

2 TEASPOONS SMOKED PAPRIKA

1 TEASPOON GROUND BLACK PEPPER

SALT, TO TASTE

1. Place all of the ingredients in a blender and pulse until combined. Use as desired.

Simple Syrup

YIELD: 1½ CUPS / **ACTIVE TIME:** 5 MINUTES / **TOTAL TIME:** 1 HOUR

1 CUP SUGAR

1 CUP WATER

1. Place the ingredients in a saucepan and bring to a boil, stirring to dissolve the sugar.

2. Remove the pan from heat and let the syrup cool completely before using.

APPENDIX

Blistered Jalapeño Syrup

YIELD: 3 CUPS / **ACTIVE TIME:** 10 MINUTES / **TOTAL TIME:** 20 MINUTES

6 JALAPEÑO CHILE PEPPERS, STEMMED AND SLICED

2 CUPS WATER

2 CUPS SUGAR

1. Warm a comal or large cast-iron skillet over medium heat. Add the jalapeños and cook until they are lightly charred, turning them occasionally.

2. Place the jalapeños in a blender, add the water and sugar, and puree on high for 30 seconds.

3. Strain the syrup into a mason jar and use as desired.

Chorizo-Washed Mezcal

YIELD: 2 CUPS / **ACTIVE TIME:** 20 MINUTES / **TOTAL TIME:** 18 HOURS

½ LB. MEXICAN CHORIZO, CASING REMOVED

MEZCAL, AS NEEDED

1. Place the chorizo in a dry skillet and cook over low heat to render the fat. When the chorizo is cooked through, remove it from the pan and use it in another preparation.

2. Place the rendered fat in a large mason jar. For every 2 oz. of fat, add a 750 ml bottle of mezcal. Let the mixture sit at room temperature for 12 hours.

3. Chill the mixture in the freezer for 6 to 8 hours.

4. Strain the mezcal through a fine-mesh sieve or cheesecloth and use as desired.

Charred Pineapple Puree

YIELD: 3 CUPS / **ACTIVE TIME:** 30 MINUTES / **TOTAL TIME:** 30 MINUTES

1 PINEAPPLE, PEELED, CORED, AND CUT INTO RINGS

WATER, AS NEEDED

1. Prepare a gas or charcoal grill for medium heat (about 400°F). Place the pineapple on the grill and cook until it is charred on both sides, about 6 minutes, turning it as necessary.
2. Place the pineapple in a blender and pulse, adding water a tablespoon at a time until the texture of the puree is similar to applesauce. Use as desired.

Jamaica Syrup

YIELD: 1½ CUPS / **ACTIVE TIME:** 20 MINUTES / **TOTAL TIME:** 1 HOUR AND 20 MINUTES

2 CUPS WATER

1 CUP DRIED HIBISCUS FLOWERS

¼ TEASPOON KOSHER SALT

1 STAR ANISE POD

1 CINNAMON STICK

1 WHOLE CLOVE

2 CUPS SUGAR

1. Place the water in a saucepan and bring it to a boil.
2. Add the hibiscus flowers, salt, star anise, cinnamon stick, and clove and boil for 2 minutes. Reduce the heat and simmer for 10 minutes.
3. Remove the pan from heat, add the sugar, and stir until it has dissolved. Cover the pan and let it sit for 1 hour. Strain before using.

APPENDIX

449

Thyme Syrup

YIELD: 1½ CUPS / **ACTIVE TIME:** 20 MINUTES / **TOTAL TIME:** 1 HOUR AND 20 MINUTES

1 CUP SUGAR

1 CUP WATER

3 SPRIGS OF FRESH THYME

1. Place the sugar and water in a saucepan and bring to a boil, stirring to dissolve the sugar.
2. Add the thyme, remove the pan from heat, and let the syrup cool. Strain before using.

Chamomile Mezcal

YIELD: 1 CUP / **ACTIVE TIME:** 5 MINUTES / **TOTAL TIME:** 35 MINUTES

¼ CUP LOOSE-LEAF CHAMOMILE TEA

1 CUP MEZCAL

1. Place the ingredients in a large mason jar and steep for 30 minutes to 1 hour, tasting the mixture every 5 minutes after the 30-minute mark to account for the varying results different mezcals will produce. Strain before using.

Ginger & Serrano Syrup

YIELD: 1 CUP / **ACTIVE TIME:** 5 MINUTES / **TOTAL TIME:** 35 MINUTES

1 CUP SUGAR

½ CUP WATER

3 SERRANO CHILE PEPPERS, STEMMED AND SLICED

2 LARGE PIECES OF FRESH GINGER, CHOPPED

1. Place all of the ingredients in a saucepan and bring to a boil, stirring to dissolve the sugar.

2. Remove the pan from heat and let the syrup cool completely. Strain before using.

Black Lava Solution

YIELD: 1 CUP / **ACTIVE TIME:** 5 MINUTES / **TOTAL TIME:** 1 HOUR

½ CUP WATER

¼ CUP BLACK LAVA SALT

1. Place the ingredients in a saucepan and bring the mixture to a boil, stirring until the salt has dissolved.

2. Remove the pan from heat and let it cool completely before using.

Lavender Agave

YIELD: 3½ CUPS / **ACTIVE TIME:** 5 MINUTES / **TOTAL TIME:** 2 HOURS AND 15 MINUTES

1 TEASPOON DRIED LAVENDER BUDS

4 CUPS AGAVE NECTAR

1. Place the lavender buds in a piece of cheesecloth and use kitchen twine to turn it into a sachet.
2. Place the agave in a saucepan and bring it to a boil.
3. Remove the pan from heat, add the lavender sachet, and let the mixture steep for 2 hours. Remove the sachet before using.

Cinnamon Syrup

YIELD: 1½ CUPS / **ACTIVE TIME:** 5 MINUTES / **TOTAL TIME:** 1 HOUR

1 CUP SUGAR

1 CUP WATER

3 CINNAMON STICKS

1. Place the sugar and water in a saucepan and bring to a boil, stirring to dissolve the sugar.
2. Add the cinnamon sticks, remove the pan from heat, and let the syrup cool completely. Strain before using.

Thai Chile Agave

YIELD: 1 CUP / **ACTIVE TIME:** 15 MINUTES / **TOTAL TIME:** 2 HOURS

2 OZ. THAI CHILE PEPPERS

2 CUPS WATER

2 CUPS AGAVE NECTAR

1. Place the chiles and water in a saucepan and bring to a boil.
2. Stir in the agave nectar and simmer the mixture for 1 hour.
3. Let the mixture cool completely. Strain before using.

Mexican Pepper Reduction

YIELD: 4 CUPS / **ACTIVE TIME:** 15 MINUTES / **TOTAL TIME:** 1 HOUR AND 30 MINUTES

2 CUPS WATER

1 DRIED CHILE DE ÁRBOL

1 ANCHO CHILE PEPPER

1 JALAPEÑO CHILE PEPPER, SLICED LENGTHWISE

3 CUPS SUGAR

1. Make sure to prepare this in a well-ventilated kitchen, as the fumes from cooking the reduction will make the air extremely peppery. Place all of the ingredients, except for the sugar, in a saucepan, bring to a boil, and cook for 20 minutes.
2. Strain the mixture into a mixing bowl, add the sugar, and stir until dissolved. Let the mixture cool completely before using.

Citrus Salt

YIELD: ½ CUP / **ACTIVE TIME:** 5 MINUTES / **TOTAL TIME:** 5 MINUTES

ZEST OF 2 LEMONS

ZEST OF 2 LIMES

½ CUP KOSHER SALT

1. Place all of the ingredients in a mixing bowl, stir to combine, and use as desired.

Avocado Mix

YIELD: 4 CUPS / **ACTIVE TIME:** 5 MINUTES / **TOTAL TIME:** 5 MINUTES

FLESH OF 1½ AVOCADOS

1 LB. PINEAPPLE, DICED

¾ LB. FRESH CILANTRO

1. Place all of the ingredients in a blender, puree until smooth, and use as desired.

Orange Bell Pepper & Beet Syrup

YIELD: 1½ CUPS / **ACTIVE TIME:** 15 MINUTES / **TOTAL TIME:** 1 HOUR

½ CUP CHOPPED ORANGE BELL PEPPER

½ CUP CHOPPED BEETS

1 CUP SUGAR

1. Juice the pepper and beets separately. Strain the remaining pulp, pressing down on it to extract as much liquid as possible.

2. Place the juices and sugar in a saucepan and bring the mixture to a boil, stirring to dissolve the sugar. Remove the pan from heat and let the syrup cool completely before using.

Pineapple Marmalade

YIELD: 5 CUPS / **ACTIVE TIME:** 30 MINUTES / **TOTAL TIME:** 6 HOURS

4 PINEAPPLES, PEELED, CORED, AND CUBED

8 CINNAMON STICKS

¼ CUP PURE VANILLA EXTRACT

4 ORANGE PEELS

2 GUAJILLO CHILES, STEMMED AND SEEDED

1 CUP SWEET VERMOUTH

1 CUP LILLET

4 CUPS SUGAR

1. Place all of the ingredients in a large saucepan and bring to a simmer. Simmer for 5 hours, stirring occasionally, until the liquid has reduced by at least half.

2. Remove the cinnamon sticks and chiles. Place the remaining mixture in a blender and puree until smooth. Let cool before using.

APPENDIX

Zeus Juice Cordial

YIELD: 2 CUPS / **ACTIVE TIME:** 10 MINUTES / **TOTAL TIME:** 10 MINUTES

3/8 OZ. CRUSHED HAY

5¼ OZ. CELERY JUICE

3½ OZ. CASTER (SUPERFINE) SUGAR

7/8 OZ. SIMPLE SYRUP (SEE PAGE 447)

8 OZ. MEZCAL

3½ OZ. GIK BLUE WINE

½ OZ. SALINE SOLUTION (SEE PAGE 446)

2 DROPS OF MSK TOASTED COCONUT FLAVOUR DROPS

1. Place the hay, celery juice, and sugar in a blender and pulse until combined.
2. Strain through cheesecloth and stir in the Simple Syrup, mezcal, wine, Saline Solution, and toasted coconut drops. Use as desired.

Silver Needle–Infused Tequila

YIELD: 1¼ CUPS / **ACTIVE TIME:** 5 MINUTES / **TOTAL TIME:** 24 HOURS

10½ OZ. TEQUILA

1/8 OZ. LOOSE-LEAF SILVER NEEDLE TEA

1. Place the ingredients in a mason jar and steep for 24 hours. Strain before using.

Peach Cordial

YIELD: 6 CUPS / **ACTIVE TIME:** 10 MINUTES / **TOTAL TIME:** 10 MINUTES

4½ LBS. PEACHES, PITTED

2 TEASPOONS PECTIN

53 OZ. CASTER (SUPERFINE) SUGAR

1 OZ. CITRIC ACID

10 DROPS OF GALBANUM TINCTURE

1. Place the peaches and pectin in a blender and puree for about 5 minutes.

2. Strain through a coffee filter, add the remaining ingredients, and stir until the sugar has dissolved. Use as desired.

Fig Cordial

YIELD: 1½ CUPS / **ACTIVE TIME:** 10 MINUTES / **TOTAL TIME:** 1 HOUR

15 FIGS, QUARTERED

3½ OZ. HONEY

1¾ OZ. WALNUTS

FIG LEAF SYRUP (SEE PAGE 458)

1 TABLESPOON CITRIC ACID

7 OZ. ROSÉ

1. Preheat the oven to 350°F. Place the figs on a parchment-lined baking sheet, cover them with the honey, and then sprinkle the walnuts around the pan. Place the pan in the oven and roast for 10 minutes.

2. Pour all of the Fig Leaf Syrup into a saucepan and warm it over medium heat. When the figs are done, add them to the syrup and simmer for 10 minutes.

3. Strain, stir in the citric acid and Rosé, and let the cordial cool completely before using.

Fig Leaf Syrup

YIELD: 3 CUPS / **ACTIVE TIME:** 5 MINUTES / **TOTAL TIME:** 30 MINUTES

30 FIG LEAVES

3 CUPS SIMPLE SYRUP (SEE PAGE 447), WARM

1. Place the fig leaves in a container and pour the syrup over them. Steep for 30 minutes and strain before using.

Demerara Syrup

YIELD: 2½ CUPS / **ACTIVE TIME:** 5 MINUTES / **TOTAL TIME:** 1 HOUR

2 CUPS DEMERARA SUGAR

1 CUP WATER

1. Place the ingredients in a saucepan and bring to a boil, stirring to dissolve the sugar.
2. Remove the pan from heat and let the syrup cool before using.

Lime Syrup

YIELD: 3½ CUPS / **ACTIVE TIME:** 10 MINUTES / **TOTAL TIME:** 1 HOUR

DEMERARA SYRUP (SEE PAGE 458)

ZEST OF 3 LIMES

1 CUP FRESH LIME JUICE

1. While the syrup is still warm, stir in the lime zest and lime juice. Steep for 15 minutes.
2. Strain and let the syrup cool completely before using.

Lemongrass Syrup

YIELD: 1½ CUPS / **ACTIVE TIME:** 5 MINUTES / **TOTAL TIME:** 1 HOUR

1 CUP WATER

1 CUP SUGAR

3 LEMONGRASS STALKS, PEELED AND BRUISED

1. Place the ingredients in a saucepan and bring to a boil, stirring to dissolve the sugar.
2. Remove the pan from heat, let the syrup cool completely, and strain before using.

Szechuan & Chipotle Honey

YIELD: 3½ CUPS / **ACTIVE TIME:** 15 MINUTES / **TOTAL TIME:** 1 HOUR

½ OZ. SZECHUAN PEPPERCORNS

4½ OZ. CHIPOTLE MECO CHILE PEPPERS, TORN

2 CUPS WATER

2 CUPS HONEY

1. Place the Szechuan peppercorns in a saucepan and toast until they are fragrant, shaking the pan frequently.
2. Add the chiles and water and bring to a boil. Reduce the heat and simmer for 5 minutes.
3. Strain, add the honey, and stir until combined. Let the mixture cool completely before using.

Snap Pea Syrup

YIELD: 1 CUP / **ACTIVE TIME:** 5 MINUTES / **TOTAL TIME:** 5 MINUTES

½ CUP FRESH SNAP PEA JUICE

½ CUP CASTER SUGAR

1. Place the ingredients in a mason jar and shake until the sugar has dissolved. You do not want to heat the syrup, as it will negatively impact the flavor of the fresh juice. Use as desired.

Ginger Syrup

YIELD: 1½ CUPS / **ACTIVE TIME:** 5 MINUTES / **TOTAL TIME:** 1 HOUR

1 CUP SUGAR

1 CUP WATER

2-INCH PIECE OF FRESH GINGER, SLICED

1. Place the sugar and water in a saucepan and bring to a boil, stirring to dissolve the sugar.
2. Add the ginger and cook for another minute.
3. Remove the pan from heat and let the syrup cool. Strain before using.

Vanilla Syrup

YIELD: 1½ CUPS / **ACTIVE TIME:** 5 MINUTES / **TOTAL TIME:** 1 HOUR

1 CUP WATER

1 CUP SUGAR

3 VANILLA BEANS, SPLIT

1. Place the ingredients in a saucepan and bring to a boil, stirring to dissolve the sugar.
2. Remove the pan from heat, let the syrup cool completely, and strain before using.

Tepache Syrup

YIELD: 4 CUPS / **ACTIVE TIME:** 30 MINUTES / **TOTAL TIME:** 4 DAYS

1 PINEAPPLE, CHOPPED
8 WHOLE CLOVES
10 ALLSPICE BERRIES
1 CINNAMON STICK, TORCHED
5 DRIED CHILES DE ÁRBOL
3 BAY LEAVES, CRUSHED
20 CUPS WATER
2 TABLESPOONS BLACK PEPPERCORNS, TOASTED
21 OZ. BROWN SUGAR

1. Place all of the ingredients, except for the brown sugar, in a large container and stir to combine.
2. Cover the container with a paper towel, secure the paper towel with a rubber band, and let the mixture ferment for 4 to 5 days at room temperature.
3. Strain and place the liquid in a saucepan. Cook over medium heat until it has reduced by half.
4. Add the brown sugar and continue to cook, stirring to dissolve the brown sugar, until approximately 4 cups of syrup remain.
5. Remove the syrup from heat and let it cool completely before using.

Honey & Basil Syrup

YIELD: 1½ CUPS / **ACTIVE TIME:** 5 MINUTES / **TOTAL TIME:** 1 HOUR

1 CUP HONEY
1 CUP WATER
2 HANDFULS OF FRESH BASIL LEAVES

1. Place the honey and water in a saucepan and bring to a simmer, stirring until the honey has emulsified.
2. Remove the pan from heat, add the basil, and let the syrup cool completely. Strain before using.

Hibiscus Ice Cubes

YIELD: 12 TO 20 ICE CUBES / **ACTIVE TIME:** 10 MINUTES / **TOTAL TIME:** 8 HOURS

8 CUPS WATER

1 CUP DRIED HIBISCUS BLOSSOMS

1 ORANGE PEEL

1. Place all of the ingredients in a saucepan and bring to a boil.
2. Remove the pan from heat and let the mixture steep for 3 hours. Strain, pour the strained liquid into ice molds, and freeze until the ice cubes are solid.

Thai Pepper Shrub

YIELD: ½ CUP / **ACTIVE TIME:** 10 MINUTES / **TOTAL TIME:** 1 HOUR

4 THAI CHILE PEPPERS, CHOPPED

¼ CUP CANE VINEGAR

¼ CUP CANE SUGAR

1. Place all of the ingredients in a saucepan and bring to a boil, stirring to dissolve the sugar. Cook for 5 minutes, remove the pan from heat, and let the shrub cool completely. Strain before using.

Thai Chile & Basil Syrup

YIELD: 2 CUPS / **ACTIVE TIME:** 5 MINUTES / **TOTAL TIME:** 2 DAYS

3 THAI CHILE PEPPERS, DICED

HANDFUL OF FRESH THAI BASIL

2 CUPS SIMPLE SYRUP (SEE PAGE 447)

1. Add the chiles and basil to the Simple Syrup and let the mixture steep in the refrigerator for 2 days. Strain before using.

Spicy Mezcal

YIELD: 4 CUPS / **ACTIVE TIME:** 5 MINUTES / **TOTAL TIME:** 24 HOURS

2 TO 3 JALAPEÑO CHILE PEPPERS, SLICED

1 (750 ML) BOTTLE OF MEZCAL

1. Place the jalapeños in the mezcal and let the mixture steep for 24 hours. Strain before using.

Tamarind Syrup

YIELD: 2 CUPS / **ACTIVE TIME:** 5 MINUTES / **TOTAL TIME:** 1 HOUR

¼ CUP TAMARIND PULP

1 CUP WATER

1 CUP SUGAR

1. Place all of the ingredients in a saucepan and bring to a simmer, stirring to dissolve the sugar and incorporate the tamarind.

2. Remove the pan from heat and let the syrup cool completely. Strain before using.

Butterfly Pea Flower–Infused Mezcal

YIELD: 4 CUPS / **ACTIVE TIME:** 5 MINUTES / **TOTAL TIME:** 3 HOURS

2 TABLESPOONS DRIED BUTTERFLY PEA FLOWERS

1 (750 ML) BOTTLE OF MEZCAL

1. Place the ingredients in a large mason jar, shake vigorously, and let the mixture steep for 3 hours. Strain before using.

APPENDIX

METRIC CONVERSION CHART

Weights

1 oz. = 28 grams

2 oz. = 57 grams

4 oz. (¼ lb.) = 113 grams

8 oz. (½ lb.) = 227 grams

16 oz. (1 lb.) = 454 grams

Volume Measures

⅛ teaspoon = 0.6 ml

¼ teaspoon = 1.23 ml

½ teaspoon = 2.5 ml

1 teaspoon = 5 ml

1 tablespoon (3 teaspoons) = ½ fluid oz. = 15 ml

2 tablespoons = 1 fluid oz. = 29.5 ml

¼ cup (4 tablespoons) = 2 fluid oz. = 59 ml

⅓ cup (5⅓ tablespoons) = 2.7 fluid oz. = 80 ml

½ cup (8 tablespoons) = 4 fluid oz. = 120 ml

⅔ cup (10⅔ tablespoons) = 5.4 fluid oz. = 160 ml

¾ cup (12 tablespoons) = 6 fluid oz. = 180 ml

1 cup (16 tablespoons) = 8 fluid oz. = 240 ml

Temperature Equivalents

°F	°C	Gas Mark
225	110	¼
250	130	½
275	140	1
300	150	2
325	170	3
350	180	4
375	190	5
400	200	6
425	220	7
450	230	8
475	240	9
500	250	10

Length Measures

1/16 inch = 1.6 mm

⅛ inch = 3 mm

¼ inch = 6.35 mm

½ inch = 1.25 cm

¾ inch = 2 cm

1 inch = 2.5 cm

INDEX

A

absinthe
- Lost in the Rain in Juárez, 391
- Mezcal Survivor, 395

Abuela's Sopes, 194

Abuelita's Chocolate Pots de Crème, 300

achiote paste
- Recado Rojo, 272

agave nectar
- Blacker the Berry, the Sweeter the Juice, 376
- Brujera, 379
- Dons of Soul, 396
- The Fifth Element, 388
- Flor de Jalisco, 374
- Habanero Agave, 436
- Lavender Agave, 452
- Mr. Kotter, 410
- Oaxaca Old Fashioned, 364
- Oaxacarajillo, 365
- Sunday Morning Coming Down, 390
- Thai Chile Agave, 453
- Vampiro Mix, 447

Agua de Jamaica, 423

Agua de Melon, 422

Agua de Tamarindo, 423

Aguachile Verde, 19

Albondigas Soup, 243

allspice leaves
- Ostiones al Tapesco, 48

almonds
- Chiles en Nogada, 132
- Mexican Chocolate Sauce, 442
- Mixed Nut Marzipan, 330
- Mole Negro, 252–253
- Mole Poblano, 154
- Muscovy Duck Breast Mole, 142
- Puerco en Pipian Verde, 126

amaro
- Desert Daisy, 384
- El Nacional, 414
- True Romance, 402

Anaheim chile peppers
- Pavo en Escabeche, 151

ancho chile peppers
- Barbacoa Adobo, 265
- Chile Colorado, 256
- Chilorio, 136
- Mexican Pepper Reduction, 453
- Mextlapique de Callo de Hacha, 169
- Mixiotes de Pollo, 150
- Mole Brownies, 327
- Mole Manchamanteles, 257
- Mole Negro, 252–253
- Muscovy Duck Breast Mole, 142
- Mushroom Barbacoa, 199
- Pescado Zarandeado, 185
- Pierna de Puerco, 124
- Pipian Rojo, 266
- Salsa Macha, 286

Ancho Reyes liqueur
- Drunken Rabbit, 378
- Ramon Bravo, 365

Angostura bitters
- Brujera, 379
- Jalisco Sour, 399
- L & N, 403
- Oaxaca Old Fashioned, 364

Aperol
- Guera, 408
- Maya Gold, 378
- Naked & Famous, 399
- Sunday Morning Coming Down, 390
- Unscalpe, 394

appetizers and sides
- Aguachile Verde, 19
- Arroz a la Mexicana, 85
- Betabel with Salsa Macha y Queso Fresco, 46
- Calabacitas con Elote y Queso Fresco, 76
- Camote con Mole Blanco, 39
- Ceviche de Pescado, 32
- Charred Escabeche, 64
- Chulibu'ul, 84
- Coctel de Camarón, 27
- Coctel de Marisco, 30
- Coffee & Ancho Carrots, 41
- Corn Tortillas, 65

- Cured Sardines, 72
- Escabeche, 86
- Esquites con Longaniza, 24
- Flor de Calabaza con Queso Fresco y Hierbabuena, 57
- Flour Tortillas, 82
- Fried Brussels Sprouts with Habanero Agave, 35
- Frijol Ayocote with Pasilla Yogurt, 49
- Frijoles de la Olla, 56
- Frijoles Negros Refritos, 56
- Guacamole, 80
- Huauzontles Relleno de Queso con Chiltomate, 40
- Koji-Fried Sardines, 73
- Koji-Marinated Sweet Potatoes with Salsa Macha, 35
- Masa-Crusted Sardines with Pickled Manzano, 34
- Ostiones al Tapesco, 48
- Pickled Manzano Peppers, 77
- Pickled Pineapple, 76
- Pickled Red Onion, 77
- Pork Toro with Salsa Macha, 70
- Puritos de Platano Macho Relleno de Frijoles Negros y Mole Negro, 38
- Quesadillas de Champiñones, 52
- Queso Fundido, 71
- Shrimp Aguachile with Avocado Panna Cotta, 28
- Striped Sea Bass Ceviche, 26
- Sweet Corn & Pepita Guacamole, 87
- Taquitos de Papa, 62
- Taquitos de Requesón con Rajas, 61
- Tetelas de Aguacate con Requesón y Nopales, 68
- Tomato Aguachile, 44
- Tortitas de Coliflor, 60
- Verdolagas en Salsa Verde, 48
- Vuelva a la Vida, 53

apple juice, green
- La Santa, 415

apples
- Mole Blanco, 260
- Mole Manchamanteles, 257

Arroz a la Mexicana
- Chilorio, 136
- recipe, 85

Arroz con Leche, 302

arugula
- Esquites con Longaniza, 24
- Guanajuato Strawberry & Beet Salad, 19

Atole, 426

avocado leaves
- Barbacoa Adobo, 265
- Michoacán-Style Carnitas, 108

Avocado Mix
- The Fifth Element, 388
- recipe, 454

avocados
- Abuela's Sopes, 194
- Aguachile Verde, 19
- Avocado Mix, 454
- Avocado Panna Cotta, 435
- Carnitas de Atun, 176
- Ceviche de Pescado, 32
- Chicken Chorizo, 148
- Coctel de Marisco, 30
- Dzik de Res, 110
- Frijol Ayocote with Pasilla Yogurt, 49
- Guacamole, 80
- Salsa Cruda Verde, 284
- Salsa de Aguacate, 274
- Shrimp Aguachile with Avocado Panna Cotta, 28
- Sweet Corn & Pepita Guacamole, 87
- Tetelas de Aguacate con Requesón y Nopales, 68
- Vuelva a la Vida, 53

ayocote beans
- Sopa de Chorizo, Ayocotes y Acelgas, 224

B

bacon
- Carne en su Jugo, 133

Baja Tortilla Soup, 229

banana leaves
- Cochinita Pibil, 99
- Mushroom Barbacoa, 199
- Ostiones al Tapesco, 48

Pescado Adobado en Hoja de Plátano, 184

Puritos de Platano Macho Relleno de Frijoles Negros y Mole Negro, 38

Tamales de Chulibu'ul, 198

Tikin Xic, 173

banana liqueur
- Home Is Where the Heat Is, 416

bananas
- Mole Poblano, 154

Barbacoa Adobo, 265

basil
- Honey & Basil Syrup, 462
- L & N, 403
- Thai Chile & Basil Syrup, 464

Batanga, 357

Bay Leaf Oil, 286

beans and legumes
- Caldo de Espinazo de Puerco, 241
- Carne en su Jugo, 133
- Chilibul, 98
- Chulibu'ul, 84
- Frijol Ayocote with Pasilla Yogurt, 49
- Frijoles de la Olla, 56
- Frijoles Negros Refritos, 56
- Pan de Cazon, 172
- Puchero de Tres Carnes, 237
- Sopa de Chorizo, Ayocotes y Acelgas, 224
- Sopa de Frijol Colado, 235
- Sopa de Lentejas, 248
- Tostadas de Cueritos, 117

beef
- Albondigas Soup, 243
- Beef Barbacoa Tacos, 212
- Beef Cheeks with Salsa Verde, 112
- Beef Machaca with Potatoes & Eggs, 144
- Caldo de Res, 245
- Carne Asada, 118
- Carne en su Jugo, 133
- Chilibul, 98
- Costilla Corta de Res con Chile Colorado, 103
- Dzik de Res, 110

INDEX 467

Milanesa de Res y Mole Blanco, 102

Picadillo de Res, 125

Puchero de Tres Carnes, 237

Beef Stock

Costilla Corta de Res con Chile Colorado, 103

Dzik de Res, 110

recipe, 440

beef tongue

Lengua en Salsa Roja, 116

beer

Michelada, 352

Michoacán-Style Carnitas, 108

Salsa Borracha, 280

beets

Betabel with Salsa Macha y Queso Fresco, 46

Desert Daisy, 384

Guanajuato Strawberry & Beet Salad, 19

Orange Bell Pepper & Beet Syrup, 455

Berries, Raicilla-Soaked, 443

Betabel with Salsa Macha y Queso Fresco, 46

beverages

Agua de Jamaica, 423

Agua de Melon, 422

Agua de Tamarindo, 423

Atole, 426

Batanga, 357

Blacker the Berry, the Sweeter the Juice, 376

Brujera, 379

Cantaritos, 398

Champagne Paloma, 391

Champurrado, 427

Cooper's Café, 364

Cornchata, 418

Desert Daisy, 384

Diablo Otoño, 394

Dons of Soul, 396

Drunken Rabbit, 378

East LA, 354

El Chavo del Ocho, 371

El Nacional, 414

El Vato Swizzle, 382

The Fifth Element, 388

Ghost in the Shell, 406

Guera, 408

Hay Zeus, 386

Home Is Where the Heat Is, 416

Horchata, 419

Horchata con Rum, 418

Jamaica Collins, 370

L & N, 403

La Cura, 415

La Diosa, 392

La Mula, 407

La Santa, 415

Lavagave, 368

Lost in the Rain in Juárez, 391

Mámù Vida, 403

Margarita, 348

Maya Gold, 378

Mexican Hot Chocolate, 426

Mezcal & Mango Float, 350

Michelada, 352

Mr. Kotter, 410

Naked & Famous, 399

Oaxaca Old Fashioned, 364

Oaxacan Bottle Rocket, 412

Oaxacarajillo, 365

Paloma, 358

Pan, 404

Peach Tea, 390

Piña Fumada, 395

Pineapple Express, 380

Pineapple Tepache Kombucha, 428

Ramon Bravo, 365

Ranch Water, 360

Rising Sun, 383

Shake Your Tamarind, 379

She's a Rainbow, 400

Spicy Margarita, 362

Sunday Morning Coming Down, 390

Tejuino, 427

Tepache de Piña, 429

True Romance, 402

Última Palabra, 356

Unscalpe, 394

Vampiro, 351

Violet Skies, 414

Xocolatl, 422

Birria de Chivo, 92

black beans

Chilibul, 98

Frijoles de la Olla, 56

Frijoles Negros Refritos, 56

Pan de Cazon, 172

Sopa de Frijol Colado, 235

Black Lava Solution

Flor de Jalisco, 374

recipe, 451

blackberries

Blacker the Berry, the Sweeter the Juice, 376

black-eyed peas

Chulibu'ul, 84

Blistered Jalapeño Syrup

recipe, 448

Spicy Margarita, 362

Blue Corn Crunchies

Horchata Ice Cream, 290

recipe, 444

bolillos

Sopa de Chorizo, Ayocotes y Acelgas, 224

Tortas de Lomo, 211

Bonbonaise, 304

Bourbon Truffles, Mayan Chocolate &, 326

brandy, strawberry

Violet Skies, 414

Brujera, 379

Brussels Sprouts with Habanero Agave, Fried, 35

Buñuelos

Coffee Flan with Buñuelos, 306

recipe, 312

Butterfly Pea Flower–Infused Mezcal

recipe, 465

Violet Skies, 414

Butternut Squash & Chorizo Bisque, 228

C

cabbage

Caldo de Res, 245

Carnitas de Atun, 176

Chicken Tinga Sopes, 205

Empanadas de Picadillo, 130

Gorditas de Picadillo de Res, 138

Masa-Battered Fish Tacos, 181

Pozole Blanco, 220

Puchero de Tres Carnes, 237

Taquitos de Papa, 62

cactus

Mixiotes de Pollo, 150

Cajeta, 445

Cake, Cinnamon & Chocolate, 317

Calabacitas con Elote y Queso Fresco, 76

Caldo de Camarón Seco, 244

Caldo de Espinazo de Puerco, 241

Caldo de Pescado, 242

Caldo de Res, 245

California chile peppers

Caldo de Espinazo de Puerco, 241

Caldo de Pescado, 242

Camarones a la Diabla, 180

Camarones en Adobo, 163

Camote con Mole Blanco, 39

Campari

El Nacional, 414

Pineapple-Infused Campari, 446

Shake Your Tamarind, 379

Campari, Pineapple-Infused

Playa Rosita, 350

Canoe Club, 372

cantaloupe

Agua de Melon, 422

Cantaritos, 398

capers

Pescado Veracruz, 179

Pollo Veracruzano, 158

Carne Adobada, 232

Carne Asada, 118

Carne en su Jugo, 133

Carnitas de Atun, 176

carrots

Albondigas Soup, 243

Arroz a la Mexicana, 85

Beef Stock, 440

Caldo de Pescado, 242

Caldo de Res, 245

Charred Escabeche, 64

Chicken Stock, 438

Coffee & Ancho Carrots, 41

Escabeche, 86

Picadillo de Res, 125

Puchero de Tres Carnes, 237

Smoked Trout Tostadas, 178

Sopa de Lentejas, 248

Vegetable Stock, 439

cascabel chile peppers

Pierna de Puerco, 124

cauliflower

Escabeche, 86

Tortitas de Coliflor, 60

Cecina de Cerdo, 105

celery

Beef Stock, 440

Caldo de Pescado, 242

Chicken Stock, 438

Sopa de Lentejas, 248

celery juice

Zeus Juice Cordial, 456

Ceviche de Pescado, 32

Chamomile Mezcal

Maya Gold, 378

recipe, 450

chamoy

Michelada, 352

Champagne Paloma, 391

Champurrado, 427

Charred Escabeche, 64

Charred Pineapple Puree

Ramon Bravo, 365

recipe, 449

Chartreuse, green

Última Palabra, 356

Chartreuse, yellow

Maya Gold, 378

Naked & Famous, 399

Rising Sun, 383

True Romance, 402

Chayote en Pipian Rojo, 188

cheese. See individual cheese types

cherry bark vanilla bitters

Lavagave, 368

468 THE ENCYCLOPEDIA OF MEXICAN FOOD

Chicharron, Chocolate-Covered, 312

Chicharron en Salsa Roja
Memelas de Chicharron, 205
recipe, 120

chicken
Chicken Chorizo, 148
Chicken de Champiñones, 139
Chicken Tinga Sopes, 205
Enchiladas de Mole, 159
Masa-Battered Fried Chicken, 155
Milanesa de Pollo, 162
Mixiotes de Pollo, 150
Mole Poblano, 154
Pollo Veracruzano, 158
Pozole Blanco, 220
Puchero de Tres Carnes, 237
Tinga de Pollo, 168

Chicken Chorizo
Abuela's Sopes, 194
Chilaquiles Verdes, 214
recipe, 148

chicken livers
Higados en Salsa Chipotle de Adobo, 113

Chicken Stock
Arroz a la Mexicana, 85
Chayote en Pipian Rojo, 188
Chilaquiles Verdes, 214
Chile Colorado, 256
Chileatole Verde, 281
Frijol Ayocote with Pasilla Yogurt, 49
Higados en Salsa Chipotle de Adobo, 113
Joroches de Chorizo y Frijoles Colados, 96
Masa for Tamales, 434
Mole Blanco, 260
Mole Manchamanteles, 257
Mole Negro, 252–253
Muscovy Duck Breast Mole, 142
Pig Ear Salad, 18
Pipian Rojo, 266
Pollo Veracruzano, 158
Puchero de Tres Carnes, 237
Pulpo al Pastor, 166

Puritos de Platano Macho Relleno de Frijoles Negros y Mole Negro, 38
recipe, 438
Sopa de Chile Poblano, 236
Sopa de Chorizo, Ayocotes y Acelgas, 224
Sopa de Conchitas, 222
Sopa de Flor de Calabaza, 234
Sopa de Frijol Colado, 235
Sopa de Lentejas, 248

chickpeas
Caldo de Espinazo de Puerco, 241
Puchero de Tres Carnes, 237

Chihuahua cheese
Molotes de Frijol y Queso, 195

Chilaquiles Rojos, 94
Chilaquiles Verdes, 214

Chile Colorado
Costilla Corta de Res con Chile Colorado, 103
recipe, 256

Chile Toreado Mayonnaise
Masa-Crusted Sardines with Pickled Manzano, 34
recipe, 439

Chileatole Verde, 281

chiles de árbol
Beef Cheeks with Salsa Verde, 112
Calabacitas con Elote y Queso Fresco, 76
Caldo de Camarón Seco, 244
Camarones a la Diabla, 180
Cecina de Cerdo, 105
Chilaquiles Rojos, 94
Chile Colorado, 256
Frijoles Negros Refritos, 56
Huaraches with Wild Mushrooms & Epazote, 191
Menudo, 226
Mexican Pepper Reduction, 453
Pickled Pineapple, 76
Pipian Rojo, 266
Pork Toro with Salsa Macha, 70
Preserved Limes with Chile de Árbol & Spices, 261

Pulpo al Pastor, 166
Quesadillas de Champiñones, 52
Salsa de Árbol, 269
Salsa Macha, 286
Sere de Pescado, 225
Strawberry Hot Sauce, 261
Tepache Syrup, 462
Tortas Ahogadas, 216
Tostadas de Cueritos, 117
Chiles en Nogada, 132
Chiles Rellenos, 190
Chiles Toreados, 270

chilhuacle negro chile peppers
Mole Negro, 252–253
Chilibul, 98
Chilorio, 136

chipotle chile peppers
Barbacoa Adobo, 265
Chilibul, 98
Mushroom Barbacoa, 199
Tinga de Pollo, 168

chipotle meco chile peppers
Mámù Vida, 403
Mole Manchamanteles, 257
Mole Negro, 252–253
Mole Poblano, 154
Szechuan & Chipotle Honey, 460

chipotle morita chile peppers
Costillitas de Puerco en Chile Rojo, 121
Fermented Chile Adobo, 276
Mole Poblano, 154
Morita Salsa, 276
Pierna de Puerco, 124
Pig Ear Salad, 18
Pulpo al Pastor, 166
Salsa Borracha, 280
Sopa de Chorizo, Ayocotes y Acelgas, 224
Verdolagas en Salsa Verde, 48

chipotles en adobo
Camarones en Adobo, 163
Chilibul, 98
Higados en Salsa Chipotle de Adobo, 113
Chocoflan, 310–311

chocolate
Abuelita's Chocolate Pots de Crème, 300
Champurrado, 427
Chocolate & Mexican Vanilla Frosting, 445
Chocolate Mole Profiteroles, 307
Chocolate Tamarind Truffles, 313
Chocolate-Covered Chicharron, 312
Cinnamon & Chocolate Cake, 317
Dark Chocolate Ganache, 443
Gluten-Free Spicy Chocolate Cookies, 331
Mayan Chocolate & Bourbon Truffles, 326
Mexican Chocolate Crinkle Cookies, 340
Mexican Hot Chocolate, 426
Mole Blanco, 260
Mole Negro, 252–253
Mole Poblano, 154
Muscovy Duck Breast Mole, 142
Spicy Chocolate Truffles, 316
Xocolatl, 422

Chocolate & Mexican Vanilla Frosting
Mole Brownies, 327
recipe, 445

Chocolate Mole
Chocolate Mole Profiteroles, 307
recipe, 441

chorizo
Abuela's Sopes, 194
Butternut Squash & Chorizo Bisque, 228
Chicken Chorizo, 148
Chilaquiles Verdes, 214
Chorizo-Washed Mezcal, 448
Huevos Motuleños, 210
Joroches de Chorizo y Frijoles Colados, 96
Queso Fundido, 71
Sopa de Chorizo, Ayocotes y Acelgas, 224
Tacos Dorados de Frijol, Chorizo y Camote, 204

Chorizo-Washed Mezcal
Ramon Bravo, 365
recipe, 448

Chulibu'ul
recipe, 84
Tamales de Chulibu'ul, 198
Churros, 320

cilantro
Aguachile Verde, 19
Avocado Mix, 454
Calabacitas con Elote y Queso Fresco, 76
Caldo de Pescado, 242
Carne Asada, 118
Carne en su Jugo, 133
Ceviche de Pescado, 32
Chilaquiles Verdes, 214
Chileatole Verde, 281
Cilantro Pesto, 434
Coconut Dressing, 435
Coctel de Camarón, 27
Coctel de Marisco, 30
Cumin & Cilantro Vinaigrette, 264
Dzik de Res, 110
Dzikil P'aak, 280
El Vato Swizzle, 382
Ensalada de Nopales, 22
Esquites con Longaniza, 24
Frijol Ayocote with Pasilla Yogurt, 49
Guacamole, 80
Huevos Rancheros, 208
La Diosa, 392
Memelas de Chicharron, 205
Mole Verde, 277
Ostiones al Tapesco, 48
Pork Toro with Salsa Macha, 70
Puerco en Pipian Verde, 126
Queso Fundido, 71
Ramon Bravo, 365
Salsa de Aguacate, 274
Salsa Verde Tatemada, 262
Shrimp Aguachile with Avocado Panna Cotta, 28
Sopa de Papa, 240
Striped Sea Bass Ceviche, 26

INDEX

469

Sweet Corn & Pepita Guacamole, 87

Taquitos de Papa, 62

Tetelas de Aguacate con Requesón y Nopales, 68

Tikin Xic, 173

Tomato Aguachile, 44

Vuelva a la Vida, 53

X'nipek, 268

Cilantro Pesto

Guanajuato Strawberry & Beet Salad, 19

recipe, 434

Cinnamon & Chocolate Cake, 317

Cinnamon Syrup

Champagne Paloma, 391

Cooper's Café, 364

Drunken Rabbit, 378

recipe, 452

Shake Your Tamarind, 379

Citrus Salt, 454

Clamato

Coctel de Camarón, 27

Coctel de Marisco, 30

Michelada, 352

Vampiro Mix, 447

Vuelva a la Vida, 53

Classic Carnitas, 128

Cocchi Americano

Mezcal Survivor, 395

Cochinita Pibil, 99

cocoa powder

Chocoflan, 310–311

Chocolate Mole, 441

Chocolate Tamarind Truffles, 313

Coconut Dressing, 435

Gluten-Free Spicy Chocolate Cookies, 331

Mayan Chocolate & Bourbon Truffles, 326

Mexican Chocolate Crinkle Cookies, 340

Mexican Chocolate Sauce, 442

Mole Brownies, 327

Spicy Chocolate Truffles, 316

coconut

Bonbonaise, 304

Striped Sea Bass Ceviche, 26

Coconut Dressing

recipe, 435

Striped Sea Bass Ceviche, 26

coconut liqueur

Violet Skies, 414

coconut milk

Coconut Tres Leches, 328

Horchata, 419

Sere de Pescado, 225

Striped Sea Bass Ceviche, 26

Coctel de Camarón, 27

Coctel de Marisco, 30

cod

Pan de Cazon, 172

Codorniz a la Parrilla, 152

Coffee Flan with Buñuelos, 306

coffee/espresso

Chocoflan, 310–311

Coffee & Ancho Carrots, 41

Coffee Flan with Buñuelos, 306

Cooper's Café, 364

Horchata con Espresso, 419

Oaxacarajillo, 365

Cointreau

Margarita, 348

Spicy Margarita, 362

cola

Batanga, 357

Classic Carnitas, 128

Conchas

Conchas Pudding, 303

recipe, 324–325

Strawberry Shortcake con Conchas, 321

conversion chart, 466

cookies

Gluten-Free Spicy Chocolate Cookies, 331

Mexican Chocolate Crinkle Cookies, 340

Mexican Wedding Cookies, 332

Cooper's Café, 364

coriander bitters

Dons of Soul, 396

corn

Calabacitas con Elote y Queso Fresco, 76

Chileatole Verde, 281

Chulibu'ul, 84

Cornchata, 418

Lobster & Street Corn Salad, 16

Sweet Corn & Pepita Guacamole, 87

Sweet Corn Pudding Pops, 338

corn husks

Mextlapique de Callo de Hacha, 169

Corn Tortillas

Albondigas Soup, 243

Baja Tortilla Soup, 229

Beef Barbacoa Tacos, 212

Beef Cheeks with Salsa Verde, 112

Birria de Chivo, 92

Blue Corn Crunchies, 444

Caldo de Camarón Seco, 244

Caldo de Res, 245

Camarones en Adobo, 163

Carne Adobada, 232

Carne Asada, 118

Carne en su Jugo, 133

Cecina de Cerdo, 105

Chicharron en Salsa Roja, 120

Chilaquiles Rojos, 94

Chilibul, 98

Chilorio, 136

Classic Carnitas, 128

Cochinita Pibil, 99

Coctel de Marisco, 30

Codorniz a la Parrilla, 152

Costillitas de Puerco en Chile Rojo, 121

Dzik de Res, 110

Enchiladas de Mole, 159

Frijol Ayocote with Pasilla Yogurt, 49

Huevos Motuleños, 210

Huevos Rancheros, 208

Lengua en Salsa Roja, 116

Lomo y Manchamanteles, 104

Masa-Battered Fish Tacos, 181

Menudo, 226

Michoacán-Style Carnitas, 108

Milanesa de Pollo, 162

Mixiotes de Pollo, 150

Mole Poblano, 154

Muscovy Duck Breast Mole, 142

Mushroom Barbacoa, 199

Pan de Cazon, 172

Pescado Adobado en Hoja de Plátano, 184

Pescado Zarandeado, 185

Pipian Rojo, 266

Puchero de Tres Carnes, 237

Puerco en Pipian Verde, 126

Pulpo al Pastor, 166

Queso Fundido, 71

Rabo de Res en Salsa Roja, 129

recipe, 65

Sopa de Chile Poblano, 236

Sopa de Frijol Colado, 235

Taquitos de Papa, 62

Taquitos de Requesón con Rajas, 61

Tikin Xic, 173

Tinga de Pollo, 168

Tostadas de Cueritos, 117

Verdolagas en Salsa Verde, 48

Cornchata, 418

Cornchata Hard Candies, 297

cornflakes

No-Fry Fried Ice Cream, 335

Costilla Corta de Res con Chile Colorado, 103

Costillitas de Puerco en Chile Rojo, 121

cotija cheese

Empanadas de Picadillo, 130

Ensalada de Nopales, 22

Gorditas de Picadillo de Res, 138

Joroches de Chorizo y Frijoles Colados, 96

Sopa de Frijol Colado, 235

Tacos Dorados de Frijol, Chorizo y Camote, 204

Taquitos de Papa, 62

Tostadas de Cueritos, 117

crabmeat

Baja Tortilla Soup, 229

Coctel de Marisco, 30

cream cheese

Coffee Flan with Buñuelos, 306

The Perfect Flan, 336

Crema, Lime, 437

crème de mure

Canoe Club, 372

Kinda Knew Anna, 398

crème de pêche

Peach Tea, 390

crème de violette

Violet Skies, 414

cucumbers

Aguachile Verde, 19

Ceviche de Pescado, 32

Coctel de Camarón, 27

Coctel de Marisco, 30

East LA, 354

La Santa, 415

Shrimp Aguachile with Avocado Panna Cotta, 28

Tomato Aguachile, 44

Cumin & Cilantro Vinaigrette, 264

Curaçao

Mr. Kotter, 410

Cured Sardines, 72

curry leaves

Pig Ear Salad, 18

D

Dark Chocolate Ganache

Churros, 320

Cinnamon & Chocolate Cake, 317

recipe, 443

Demerara Syrup

Lime Syrup, 459

Lost in the Rain in Juárez, 391

recipe, 458

Desert Daisy, 384

desserts

Abuelita's Chocolate Pots de Crème, 300

Arroz con Leche, 302

Bonbonaise, 304

Buñuelos, 312

Chocoflan, 310–311

470   THE ENCYCLOPEDIA OF MEXICAN FOOD

Chocolate Mole Profiteroles, 307

Chocolate Tamarind Truffles, 313

Chocolate-Covered Chicharron, 312

Churros, 320

Cinnamon & Chocolate Cake, 317

Coconut Tres Leches, 328

Coffee Flan with Buñuelos, 306

Conchas Pudding, 303

Cornchata Hard Candies, 297

Gluten-Free Spicy Chocolate Cookies, 331

Horchata Ice Cream, 290

Leche Quemada, 292

Mango con Chile Pate de Fruit, 318

Mayan Chocolate & Bourbon Truffles, 326

Mexican Chocolate Crinkle Cookies, 340

Mexican Vanilla Ice Cream, 344

Mexican Wedding Cookies, 332

Mezcal Ice Cream, 321

Mixed Nut Marzipan, 330

Mole Brownies, 327

No-Fry Fried Ice Cream, 335

Orejas, 296

Pan de Hoja Santa, 334

The Perfect Flan, 336

Sopaipillas, 342

Spicy Chocolate Truffles, 316

Strawberry Shortcake con Conchas, 321

Sweet Corn Pudding Pops, 338

Sweet Empanadas, 293

Diablo Otoño, 394

dogfish

Pan de Cazon, 172

Domaine de Canton

La Mula, 407

Dons of Soul, 396

Drunken Rabbit, 378

Duck Breast Mole, Muscovy, 142

Dzik de Res, 110

Dzikil P'aak, 280

E

East LA, 354

eggs/egg whites

Abuelita's Chocolate Pots de Crème, 300

Arroz con Leche, 302

Beef Machaca with Potatoes & Eggs, 144

Chicken Chorizo, 148

Chilaquiles Rojos, 94

Chilaquiles Verdes, 214

Chiles Rellenos, 190

Chocoflan, 310–311

Chocolate Mole Profiteroles, 307

Churros, 320

Coconut Tres Leches, 328

Coffee Flan with Buñuelos, 306

Conchas, 324–325

Conchas Pudding, 303

Cumin & Cilantro Vinaigrette, 264

El Chavo del Ocho, 371

The Fifth Element, 388

Horchata Ice Cream, 290

Huauzontles Relleno de Queso con Chiltomate, 40

Huevos Motuleños, 210

Huevos Rancheros, 208

La Diosa, 392

Lavagave, 368

Lost in the Rain in Juárez, 391

Milanesa de Pollo, 162

Milanesa de Res y Mole Blanco, 102

Mole Brownies, 327

The Perfect Flan, 336

Pork Milanesa, 145

Sweet Corn Pudding Pops, 338

Tortitas de Coliflor, 60

El Chavo del Ocho, 371

El Nacional, 414

El Vato Swizzle, 382

Empanadas de Picadillo, 130

Enchiladas de Mole, 159

Ensalada de Nopales

Milanesa de Pollo, 162

recipe, 22

entrees

Abuela's Sopes, 194

Beef Barbacoa Tacos, 212

Beef Cheeks with Salsa Verde, 112

Beef Machaca with Potatoes & Eggs, 144

Birria de Chivo, 92

Camarones a la Diabla, 180

Camarones en Adobo, 163

Carne Asada, 118

Carne en su Jugo, 133

Carnitas de Atun, 176

Cecina de Cerdo, 105

Chayote en Pipian Rojo, 188

Chicharron en Salsa Roja, 120

Chicken Chorizo, 148

Chicken de Champiñones, 139

Chicken Tinga Sopes, 205

Chilaquiles Rojos, 94

Chilaquiles Verdes, 214

Chiles en Nogada, 132

Chiles Rellenos, 190

Chilibul, 98

Chilorio, 136

Classic Carnitas, 128

Cochinita Pibil, 99

Codorniz a la Parrilla, 152

Costilla Corta de Res con Chile Colorado, 103

Costillitas de Puerco en Chile Rojo, 121

Dzik de Res, 110

Empanadas de Picadillo, 130

Enchiladas de Mole, 159

Gorditas de Picadillo de Res, 138

Higados en Salsa Chipotle de Adobo, 113

Huaraches with Wild Mushrooms & Epazote, 191

Huevos Motuleños, 210

Huevos Rancheros, 208

Joroches de Chorizo y Frijoles Colados, 96

Lengua en Salsa Roja, 116

Lomo y Manchamanteles, 104

Masa-Battered Fish Tacos, 181

Masa-Battered Fried Chicken, 155

Memelas de Chicharron, 205

Mextlapique de Callo de Hacha, 169

Michoacán-Style Carnitas, 108

Milanesa de Pollo, 162

Milanesa de Res y Mole Blanco, 102

Mixiotes de Pollo, 150

Mole Poblano, 154

Molotes de Frijol y Queso, 195

Muscovy Duck Breast Mole, 142

Mushroom Barbacoa, 199

Pan de Cazon, 172

Pavo en Escabeche, 151

Pescado Adobado en Hoja de Plátano, 184

Pescado Veracruz, 179

Pescado Zarandeado, 185

Picadillo de Res, 125

Pierna de Puerco, 124

Pollo Veracruzano, 158

Pork Milanesa, 145

Puerco en Pipian Verde, 126

Pulpo al Pastor, 166

Rabo de Res en Salsa Roja, 129

Smoked Trout Tostadas, 178

Tacos Dorados de Frijol, Chorizo y Camote, 204

Tamales de Chulibu'ul, 198

Tikin Xic, 173

Tinga de Pollo, 168

Tlacoyos de Hongos, 202

Tortas Ahogadas, 216

Tortas de Lomo, 211

Tortilla Gruesa de Hoja Santa y Queso, 194

Tostadas de Cueritos, 117

epazote

Caldo de Camarón Seco, 244

Chileatole Verde, 281

Epazote Oil, 265

Frijol Ayocote with Pasilla Yogurt, 49

Frijoles de la Olla, 56

Frijoles Negros Refritos, 56

Huaraches with Wild Mushrooms & Epazote, 191

Mextlapique de Callo de Hacha, 169

Mole Verde, 277

Molotes de Frijol y Queso, 195

Pan de Cazon, 172

Puerco en Pipian Verde, 126

Pulpo al Pastor, 166

Quesadillas de Champiñones, 52

Sopa de Chorizo, Ayocotes y Acelgas, 224

Sopa de Flor de Calabaza, 234

Sopa de Frijol Colado, 235

Sopa de Hongos, 223

Verdolagas en Salsa Verde, 48

Epazote Oil, 265

Escabeche

Chilibul, 98

Costilla Corta de Res con Chile Colorado, 103

Pavo en Escabeche, 151

recipe, 86

Tortas de Lomo, 211

Tostadas de Cueritos, 117

espresso/coffee

Chocoflan, 310–311

Coffee & Ancho Carrots, 41

Coffee Flan with Buñuelos, 306

Cooper's Café, 364

Horchata con Espresso, 419

Oaxacarajillo, 365

Esquites con Longaniza, 24

evaporated milk

Chocoflan, 310–311

Coconut Tres Leches, 328

Coffee Flan with Buñuelos, 306

Leche Quemada, 292

The Perfect Flan, 336

F

fennel

Mole Blanco, 260

Fermented Chile Adobo, 276

feta cheese

Esquites con Longaniza, 24

Fifth Element, The, 388

Fig Cordial

Diablo Otoño, 394

recipe, 457

Fig Leaf Syrup

Fig Cordial, 457

recipe, 458

fig liqueur

Diablo Otoño, 394

Fire Walk with Me, 402

fish and seafood

Aguachile Verde, 19

Caldo de Camarón Seco, 244

Caldo de Pescado, 242

Camarones a la Diabla, 180

Camarones en Adobo, 163

Carnitas de Atun, 176

Ceviche de Pescado, 32

Coctel de Camarón, 27

Coctel de Marisco, 30

Cured Sardines, 72

Koji-Fried Sardines, 73

Lobster Mojo de Ajo, 156

Masa-Battered Fish Tacos, 181

Masa-Crusted Sardines with Pickled Manzano, 34

Mextlapique de Callo de Hacha, 169

Ostiones al Tapesco, 48

Pan de Cazon, 172

Pescado Adobado en Hoja de Plátano, 184

Pescado Veracruz, 179

Pescado Zarandeado, 185

Pulpo al Pastor, 166

Sere de Pescado, 225

Shrimp Aguachile with Avocado Panna Cotta, 28

Smoked Trout Tostadas, 178

Striped Sea Bass Ceviche, 26

Tikin Xic, 173

Vuelva a la Vida, 53

fish sauce

Striped Sea Bass Ceviche, 26

Vuelva a la Vida, 53

Flan, The Perfect, 336

Flor de Calabaza con Queso Fresco y Hierbabuena, 57

Flor de Jalisco, 374

Flour Tortillas

Beef Machaca with Potatoes & Eggs, 144

Costilla Corta de Res con Chile Colorado, 103

recipe, 82

Fried Brussels Sprouts with Habanero Agave, 35

Frijol Ayocote with Pasilla Yogurt, 49

Frijoles de la Olla

Beef Machaca with Potatoes & Eggs, 144

Costillitas de Puerco en Chile Rojo, 121

Huevos Rancheros, 208

recipe, 56

Frijoles Negros Refritos

Abuela's Sopes, 194

Chicken Tinga Sopes, 205

Chilaquiles Verdes, 214

Huaraches with Wild Mushrooms & Epazote, 191

Huevos Motuleños, 210

Memelas de Chicharron, 205

Molotes de Frijol y Queso, 195

Puritos de Platano Macho Relleno de Frijoles Negros y Mole Negro, 38

recipe, 56

Tacos Dorados de Frijol, Chorizo y Camote, 204

Tostadas de Cueritos, 117

G

garlic

Barbacoa Adobo, 265

Beef Cheeks with Salsa Verde, 112

Birria de Chivo, 92

Calabacitas con Elote y Queso Fresco, 76

Caldo de Camarón Seco, 244

Camarones a la Diabla, 180

Camarones en Adobo, 163

Carne Adobada, 232

Carne Asada, 118

Carne en su Jugo, 133

Cecina de Cerdo, 105

Chicharron en Salsa Roja, 120

Chilaquiles Verdes, 214

Chile Colorado, 256

Chileatole Verde, 281

Chilibul, 98

Chilorio, 136

Classic Carnitas, 128

Costillitas de Puerco en Chile Rojo, 121

Dzik de Res, 110

Dzikil P'aak, 280

Fermented Chile Adobo, 276

Frijol Ayocote with Pasilla Yogurt, 49

Frijoles de la Olla, 56

Frijoles Negros Refritos, 56

Huaraches with Wild Mushrooms & Epazote, 191

Lengua en Salsa Roja, 116

Lobster Mojo de Ajo, 156

Menudo, 226

Michoacán-Style Carnitas, 108

Mixiotes de Pollo, 150

Mole Manchamanteles, 257

Mole Negro, 252–253

Mole Poblano, 154

Mole Verde, 277

Morita Salsa, 276

Mushroom Barbacoa, 199

Pan de Cazon, 172

Pavo en Escabeche, 151

Pescado Adobado en Hoja de Plátano, 184

Pescado Veracruz, 179

Pescado Zarandeado, 185

Pierna de Puerco, 124

Pig Ear Salad, 18

Pipian Rojo, 266

Pozole Blanco, 220

Puchero de Tres Carnes, 237

Puerco en Pipian Verde, 126

Pulpo al Pastor, 166

Rabo de Res en Salsa Roja, 129

Recado Rojo, 272

Salsa Borracha, 280

Salsa de Aguacate, 274

Salsa de Árbol, 269

Salsa de Chiltomate, 258

Salsa Macha, 286

Salsa Verde Tatemada, 262

Sere de Pescado, 225

Smoked Trout Tostadas, 178

Sopa de Chile Poblano, 236

Sopa de Chorizo, Ayocotes y Acelgas, 224

Sopa de Flor de Calabaza, 234

Sopa de Frijol Colado, 235

Sopa de Hongos, 223

Striped Sea Bass Ceviche, 26

Tortas de Lomo, 211

Vegetable Stock, 439

Verdolagas en Salsa Verde, 48

Vuelva a la Vida, 53

Ghost in the Shell, 406

Giffard Banane du Brésil

Home Is Where the Heat Is, 416

gin

Jamaica Collins, 370

Violet Skies, 414

ginger, fresh

Beef Barbacoa Tacos, 212

Coconut Dressing, 435

Ginger & Serrano Syrup, 451

Ginger Syrup, 461

Pan, 404

Striped Sea Bass Ceviche, 26

Ginger & Serrano Syrup

Canoe Club, 372

recipe, 451

ginger beer

Kinda Knew Anna, 398

La Mula, 407

Mezcal & Mango Float, 350

Ginger Syrup

Blacker the Berry, the Sweeter the Juice, 376

Ghost in the Shell, 406

La Cura, 415

recipe, 461

Gluten-Free Spicy Chocolate Cookies, 331

goat

Birria de Chivo, 92

goat cheese

Esquites con Longaniza, 24

goat milk

Cajeta, 445

Gorditas de Picadillo de Res, 138

grapefruit bitters

Violet Skies, 414

grapefruit juice

Cantaritos, 398

Champagne Paloma, 391

Guera, 408

Lavagave, 368

Paloma, 358

Recado Rojo, 272

She's a Rainbow, 400

Vampiro, 351

grapefruit soda

Cantaritos, 398

green onions

Puerco en Pipian Verde, 126

greens

Betabel with Salsa Macha y Queso Fresco, 46

Guacamole

recipe, 80

Sweet Corn & Pepita Guacamole, 87

Taquitos de Requesón con Rajas, 61

guajillo chile peppers

Barbacoa Adobo, 265

Beef Cheeks with Salsa Verde, 112

Birria de Chivo, 92

Caldo de Camarón Seco, 244

Camarones a la Diabla, 180

Camarones en Adobo, 163

Cecina de Cerdo, 105

Chicken Chorizo, 148

Chilaquiles Rojos, 94

Chile Colorado, 256

Chilorio, 136

Costillitas de Puerco en Chile Rojo, 121

Menudo, 226

Mixiotes de Pollo, 150

Mole Manchamanteles, 257

Mole Negro, 252–253

Mole Poblano, 154

Muscovy Duck Breast Mole, 142

Mushroom Barbacoa, 199

Pescado Adobado en Hoja de Plátano, 184

Pescado Zarandeado, 185

Pierna de Puerco, 124

Pineapple Marmalade, 455

Pipian Rojo, 266

Pulpo al Pastor, 166

Salsa de Árbol, 269

Salsa Macha, 286

Sopa de Chorizo, Ayocotes y Acelgas, 224

Spicy Chocolate Truffles, 316

Tomato Aguachile, 44

Guanajuato Strawberry & Beet Salad, 19

guava juice

Drunken Rabbit, 378

Guera, 408

guero chile peppers

Sopa de Flor de Calabaza, 234

H

Habanero Agave

Fried Brussels Sprouts with Habanero Agave, 35

recipe, 436

habanero chile peppers

Dzik de Res, 110

Dzikil P'aak, 280

Habanero Honey, 287

Huevos Motuleños, 210

Mole Blanco, 260

Pan de Cazon, 172

Recado Rojo, 272

Salpicon de Rabano y Chile Habanero, 264

Salsa de Chiltomate, 258

Tikin Xic, 173

X'nipek, 268

habanero shrub

Blacker the Berry, the Sweeter the Juice, 376

Desert Daisy, 384

Flor de Jalisco, 374

halibut

Ceviche de Pescado, 32

Sere de Pescado, 225

Ham Stock

Carne Adobada, 232

recipe, 440

hay

Zeus Juice Cordial, 456

Hay Zeus, 386

hibiscus blossoms

Agua de Jamaica, 423

Hibiscus Ice Cubes, 463

Jamaica Syrup, 449

hierbabuena

Albondigas Soup, 243

Flor de Calabaza con Queso Fresco y Hierbabuena, 57

Higados en Salsa Chipotle de Adobo, 113

hoja santa

Chileatole Verde, 281

La Santa, 415

Mixiotes de Pollo, 150

Mole Negro, 252–253

Mole Verde, 277

Pan de Hoja Santa, 334

Tortilla Gruesa de Hoja Santa y Queso, 194

Home Is Where the Heat Is, 416

hominy

Menudo, 226

Pozole Blanco, 220

honey

Agua de Melon, 422

Chileatole Verde, 281

Fig Cordial, 457

Flor de Calabaza con Queso Fresco y Hierbabuena, 57

Habanero Honey, 287

Honey & Basil Syrup, 462

L & N, 403

Lomo y Manchamanteles, 104

Mámù Vida, 403

Piña Fumada, 395

Szechuan & Chipotle Honey, 460

Honey & Basil Syrup

L & N, 403

recipe, 462

honeydew melon

Agua de Melon, 422

Horchata

Horchata con Espresso, 419

Horchata con Rum, 418

recipe, 419

Horchata Ice Cream, 290

hot sauce

Strawberry Hot Sauce, 261

Vuelva a la Vida, 53

Huaraches with Wild Mushrooms & Epazote, 191

Huauzontles Relleno de Queso con Chiltomate, 40

Huevos Motuleños, 210

Huevos Rancheros, 208

I

ice cream

Horchata Ice Cream, 290

Mexican Vanilla Ice Cream, 344

Mezcal & Mango Float, 350

Mezcal Ice Cream, 321

No-Fry Fried Ice Cream, 335

iced tea, mint

La Cura, 415

Islay Cask Bitters

Unscalpe, 394

J

jalapeño chile peppers

Albondigas Soup, 243

Baja Tortilla Soup, 229

Beef Machaca with Potatoes & Eggs, 144

Blistered Jalapeño Syrup, 448

Carne Asada, 118

Ceviche de Pescado, 32

Charred Escabeche, 64

Chilaquiles Verdes, 214

Chiles Toreados, 270

Coctel de Marisco, 30

Escabeche, 86

Esquites con Longaniza, 24

Fire Walk with Me, 402

La Mula, 407

Lengua en Salsa Roja, 116

Mexican Pepper Reduction, 453

Mextlapique de Callo de Hacha, 169

Puerco en Pipian Verde, 126

Shrimp Aguachile with Avocado Panna Cotta, 28

Sopa de Chile Poblano, 236

Spicy Mezcal, 464

Taquitos de Papa, 62

Vuelva a la Vida, 53

Jalisco Sour, 399

Jamaica Collins, 370

Jamaica Syrup

Jamaica Collins, 370

recipe, 449

Joroches de Chorizo y Frijoles Colados, 96

K

kale

Mole Verde, 277

Sopa de Chile Poblano, 236

ketchup

Coctel de Camarón, 27

Coctel de Marisco, 30

Kinda Knew Anna, 398

Koji-Fried Sardines, 73

Koji-Marinated Sweet Potatoes with Salsa Macha, 35

Kombucha, Pineapple Tepache, 428

L

L & N, 403

La Cura, 415

La Diosa, 392

La Mula, 407

La Santa, 415

lamb

Birria de Chivo, 92

Lavagave, 368

Lavender Agave

Lavagave, 368

recipe, 452

Leche Quemada, 292

leeks

Vegetable Stock, 439

lemon juice

Coconut Dressing, 435

Dons of Soul, 396

Flor de Calabaza con Queso Fresco y Hierbabuena, 57

La Cura, 415

Mámù Vida, 403

Mezcal Survivor, 395

Piña Fumada, 395

Striped Sea Bass Ceviche, 26

Violet Skies, 414

lemon soda

Guera, 408

lemon zest

Flor de Calabaza con Queso Fresco y Hierbabuena, 57

lemongrass stalks

Lemongrass Syrup, 459

Striped Sea Bass Ceviche, 26

Lemongrass Syrup

Pan, 404

recipe, 459

lemons

Citrus Salt, 454

Lengua en Salsa Roja, 116

lentils

Sopa de Lentejas, 248

lettuce

Abuela's Sopes, 194

Chicken Tinga Sopes, 205

Esquites con Longaniza, 24

Puerco en Pipian Verde, 126

Tostadas de Cueritos, 117

Licor 43

El Chavo del Ocho, 371

Oaxacarajillo, 365

Lillet

Pineapple Marmalade, 455

lime cordial

Rising Sun, 383

Lime Crema

Baja Tortilla Soup, 229

recipe, 437

Sopa de Conchitas, 222

lime juice

Aguachile Verde, 19

Barbacoa Adobo, 265

Batanga, 357

Blacker the Berry, the Sweeter the Juice, 376

Canoe Club, 372

Cantaritos, 398

Carnitas de Atun, 176

Chiles Toreados, 270

INDEX

473

Coctel de Camarón, 27

Codorniz a la Parrilla, 152

Desert Daisy, 384

Dons of Soul, 396

Dzik de Res, 110

Dzikil P'aak, 280

East LA, 354

El Chavo del Ocho, 371

El Vato Swizzle, 382

The Fifth Element, 388

Fire Walk with Me, 402

Flor de Jalisco, 374

Frijol Ayocote with Pasilla Yogurt, 49

Ghost in the Shell, 406

Guacamole, 80

Guera, 408

Hay Zeus, 386

Home Is Where the Heat Is, 416

Jalisco Sour, 399

Jamaica Collins, 370

Kinda Knew Anna, 398

La Diosa, 392

La Mula, 407

La Santa, 415

Lavagave, 368

Lime Syrup, 459

Lost in the Rain in Juárez, 391

Margarita, 348

Michelada, 352

Michoacán-Style Carnitas, 108

Mixiotes de Pollo, 150

Mr. Kotter, 410

Mushroom Barbacoa, 199

Naked & Famous, 399

Oaxacan Bottle Rocket, 412

Ostiones al Tapesco, 48

Paloma, 358

Pan de Cazon, 172

Pescado Zarandeado, 185

Pineapple Express, 380

Pulpo al Pastor, 166

Ramon Bravo, 365

Ranch Water, 360

Recado Rojo, 272

Salpicon de Rabano y Chile Habanero, 264

Sere de Pescado, 225

Shake Your Tamarind, 379

Shrimp Aguachile with Avocado Panna Cotta, 28

Spicy Margarita, 362

Tejuino, 427

Tomato Aguachile, 44

Última Palabra, 356

Vampiro, 351

Vampiro Mix, 447

Vuelva a la Vida, 53

X'nipek, 268

Lime Syrup

Mezcal Survivor, 395

recipe, 459

limes

Ceviche de Pescado, 32

Citrus Salt, 454

Cochinita Pibil, 99

Lime Syrup, 459

Milanesa de Res y Mole Blanco, 102

Pig Ear Salad, 18

Preserved Limes with Chile de Árbol & Spices, 261

livers, chicken

Higados en Salsa Chipotle de Adobo, 113

lobster

Lobster & Street Corn Salad, 16

Lobster Mojo de Ajo, 156

Lomo y Manchamanteles, 104

Longaniza, Esquites con, 24

Lost in the Rain in Juárez, 391

M

Maggi seasoning sauce

Chiles Toreados, 270

Dzikil P'aak, 280

Michelada, 352

Pescado Zarandeado, 185

Salsa Borracha, 280

Mámù Vida, 403

Mango con Chile Pate de Fruit, 318

mango puree

Mezcal & Mango Float, 350

manzano chile peppers

Pickled Manzano Peppers, 77

Sopa de Flor de Calabaza, 234

maraschino cherries

Mezcal Survivor, 395

Rising Sun, 383

maraschino liqueur

Última Palabra, 356

Margarita, 348

marrow bones

Menudo, 226

Roasted Bone Marrow, 437

masa/masa harina

Abuela's Sopes, 194

Atole, 426

Champurrado, 427

Chicken Tinga Sopes, 205

Chileatole Verde, 281

Corn Tortillas, 65

Empanadas de Picadillo, 130

Gorditas de Picadillo de Res, 138

Huaraches with Wild Mushrooms & Epazote, 191

Huauzontles Relleno de Queso con Chiltomate, 40

Joroches de Chorizo y Frijoles Colados, 96

Masa for Tamales, 434

Masa-Battered Fish Tacos, 181

Masa-Battered Fried Chicken, 155

Masa-Crusted Sardines with Pickled Manzano, 34

Memelas de Chicharron, 205

Mole Blanco, 260

Molotes de Frijol y Queso, 195

Quesadillas de Champiñones, 52

Tacos Dorados de Frijol, Chorizo y Camote, 204

Tamales de Chulibu'ul, 198

Tejuino, 427

Tetelas de Aguacate con Requesón y Nopales, 68

Tlacoyos de Hongos, 202

Tomato Aguachile, 44

Tortilla Gruesa de Hoja Santa y Queso, 194

Maya Gold, 378

Mayan Chocolate & Bourbon Truffles, 326

Memelas de Chicharron, 205

Menudo, 226

Mexican Chocolate Crinkle Cookies, 340

Mexican Chocolate Sauce, 442

Mexican Hot Chocolate, 426

Mexican Pepper Reduction

El Vato Swizzle, 382

recipe, 453

Mexican Vanilla Ice Cream, 344

Mexican Wedding Cookies, 332

Mextlapique de Callo de Hacha, 169

mezcal

Blacker the Berry, the Sweeter the Juice, 376

Butterfly Pea Flower–Infused Mezcal, 465

Canoe Club, 372

Chamomile Mezcal, 450

Chorizo-Washed Mezcal, 448

Cooper's Café, 364

Drunken Rabbit, 378

El Nacional, 414

Flor de Jalisco, 374

Ghost in the Shell, 406

Home Is Where the Heat Is, 416

Lavagave, 368

Lost in the Rain in Juárez, 391

Mámù Vida, 403

Maya Gold, 378

Mezcal & Mango Float, 350

Mezcal Ice Cream, 321

Mezcal Survivor, 395

Naked & Famous, 399

Oaxaca Old Fashioned, 364

Oaxacan Bottle Rocket, 412

Oaxacarajillo, 365

Pierna de Puerco, 124

Piña Fumada, 395

Pineapple Express, 380

Playa Rosita, 350

Ramon Bravo, 365

Salsa Borracha, 280

Shake Your Tamarind, 379

Spicy Mezcal, 464

True Romance, 402

Última Palabra, 356

Unscalpe, 394

Vampiro, 351

Violet Skies, 414

Zeus Juice Cordial, 456

See also tequila

Michelada, 352

Michoacán-Style Carnitas, 108

Midori

She's a Rainbow, 400

Milanesa de Pollo, 162

Milanesa de Res y Mole Blanco, 102

mint

East LA, 354

Flor de Calabaza con Queso Fresco y Hierbabuena, 57

Mole Verde, 277

Oaxacan Bottle Rocket, 412

Mixed Nut Marzipan, 330

Mixiotes de Pollo, 150

mole bitters

El Nacional, 414

L & N, 403

Mole Blanco

Camote con Mole Blanco, 39

Milanesa de Res y Mole Blanco, 102

recipe, 260

Mole Brownies, 327

Mole Manchamanteles

Lomo y Manchamanteles, 104

recipe, 257

Mole Negro

Enchiladas de Mole, 159

Puritos de Platano Macho Relleno de Frijoles Negros y Mole Negro, 38

recipe, 252–253

Mole Poblano, 154

Mole Spice

Masa-Crusted Sardines with Pickled Manzano, 34

recipe, 436

Mole Verde, 277

Molotes de Frijol y Queso, 195

monkfish

Pan de Cazon, 172

Monterey Jack cheese

Chiles Rellenos, 190

Queso Fundido, 71

Morita Salsa
  recipe, 276
  Tacos Dorados de Frijol, Chorizo y Camote, 204

Mr. Kotter, 410

mulato chile peppers
  Mole Poblano, 154

Muscovy Duck Breast Mole, 142

mushrooms
  Chicken de Champiñones, 139
  Huaraches with Wild Mushrooms & Epazote, 191
  Mushroom Barbacoa, 199
  Quesadillas de Champiñones, 52
  Sopa de Hongos, 223
  Tlacoyos de Hongos, 202

N

Naked & Famous, 399

negro chile peppers
  Mole Poblano, 154

New Mexico chile peppers
  Beef Barbacoa Tacos, 212
  Caldo de Espinazo de Puerco, 241

No-Fry Fried Ice Cream, 335

nopales
  Ensalada de Nopales, 22
  Tetelas de Aguacate con Requesón y Nopales, 68

nuts. See individual nut types

O

Oaxaca cheese
  Beef Barbacoa Tacos, 212
  Chicken de Champiñones, 139
  Chiles Rellenos, 190
  Huauzontles Relleno de Queso con Chiltomate, 40
  Memelas de Chicharron, 205
  Molotes de Frijol y Queso, 195
  Quesadillas de Champiñones, 52
  Queso Fundido, 71
  Tortilla Gruesa de Hoja Santa y Queso, 194

Oaxaca Old Fashioned, 364

Oaxacan Bottle Rocket, 412

Oaxacarajillo, 365

octopus
  Coctel de Marisco, 30
  Pulpo al Pastor, 166

olive brine
  Michelada, 352

olives
  Pescado Veracruz, 179
  Pollo Veracruzano, 158
  Smoked Trout Tostadas, 178

onions
  Aguachile Verde, 19
  Arroz a la Mexicana, 85
  Baja Tortilla Soup, 229
  Barbacoa Adobo, 265
  Beef Barbacoa Tacos, 212
  Beef Cheeks with Salsa Verde, 112
  Beef Machaca with Potatoes & Eggs, 144
  Beef Stock, 440
  Birria de Chivo, 92
  Butternut Squash & Chorizo Bisque, 228
  Calabacitas con Elote y Queso Fresco, 76
  Caldo de Camarón Seco, 244
  Camarones a la Diabla, 180
  Camarones en Adobo, 163
  Carne en su Jugo, 133
  Ceviche de Pescado, 32
  Chicken Stock, 438
  Chilaquiles Rojos, 94
  Chilaquiles Verdes, 214
  Chile Colorado, 256
  Chileatole Verde, 281
  Chiles Rellenos, 190
  Chiles Toreados, 270
  Chilibul, 98
  Chilorio, 136
  Chulibu'ul, 84
  Classic Carnitas, 128
  Cochinita Pibil, 99
  Coctel de Camarón, 27
  Coctel de Marisco, 30
  Costilla Corta de Res con Chile Colorado, 103
  Costillitas de Puerco en Chile Rojo, 121

Dzik de Res, 110

Dzikil P'aak, 280

Ensalada de Nopales, 22

Escabeche, 86

Frijol Ayocote with Pasilla Yogurt, 49

Frijoles de la Olla, 56

Guacamole, 80

Ham Stock, 440

Higados en Salsa Chipotle de Adobo, 113

Huaraches with Wild Mushrooms & Epazote, 191

Huevos Motuleños, 210

Huevos Rancheros, 208

Lengua en Salsa Roja, 116

Mextlapique de Callo de Hacha, 169

Michoacán-Style Carnitas, 108

Mixiotes de Pollo, 150

Mole Manchamanteles, 257

Mole Negro, 252–253

Mole Poblano, 154

Mole Verde, 277

Morita Salsa, 276

Mushroom Barbacoa, 199

Pan de Cazon, 172

Pescado Veracruz, 179

Picadillo de Res, 125

Pickled Red Onion, 77

Pierna de Puerco, 124

Pig Ear Salad, 18

Pipian Rojo, 266

Pollo Veracruzano, 158

Pozole Blanco, 220

Puchero de Tres Carnes, 237

Puerco en Pipian Verde, 126

Pulpo al Pastor, 166

Quesadillas de Champiñones, 52

Queso Fundido, 71

Rabo de Res en Salsa Roja, 129

Salsa Borracha, 280

Salsa de Aguacate, 274

Salsa de Chiltomate, 258

Salsa Verde Tatemada, 262

Sere de Pescado, 225

Smoked Trout Tostadas, 178

Sopa de Chile Poblano, 236

Sopa de Chorizo, Ayocotes y Acelgas, 224

Sopa de Conchitas, 222

Sopa de Flor de Calabaza, 234

Sopa de Frijol Colado, 235

Sopa de Hongos, 223

Sopa de Lentejas, 248

Sweet Corn & Pepita Guacamole, 87

Tacos Dorados de Frijol, Chorizo y Camote, 204

Taquitos de Papa, 62

Tinga de Pollo, 168

Tlacoyos de Hongos, 202

Tomato Aguachile, 44

Tortas de Lomo, 211

Tortitas de Coliflor, 60

Tostadas de Cueritos, 117

Vegetable Stock, 439

Verdolagas en Salsa Verde, 48

Vuelva a la Vida, 53

X'nipek, 268

Orange Bell Pepper & Beet Syrup
  Desert Daisy, 384
  recipe, 455

orange juice
  Barbacoa Adobo, 265
  Cantaritos, 398
  Carne Asada, 118
  Carnitas de Atun, 176
  Chilorio, 136
  Classic Carnitas, 128
  Codorniz a la Parrilla, 152
  Dzik de Res, 110
  Dzikil P'aak, 280
  Michoacán-Style Carnitas, 108
  Mixiotes de Pollo, 150
  Mushroom Barbacoa, 199
  Oaxacan Bottle Rocket, 412
  Pan de Cazon, 172
  Recado Rojo, 272
  Salpicon de Rabano y Chile Habanero, 264
  Vuelva a la Vida, 53
  X'nipek, 268

orange zest
  Mole Brownies, 327

Orejas, 296

orgeat
  Fire Walk with Me, 402
  Ghost in the Shell, 406

Ostiones al Tapesco, 48

oxtail
  Rabo de Res en Salsa Roja, 129

oysters
  Ostiones al Tapesco, 48

P

Paloma, 358

Pan, 404

Pan de Cazon, 172

Pan de Hoja Santa, 334

parsley
  Albondigas Soup, 243
  Mole Verde, 277

pasilla chile peppers
  Barbacoa Adobo, 265
  Chicken Chorizo, 148
  Costillitas de Puerco en Chile Rojo, 121
  Frijol Ayocote with Pasilla Yogurt, 49
  Mextlapique de Callo de Hacha, 169
  Mole Negro, 252–253
  Mole Poblano, 154
  Mushroom Barbacoa, 199
  Puerco en Pipian Verde, 126
  Puritos de Platano Macho Relleno de Frijoles Negros y Mole Negro, 38
  Salsa Borracha, 280
  Sopa de Hongos, 223

passion fruit puree
  El Chavo del Ocho, 371

pasta
  Sopa de Conchitas, 222
  Sopa de Fideo, 240

Pavo en Escabeche, 151

Peach Cordial
  Peach Tea, 390
  recipe, 457

Peach Tea, 390

peaches

INDEX

475

Lomo y Manchamanteles, 104

Mole Manchamanteles, 257

Peach Cordial, 457

peanut butter

Chocolate Mole, 441

Mixed Nut Marzipan, 330

Mole Brownies, 327

peanuts

Mixed Nut Marzipan, 330

Puerco en Pipian Verde, 126

Salsa Macha, 286

Striped Sea Bass Ceviche, 26

pears/pear puree

Mole Manchamanteles, 257

Pan, 404

peas

Arroz a la Mexicana, 85

Picadillo de Res, 125

pecans

Mexican Wedding Cookies, 332

Mixed Nut Marzipan, 330

Mole Negro, 252–253

peppers, bell

Chulibu'ul, 84

Desert Daisy, 384

Orange Bell Pepper & Beet Syrup, 455

Pescado Veracruz, 179

Pollo Veracruzano, 158

peppers, chile. See individual peppers

peppers, red chile

Mexican Hot Chocolate, 426

pequin chile peppers

Chilaquiles Verdes, 214

Perfect Caramel

Churros, 320

Coffee Flan with Buñuelos, 306

recipe, 444

Perfect Flan, The, 336

Pescado Adobado en Hoja de Plátano, 184

Pescado Veracruz, 179

Pescado Zarandeado, 185

Peychaud's bitters

Canoe Club, 372

El Vato Swizzle, 382

Oaxacan Bottle Rocket, 412

Picadillo de Res

Chiles en Nogada, 132

Empanadas de Picadillo, 130

Gorditas de Picadillo de Res, 138

recipe, 125

Pickled Manzano Peppers

Masa-Crusted Sardines with Pickled Manzano, 34

recipe, 77

Pickled Pineapple, 76

Pickled Red Onion

Beef Barbacoa Tacos, 212

Birria de Chivo, 92

Chicken Chorizo, 148

Classic Carnitas, 128

Empanadas de Picadillo, 130

Enchiladas de Mole, 159

Gorditas de Picadillo de Res, 138

Huaraches with Wild Mushrooms & Epazote, 191

Memelas de Chicharron, 205

Mole Poblano, 154

Pescado Adobado en Hoja de Plátano, 184

recipe, 77

Tinga de Pollo, 168

Tortas Ahogadas, 216

Pierna de Puerco, 124

Pig Ear Salad, 18

piloncillo

Atole, 426

Blue Corn Crunchies, 444

Champurrado, 427

Mole Manchamanteles, 257

Piloncillo Syrup, 441

Tejuino, 427

Tepache de Piña, 429

Piloncillo Syrup

Arroz con Leche, 302

recipe, 441

Piña Fumada, 395

pine nuts

Mole Blanco, 260

pineapple

Avocado Mix, 454

Charred Pineapple Puree, 449

Pickled Pineapple, 76

Pineapple Express, 380

Pineapple Marmalade, 455

Pineapple-Infused Campari, 446

Ramon Bravo, 365

Tepache de Piña, 429

Tepache Syrup, 462

pineapple juice

Drunken Rabbit, 378

Lost in the Rain in Juárez, 391

Pineapple Express, 380

Pineapple Marmalade

La Diosa, 392

recipe, 455

Pineapple Tepache Kombucha, 428

pinto beans

Carne en su Jugo, 133

Pipian Rojo

Chayote en Pipian Rojo, 188

recipe, 266

pisco

Jalisco Sour, 399

plantains

Huevos Motuleños, 210

Mole Blanco, 260

Mole Manchamanteles, 257

Mole Negro, 252–253

Puchero de Tres Carnes, 237

Puritos de Platano Macho Relleno de Frijoles Negros y Mole Negro, 38

Playa Rosita, 350

poblano chile peppers

Chiles en Nogada, 132

Chiles Rellenos, 190

Taquitos de Requesón con Rajas, 61

Pollo Veracruzano, 158

pomegranate seeds/arils

Chiles en Nogada, 132

Sweet Corn & Pepita Guacamole, 87

pork

Caldo de Espinazo de Puerco, 241

Carne Adobada, 232

Cecina de Cerdo, 105

Chilorio, 136

Classic Carnitas, 128

Cochinita Pibil, 99

Costillitas de Puerco en Chile Rojo, 121

Lomo y Manchamanteles, 104

Michoacán-Style Carnitas, 108

Pierna de Puerco, 124

Pork Milanesa, 145

Pork Toro with Salsa Macha, 70

Pozole Blanco, 220

Puchero de Tres Carnes, 237

Puerco en Pipian Verde, 126

Tortas Ahogadas, 216

Tortas de Lomo, 211

pork belly

Chicharron en Salsa Roja, 120

Tostadas de Cueritos, 117

potatoes

Beef Machaca with Potatoes & Eggs, 144

Caldo de Pescado, 242

Caldo de Res, 245

Picadillo de Res, 125

Puchero de Tres Carnes, 237

Sopa de Papa, 240

Taquitos de Papa, 62

Pozole Blanco, 220

Preserved Limes with Chile de Árbol & Spices, 261

Puchero de Tres Carnes, 237

Puerco en Pipian Verde, 126

puff pastry

Orejas, 296

Pulpo al Pastor, 166

pumpkin puree

Sweet Empanadas, 293

pumpkin seeds

Dzikil P'aak, 280

Mole Verde, 277

Muscovy Duck Breast Mole, 142

Pipian Rojo, 266

Puerco en Pipian Verde, 126

Sweet Corn & Pepita Guacamole, 87

Puritos de Platano Macho Relleno de Frijoles Negros y Mole Negro, 38

purslane

Camote con Mole Blanco, 39

Verdolagas en Salsa Verde, 48

puya chile peppers

Rabo de Res en Salsa Roja, 129

Q

quail

Codorniz a la Parrilla, 152

Quesadillas de Champiñones, 52

queso enchilado

Abuela's Sopes, 194

Chicken Chorizo, 148

Cilantro Pesto, 434

Fried Brussels Sprouts with Habanero Agave, 35

Lobster & Street Corn Salad, 16

Queso Fresco

Betabel with Salsa Macha y Queso Fresco, 46

Calabacitas con Elote y Queso Fresco, 76

Chicken Tinga Sopes, 205

Chilaquiles Rojos, 94

Chiles en Nogada, 132

Enchiladas de Mole, 159

Ensalada de Nopales, 22

Flor de Calabaza con Queso Fresco y Hierbabuena, 57

Guanajuato Strawberry & Beet Salad, 19

Huaraches with Wild Mushrooms & Epazote, 191

Huevos Motuleños, 210

Huevos Rancheros, 208

Puritos de Platano Macho Relleno de Frijoles Negros y Mole Negro, 38

Quesadillas de Champiñones, 52

recipe, 287

Sopa de Flor de Calabaza, 234

Sopa de Papa, 240

Tinga de Pollo, 168

Tomato Aguachile, 44

476 THE ENCYCLOPEDIA OF MEXICAN FOOD

Verdolagas en Salsa Verde, 48

Queso Fundido, 71

queso panela

Tortas de Lomo, 211

R

Rabo de Res en Salsa Roja, 129

radishes

Chicken Tinga Sopes, 205

Dzik de Res, 110

Pozole Blanco, 220

Salpicon de Rabano y Chile Habanero, 264

Sere de Pescado, 225

Raicilla-Soaked Berries

Coconut Tres Leches, 328

recipe, 443

raisins

Mole Blanco, 260

Mole Manchamanteles, 257

Mole Negro, 252–253

Muscovy Duck Breast Mole, 142

Ramon Bravo, 365

Ranch Water, 360

rancho gordo ayocote beans

Frijol Ayocote with Pasilla Yogurt, 49

Recado Rojo

Chicken Chorizo, 148

Cochinita Pibil, 99

Pescado Adobado en Hoja de Plátano, 184

Pulpo al Pastor, 166

recipe, 272

Tikin Xic, 173

red snapper

Caldo de Pescado, 242

Ceviche de Pescado, 32

Pescado Adobado en Hoja de Plátano, 184

Pescado Veracruz, 179

Pescado Zarandeado, 185

Tikin Xic, 173

Requesón con Rajas, Taquitos de, 61

rice

Albondigas Soup, 243

Arroz a la Mexicana, 85

Arroz con Leche, 302

Camarones a la Diabla, 180

Costillitas de Puerco en Chile Rojo, 121

Horchata, 419

Horchata Ice Cream, 290

Milanesa de Pollo, 162

Pierna de Puerco, 124

Rabo de Res en Salsa Roja, 129

Toasted Rice Powder, 438

rice flour

Pig Ear Salad, 18

ricotta cheese

Taquitos de Requesón con Rajas, 61

Tetelas de Aguacate con Requesón y Nopales, 68

Rising Sun, 383

Roasted Bone Marrow

recipe, 437

Sopa de Conchitas, 222

rosé

Fig Cordial, 457

rosewater

Jamaica Collins, 370

rum

Brujera, 379

Horchata con Rum, 418

Oaxacan Bottle Rocket, 412

S

sage tincture

Peach Tea, 390

salads

Ensalada de Nopales, 22

Esquites con Longaniza, 24

Guanajuato Strawberry & Beet Salad, 19

Lobster & Street Corn Salad, 16

Pig Ear Salad, 18

Saline Solution

Desert Daisy, 384

East LA, 354

Margarita, 348

recipe, 446

Spicy Margarita, 362

Zeus Juice Cordial, 456

Salpicon de Rabano y Chile Habanero

Milanesa de Res y Mole Blanco, 102

Puchero de Tres Carnes, 237

recipe, 264

salsa

Abuela's Sopes, 194

Caldo de Res, 245

Huaraches with Wild Mushrooms & Epazote, 191

Salsa Borracha

Mixiotes de Pollo, 150

recipe, 280

Salsa Cruda Verde

Beef Cheeks with Salsa Verde, 112

Gorditas de Picadillo de Res, 138

Molotes de Frijol y Queso, 195

recipe, 284

Verdolagas en Salsa Verde, 48

Salsa de Aguacate

recipe, 274

Tlacoyos de Hongos, 202

Salsa de Árbol

recipe, 269

Tortilla Gruesa de Hoja Santa y Queso, 194

Salsa de Chiltomate

Chilibul, 98

Cochinita Pibil, 99

Huauzontles Relleno de Queso con Chiltomate, 40

recipe, 258

Tamales de Chulibu'ul, 198

Tikin Xic, 173

Salsa Macha

Betabel with Salsa Macha y Queso Fresco, 46

Koji-Marinated Sweet Potatoes with Salsa Macha, 35

Pork Toro with Salsa Macha, 70

recipe, 286

Salsa Verde Tatemada

Chicken Chorizo, 148

Classic Carnitas, 128

Michoacán-Style Carnitas, 108

Mushroom Barbacoa, 199

recipe, 262

Tetelas de Aguacate con Requesón y Nopales, 68

sardines

Cured Sardines, 72

Koji-Fried Sardines, 73

Masa-Crusted Sardines with Pickled Manzano, 34

sauces and condiments

Barbacoa Adobo, 265

Bay Leaf Oil, 286

Chile Colorado, 256

Chileatole Verde, 281

Chiles Toreados, 270

Cumin & Cilantro Vinaigrette, 264

Dzikil P'aak, 280

Epazote Oil, 265

Fermented Chile Adobo, 276

Habanero Honey, 287

Mole Blanco, 260

Mole Manchamanteles, 257

Mole Negro, 252–253

Mole Verde, 277

Morita Salsa, 276

Pipian Rojo, 266

Preserved Limes with Chile de Árbol & Spices, 261

Queso Fresco, 287

Recado Rojo, 272

Salpicon de Rabano y Chile Habanero, 264

Salsa Borracha, 280

Salsa Cruda Verde, 284

Salsa de Aguacate, 274

Salsa de Árbol, 269

Salsa de Chiltomate, 258

Salsa Macha, 286

Salsa Verde Tatemada, 262

Strawberry Hot Sauce, 261

X'nipek, 268

sauerkraut

Smoked Trout Tostadas, 178

sausage/chorizo

Abuela's Sopes, 194

Butternut Squash & Chorizo Bisque, 228

Chicken Chorizo, 148

Chilaquiles Verdes, 214

Chorizo-Washed Mezcal, 448

Huevos Motuleños, 210

Joroches de Chorizo y Frijoles Colados, 96

Queso Fundido, 71

Sopa de Chorizo, Ayocotes y Acelgas, 224

Tacos Dorados de Frijol, Chorizo y Camote, 204

scallions

Striped Sea Bass Ceviche, 26

scallops

Mextlapique de Callo de Hacha, 169

scoby/scoby liquid

Pineapple Tepache Kombucha, 428

Scotch whisky

El Nacional, 414

sea bass

Pescado Adobado en Hoja de Plátano, 184

Striped Sea Bass Ceviche, 26

seafood. See fish and seafood

Sere de Pescado, 225

serrano chile peppers

Aguachile Verde, 19

Albondigas Soup, 243

Carne en su Jugo, 133

Ceviche de Pescado, 32

Chicharron en Salsa Roja, 120

Chile Toreado Mayonnaise, 439

Chileatole Verde, 281

Chiles Toreados, 270

Coctel de Camarón, 27

Coffee & Ancho Carrots, 41

Ginger & Serrano Syrup, 451

Guacamole, 80

Huevos Rancheros, 208

Mole Verde, 277

Ostiones al Tapesco, 48

Pescado Adobado en Hoja de Plátano, 184

Picadillo de Res, 125

Puerco en Pipian Verde, 126

Salsa Cruda Verde, 284

Salsa Verde Tatemada, 262

Sere de Pescado, 225

INDEX

477

Sopa de Chile Poblano, 236

Striped Sea Bass Ceviche, 26

Tetelas de Aguacate con Requesón y Nopales, 68

Tomato Aguachile, 44

sesame seeds

Chocolate Mole, 441

Mexican Chocolate Sauce, 442

Mole Brownies, 327

Mole Manchamanteles, 257

Mole Negro, 252–253

Mole Poblano, 154

Mole Verde, 277

Muscovy Duck Breast Mole, 142

Pipian Rojo, 266

Shake Your Tamarind, 379

shallots

Chicken de Champiñones, 139

Salsa Macha, 286

Striped Sea Bass Ceviche, 26

sherry, amontillado

Ghost in the Shell, 406

sherry, fino

Maya Gold, 378

sherry, manzanilla

Home Is Where the Heat Is, 416

She's a Rainbow, 400

shio koji

Koji-Marinated Sweet Potatoes with Salsa Macha, 35

shrimp

Aguachile Verde, 19

Caldo de Camarón Seco, 244

Caldo de Pescado, 242

Camarones a la Diabla, 180

Camarones en Adobo, 163

Coctel de Camarón, 27

Coctel de Marisco, 30

Shrimp Aguachile with Avocado Panna Cotta, 28

Vuelva a la Vida, 53

Silver Needle–Infused Tequila

Peach Tea, 390

recipe, 456

Simple Syrup

East LA, 354

Fig Leaf Syrup, 458

Horchata, 419

Jalisco Sour, 399

La Cura, 415

La Santa, 415

Margarita, 348

Paloma, 358

Ramon Bravo, 365

recipe, 447

Tejuino, 427

Thai Chile & Basil Syrup, 464

Vampiro, 351

Zeus Juice Cordial, 456

sloe gin

Rising Sun, 383

Smoked Trout Tostadas, 178

Snap Pea Syrup

La Santa, 415

recipe, 460

Sopa de Chile Poblano, 236

Sopa de Chorizo, Ayocotes y Acelgas, 224

Sopa de Conchitas, 222

Sopa de Fideo, 240

Sopa de Flor de Calabaza, 234

Sopa de Frijol Colado

Joroches de Chorizo y Frijoles Colados, 96

recipe, 235

Sopa de Hongos, 223

Sopa de Lentejas, 248

Sopa de Papa, 240

Sopaipillas, 342

sorrel

Betabel with Salsa Macha y Queso Fresco, 46

soups and stews

Albondigas Soup, 243

Baja Tortilla Soup, 229

Butternut Squash & Chorizo Bisque, 228

Caldo de Camarón Seco, 244

Caldo de Pescado, 242

Caldo de Res, 245

Carne Adobada, 232

Menudo, 226

Pozole Blanco, 220

Puchero de Tres Carnes, 237

Sere de Pescado, 225

Sopa de Chile Poblano, 236

Sopa de Chorizo, Ayocotes y Acelgas, 224

Sopa de Conchitas, 222

Sopa de Fideo, 240

Sopa de Flor de Calabaza, 234

Sopa de Frijol Colado, 235

Sopa de Hongos, 223

Sopa de Lentejas, 248

Sopa de Papa, 240

sour cream

Chiles en Nogada, 132

Empanadas de Picadillo, 130

Esquites con Longaniza, 24

Gorditas de Picadillo de Res, 138

Lobster & Street Corn Salad, 16

Masa-Battered Fish Tacos, 181

Picadillo de Res, 125

soy sauce

Chiles Toreados, 270

Michelada, 352

Pork Toro with Salsa Macha, 70

Striped Sea Bass Ceviche, 26

Spicy Chocolate Truffles, 316

Spicy Margarita, 362

Spicy Mezcal

Home Is Where the Heat Is, 416

recipe, 464

spinach

Puerco en Pipian Verde, 126

Sopa de Chile Poblano, 236

Sopa de Lentejas, 248

squash

Butternut Squash & Chorizo Bisque, 228

Caldo de Res, 245

Puchero de Tres Carnes, 237

Sopa de Flor de Calabaza, 234

squash blossoms

Flor de Calabaza con Queso Fresco y Hierbabuena, 57

Sopa de Flor de Calabaza, 234

St-Germain

Blacker the Berry, the Sweeter the Juice, 376

Guera, 408

strawberries

Guanajuato Strawberry & Beet Salad, 19

Strawberry Hot Sauce, 261

Strawberry Shortcake con Conchas, 321

strawberry brandy

Violet Skies, 414

strawberry jam

Flor de Jalisco, 374

Striped Sea Bass Ceviche, 26

sumac

Coffee & Ancho Carrots, 41

Sunday Morning Coming Down, 390

sunflower seeds

Cilantro Pesto, 434

Fried Brussels Sprouts with Habanero Agave, 35

Salsa Macha, 286

Sweet Corn & Pepita Guacamole, 87

Sweet Corn Pudding Pops, 338

Sweet Empanadas, 293

sweet potatoes

Camote con Mole Blanco, 39

Koji-Marinated Sweet Potatoes with Salsa Macha, 35

Puchero de Tres Carnes, 237

Tacos Dorados de Frijol, Chorizo y Camote, 204

sweetened condensed milk

Chocoflan, 310–311

Coconut Tres Leches, 328

Coffee Flan with Buñuelos, 306

Horchata, 419

The Perfect Flan, 336

Swiss chard

Sopa de Chorizo, Ayocotes y Acelgas, 224

Szechuan & Chipotle Honey

Mámù Vida, 403

recipe, 460

T

Tacos Dorados de Frijol, Chorizo y Camote, 204

tajín

Coctel de Marisco, 30

East LA, 354

La Diosa, 392

Lobster & Street Corn Salad, 16

Michelada, 352

Spicy Margarita, 362

Tamales de Chulibu'ul, 198

tamarind paste/concentrate

Chocolate Tamarind Truffles, 313

Shake Your Tamarind, 379

tamarind pods/pulp

Agua de Tamarindo, 423

Tamarind Syrup, 465

Tamarind Syrup

Home Is Where the Heat Is, 416

recipe, 465

Taquitos de Papa, 62

Taquitos de Requesón con Rajas, 61

Tejuino, 427

telera

Sopa de Chorizo, Ayocotes y Acelgas, 224

Tepache de Piña, 429

Tepache Syrup

Pineapple Tepache Kombucha, 428

recipe, 462

tequila

Batanga, 357

Brujera, 379

Cantaritos, 398

Champagne Paloma, 391

Desert Daisy, 384

Diablo Otoño, 394

Dons of Soul, 396

East LA, 354

El Chavo del Ocho, 371

El Vato Swizzle, 382

The Fifth Element, 388

Fire Walk with Me, 402

Flor de Jalisco, 374

Guera, 408

Hay Zeus, 386

Jalisco Sour, 399

Kinda Knew Anna, 398

L & N, 403

La Diosa, 392

La Mula, 407

Lavagave, 368

Margarita, 348

Mr. Kotter, 410

Oaxaca Old Fashioned, 364

Paloma, 358

Pan, 404

Peach Tea, 390

Pineapple Express, 380

Playa Rosita, 350

Ranch Water, 360

Rising Sun, 383

Salsa Borracha, 280

Shake Your Tamarind, 379

She's a Rainbow, 400

Silver Needle–Infused Tequila, 456

Spicy Margarita, 362

Sunday Morning Coming Down, 390

See also mezcal

Tetelas de Aguacate con Requesón y Nopales, 68

Thai Chile & Basil Syrup

Oaxacan Bottle Rocket, 412

recipe, 464

Thai Chile Agave

Pineapple Express, 380

recipe, 453

Thai chile peppers

Thai Chile & Basil Syrup, 464

Thai Chile Agave, 453

Thai Pepper Shrub, 463

Thai Pepper Shrub

Guera, 408

recipe, 463

Thyme Syrup

El Chavo del Ocho, 371

recipe, 450

tiki bitters

Playa Rosita, 350

Tikin Xic, 173

tilapia

Masa-Battered Fish Tacos, 181

Tinga de Pollo

Chicken Tinga Sopes, 205

recipe, 168

Tlacoyos de Hongos, 202

Toasted Rice Powder

Pig Ear Salad, 18

recipe, 438

tomatillos

Baja Tortilla Soup, 229

Carne en su Jugo, 133

Chilaquiles Verdes, 214

Dzikil P'aak, 280

Mole Blanco, 260

Mole Verde, 277

Puerco en Pipian Verde, 126

Salsa Borracha, 280

Salsa Cruda Verde, 284

Salsa de Aguacate, 274

Salsa Verde Tatemada, 262

Striped Sea Bass Ceviche, 26

tomatoes

Abuela's Sopes, 194

Albondigas Soup, 243

Baja Tortilla Soup, 229

Beef Machaca with Potatoes & Eggs, 144

Birria de Chivo, 92

Calabacitas con Elote y Queso Fresco, 76

Caldo de Pescado, 242

Camarones a la Diabla, 180

Camarones en Adobo, 163

Ceviche de Pescado, 32

Chicharron en Salsa Roja, 120

Chilaquiles Rojos, 94

Chiles Rellenos, 190

Chulibu'ul, 84

Coctel de Camarón, 27

Coctel de Marisco, 30

Dons of Soul, 396

Dzik de Res, 110

Dzikil P'aak, 280

Ensalada de Nopales, 22

Guacamole, 80

Huevos Motuleños, 210

Huevos Rancheros, 208

Lengua en Salsa Roja, 116

Menudo, 226

Mextlapique de Callo de Hacha, 169

Mole Manchamanteles, 257

Mole Negro, 252–253

Morita Salsa, 276

Pan de Cazon, 172

Pescado Veracruz, 179

Picadillo de Res, 125

Pig Ear Salad, 18

Pipian Rojo, 266

Pollo Veracruzano, 158

Quesadillas de Champiñones, 52

Rabo de Res en Salsa Roja, 129

Salsa de Chiltomate, 258

Sere de Pescado, 225

Sopa de Conchitas, 222

Sopa de Fideo, 240

Sopa de Lentejas, 248

Sopa de Papa, 240

Taquitos de Papa, 62

Tinga de Pollo, 168

Tomato Aguachile, 44

Tortas Ahogadas, 216

Tortitas de Coliflor, 60

Vuelva a la Vida, 53

X'nipek, 268

tongue, beef

Lengua en Salsa Roja, 116

Topo Chico

Huauzontles Relleno de Queso con Chiltomate, 40

Jamaica Collins, 370

Ranch Water, 360

Tortas Ahogadas, 216

Tortas de Lomo, 211

Tortilla Gruesa de Hoja Santa y Queso, 194

Tortitas de Coliflor, 60

Tostadas

Smoked Trout Tostadas, 178

Tinga de Pollo, 168

Tostadas de Cueritos, 117

tripe

Menudo, 226

triple sec

La Diosa, 392

Trout Tostadas, Smoked, 178

True Romance, 402

tuna

Carnitas de Atun, 176

turkey

Pavo en Escabeche, 151

turnip

Mole Blanco, 260

U

Última Palabra, 356

Unscalpe, 394

V

Vampiro, 351

Vampiro Mix, 447

Vanilla Syrup

Horchata con Espresso, 419

recipe, 461

Vegetable Stock

Baja Tortilla Soup, 229

Butternut Squash & Chorizo Bisque, 228

Chile Colorado, 256

Frijol Ayocote with Pasilla Yogurt, 49

Masa for Tamales, 434

Muscovy Duck Breast Mole, 142

Pipian Rojo, 266

recipe, 439

Sere de Pescado, 225

Sopa de Chile Poblano, 236

Sopa de Chorizo, Ayocotes y Acelgas, 224

Sopa de Flor de Calabaza, 234

Sopa de Frijol Colado, 235

velvet falernum

Fire Walk with Me, 402

Oaxacan Bottle Rocket, 412

Piña Fumada, 395

Verdolagas en Salsa Verde, 48

vermouth, dry

El Nacional, 414

Pan, 404

Playa Rosita, 350

Sunday Morning Coming Down, 390

vermouth, sweet

Pineapple Marmalade, 455

Playa Rosita, 350

Violet Skies, 414

vodka

Huauzontles Relleno de Queso con Chiltomate, 40

Vuelva a la Vida, 53

W

walnuts

Chiles en Nogada, 132

Fig Cordial, 457

watercress

Caldo de Espinazo de Puerco, 241

watermelon juice

El Vato Swizzle, 382

wine, blue

Zeus Juice Cordial, 456

wine, red

Beef Stock, 440

wine, sparkling

Champagne Paloma, 391

wine, white

Chicken de Champiñones, 139

Chicken Stock, 438

Pollo Veracruzano, 158

X

xcatic chile peppers

Pavo en Escabeche, 151

X'nipek

Cochinita Pibil, 99

Joroches de Chorizo y Frijoles Colados, 96

recipe, 268

Xocolatl, 422

Y

yogurt

Frijol Ayocote with Pasilla Yogurt, 49

Sopa de Chile Poblano, 236

Z

Zeus Juice Cordial

Hay Zeus, 386

recipe, 456

zucchini

Albondigas Soup, 243

Calabacitas con Elote y Queso Fresco, 76

INDEX

ABOUT CIDER MILL PRESS BOOK PUBLISHERS

Good ideas ripen with time. From seed to harvest, Cider Mill Press brings fine reading, information, and entertainment together between the covers of its creatively crafted books. Our Cider Mill bears fruit twice a year, publishing a new crop of titles each spring and fall.

"Where Good Books Are Ready for Press"

501 Nelson Place
Nashville, TN 37214

cidermillpress.com